A Man of all Tribes

A Man of all Tribes

THE LIFE OF
Alick Jakomos

Richard Broome & Corinne Manning

Aboriginal Studies Press

First published in 2006
by Aboriginal Studies Press

© Richard Broome and Corinne Manning 2006

All rights reserved. No part of this book may be reproduced or transmitted in any form or by any means, electronic or mechanical, including photocopying, recording or by any information storage and retrieval system, without prior permission in writing from the publisher. The *Australian Copyright Act 1968* (the Act) allows a maximum of one chapter or 10 per cent of this book, whichever is the greater, to be photocopied by any educational institution for its education purposes provided that the educational institution (or body that administers it) has given a remuneration notice to Copyright Agency Limited (CAL) under the Act.

Aboriginal Studies Press
the publishing arm of the
Australian Institute of Aboriginal
and Torres Strait Islander Studies
GPO Box 553, Canberra, ACT 2601
Phone: (61 2) 6246 1183
Fax: (61 2) 6261 4288
Email: asp@aiatsis.gov.au
Web: www.aiatsis.gov.au/aboriginal_studies_press

National Library of Australia Cataloguing-In-Publication data:

> Broome, Richard, 1948- .
> A man of all tribes : the life of Alick Jackomos.
> ISBN 0 85575 501 6.
>
> 1. Jackomos, Alick, 1924-1999.
> 2. Political activists — Victoria — Melbourne — Biography. 3. Aboriginal Australians — Civil rights — Victoria.
> 4. Historians — Victoria — Melbourne — Biography. I. Manning, Corinne. II. Title.

323.1199150092

Printed in Australia by Ligare Pty Ltd

Cover photograph of Alick Jackomos by Lindsay Howe, 1997 (La Trobe University Collection)

This project has been assisted by the Australian Government through the Australia Council, its arts funding and advisory body.

Aboriginal and Torres Strait Islander people are respectfully advised that this book contains names and images of deceased persons, and culturally sensitive material.

To Merle Jackomos, Alick's partner in life,
and in the struggle for Aboriginal rights

Contents

Preface		xii
1	Growing up Greek	1
2	Youth and the Great Depression	15
3	Off to War	27
4	Tent Wrestler	41
5	Just Like Hollywood	64
6	Entrepreneur and Family Man	75
7	The 'Greek Grappler'	95
8	Teaming with Doug Nicholls	106
9	Political Activism	117
10	Welfare Board Officer	141
11	Public Servant	154
12	Boomerang Diplomacy	172
13	In the Thick of Things	185
14	A Passion for Photographs	204
15	Community Historian	215
16	In Retirement	233
17	Watching the Hour-Glass	254
Notes		263
Select Bibliography		278
Index		281

Illustrations

Unless otherwise stated all illustrations in this book are from the collection of Alick and Merle Jackomos and used with the kind permission of Merle Jackomos.

Postcard scene of Castellorizo, island of Alick's forefathers	2
Castellorizo family picnic, 1928	3
Andrew and Asimina (née Augustes) Jackomos and their children, c. 1928	6
The Jackomos children, c. 1935	11
Alick Jackomos at Camberwell, c. 1932	16
John Augustes (Alick's uncle), 1927	19
Albert ('Bert') Clarke and Alick at the Exhibition Police Boys' Club, c. 1939	20
Workmates at Shields Motors, 1940	22
In uniform at last, 1942	29
Alick in uniform	30
At Luna Park, 1942	30
In training at Morphett Creek, Northern Territory, 1942	32
Scenes of devastation, Balikpapan, Borneo, 1945	36
Alick and his uncle Theo Augustes at Balikpapan	37
The joy of homecoming, early 1946	39
Alick on Harry Johns' line-up board at the Bombala Show, 1949	42
Alick with showmen in north Queensland, c. 1947	44
With his brother Michael on the showgrounds, c. 1948	46
Alick at the Adelaide Show, early 1950s	47
With Australian lightweight champion, Frankie Flannery, early 1950s	53

Rud Kee in later life	58
Alick at the Brisbane Show in the 1950s	59
Clowning around	61
Merle Morgan at Taronga Park Zoo, Sydney, 1949	66
Alick and Merle on their wedding day, 31 March 1951	71
The wedding party	72
At the reception, St Mary's Hall, Mooroopna	72
Russell Street between 1940 and 1960 (State Library of Victoria)	76
Alick on Anzac Day with members of the 21st Infantry Brigade, 2/14th Battalion	79
Alick on his 'potato run' photographed by the *Coburg Courier*, c. 1960	82
Proud parents at the Dandenongs, 1952	85
Twenty-first birthday party for Queensland Aboriginal boxer and Australian lightweight champion, George Bracken	87
The family at Jackson's Track, Drouin, in 1957	91
Holiday stopover, Ipswich, Queensland, in the early 1960s	92
Wrestling with mates at Castellorizo ('Cassie') picnic in the 1950s	96
At the Stadium with Clive Coram	99
The 'Greek Grappler' poses for a fan photograph.	99
Alick at Festival Hall, Melbourne	103
Alick and his mentor, Pastor Doug Nicholls	107
On the road with Doug Nicholls, 1960s	109
Alick and Merle Jackomos with their close friends Winnie and Eric Onus	110
At Barmah Lakes, 1958	112
Aboriginal picnic at Jackson's Track, Drouin, in the late 1950s	113
The Jackomos family at the Aboriginal Ball, Northcote Town Hall, 1970	115
Bill Onus at Belgrave, c. 1960	120
Alick as Santa at the Aboriginal Children's Christmas tree	122
With Merle at an Advancement League dinner dance, c. 1970	126
Gathering mussels at Dunwich, Stradbroke Island, c. 1960	131

Adventures at Pine Creek, Northern Territory, early 1960s	136
Charlie Huggard collects the rent from Joyce Atkinson at Rumbalara, 1960s.	142
Manatunga Housing settlement, Robinvale, 1960 (Aborigines Welfare Board, *Annual Report*, 1963)	146
Alick and Reg Worthy with Chaplain Arthur Malcolm outside Lake Tyers church, 1967	150
At the Ministry of Aboriginal Affairs, *c.* 1970	160
Alick at the Aboriginal Studies short course, Australian National University, 1971	162
With work mates at the Ministry of Aboriginal Affairs, early 1970s	163
Alick and Senator Neville Bonner	167
Choctaw Indian dancers (*Aboriginal and Islander Identity*, July 1978)	175
Alick's Brunei friends (courtesy Ambran Noor Aston and family)	180
Alick at Kuala Belait, Brunei, 1977 (courtesy Ambran Noor Aston and family)	181
Alick at a Chinese restaurant dinner, Brunei, September 1977 (courtesy Ambran Noor Aston and family)	183
Alick heading for Papua New Guinea as manager of the Australian Aboriginal Football team, 1973	188
Socialising after the Australia v. Papua New Guinea match, 1973 (*Aboriginal and Islander Identity*, June 1974)	189
At a Gippsland cultural gathering, Bairnsdale, 1985	192
At the Aboriginal Child Care Agency Conference, St Kilda, April 1979	194
Alick and Merle at an Advancement League function, 1975	198
Alick with boxers Graeme Brooks and Tony Mundine	199
Alick with his siblings, *c.* 1985	201
Escorting Doug Nicholls to the graveside at Cummeragunja, 1988	202
One of Alick's favourite fan photographs from his pal, 'Chief Little Wolf'	205
Alick with Richard Broome at Genealogical Expo at Ballarat, 1996	209

Community photographs found in Alick's magnificent albums	212
Launch of *Forgotten Heroes* at the Advancement League, April 1993	229
Interviewing old friends for the book *Sideshow Alley*, 1995 (photograph by Richard Broome)	230
Alick speaking at the launch of *Sideshow Alley*, August 1998 (photograph by Margaret Donnan)	231
On the eve of Andrew's departure to the US in 1971	234
Some of the grandchildren in 1986	235
Alick's 70th birthday at 34 Violet Grove in 1994	237
Unsuccessfully asserting the right for Aboriginal returned servicemen to march on Anzac Day as an Aboriginal group, *c.* 1988	239
Alick at the Advancement League, early 1990s	241
Alick and Merle at the Referendum 30th Anniversary Dinner, 1997	245
Alick on a sewing machine at ACES, photograph taken in the early 1990s	246
Alick with Prime Minister Paul Keating, Canberra, in 1992	247
Alick with his Australia Day medal, 1984	248
Alick on a train from Kota Kinabalu, Sabah	252
Alick and Merle beside their beloved house name — 'Cummeragunja' — October 1998	256
Alick on the 'Last Parade' at Isurava, Kokoda Trail, New Guinea	257
Alick in the 2nd AIF in 1944, a man of all tribes	261

Preface

Alick Jackomos was a living legend when we first heard of him. He reputedly knew all about Aboriginal history in Victoria, held a treasure trove of pictures and was a genuine 'gubbah-iginal', that is, one who was both gubbah (European) and Aboriginal in understanding. Richard had initially exchanged information about Aboriginal boxing with Alick in the late 1970s. They eventually collaborated on a book about the boxing tents and shows, *Sideshow Alley* (1998) and began planning Alick's life story just before Alick's death in 1999. Corinne had met Alick briefly while a university undergraduate in the mid-1990s. The true extent and worth of Alick Jackomos' life, however, only became apparent once we worked on this book. Alick was revealed as a very moral man, whose presence, in the words of a friend, left you 'feeling cleansed'. He trod lightly on the world, leaving it a better place. Alick was also a man of great tolerance and compassion, who was fascinated by other cultures. He was, as Arnold Zable called him in an obituary, 'a man of all tribes'.

Alick began writing his own story in the 1980s, but it proved difficult for the son of Greek migrants who owned the 'Magpie Fish', a fish and chip shop in Carlton, and who left school at twelve. Alick attained great achievements in research, writing and collecting during his life, but writing an extended autobiography seemed beyond him, although he left an amazing legacy of his own incidental writings, an autobiographical manuscript of fifty pages written in 1987, a host of papers and interviews with various people about his life and experiences. Some of these, especially tapes by Barry York for the National Library of Australia, fortuitously were done during his final six months.

Alick's voice is therefore strong and is clear in this book. His meticulous recording has enabled us to re-create much of his intriguing career, including his youth as a child of Greek immigrants in the Great Depression, his war service, his marriage into the Aboriginal community, his wrestling career, his thirty-year apprenticeship to Sir Doug Nicholls in Aboriginal activism and voluntary work, his paid work in Aboriginal affairs, work as a community historian and his fascination with Brunei. He became an honorary Koori, 'Uncle Alick' to almost all Aboriginal people in Victoria, yet jealousy and intolerance occasionally stalked him.

The writing of a book, like building a house, creates many debts. This book would have taken much longer, but for a vital and generous one-year grant in 2003 by the Australian Institute of Aboriginal and Torres Strait Islander Studies, for which Alick did so much. The Institute was pleased to assist, as it holds copies of Alick's collections, and has named a research room in his honour. This grant and study leave kindly provided by La Trobe University allowed us to research and write the manuscript.

People as well as institutions are the rock on which this book was built. Merle Jackomos and her children Esmai Manahan, and Andrew and Michael Jackomos, have been of immeasurable assistance in creating this life story. They have provided many memories and free access to papers and photographs. Some of Alick's grandchildren have also provided recollections. Family members, friends and work colleagues have also generously recorded memories, through taped interviews, or in the case of those interstate and overseas, written communications. These specific contributions are set out in the notes that relate to each chapter and all those who assisted are listed with great thanks in the bibliography. Without these memories of Alick's life this book would have been much the poorer.

Many others have supported us by their interest and encouragement to write this life. Our La Trobe colleagues have inspired us to push harder to fathom the man and his times. Sue Taffe of Monash University must be warmly thanked for her material on the Federal Council for the Advancement of Aboriginal and Torres Strait Islanders and her suggestions of other sources. The photographs in this book are from Alick's own collection unless otherwise captioned. Dimi Delimitrou kindly translated several Greek language articles concerning Alick, and Chris Fifis read the early chapters on Alick's place in the Greek community. The late Lorraine Dumsday transcribed five 1995 tapes of conversations between Richard and Alick on boxing tents, and Mandy Rooke expertly transcribed over thirty tapes during 2003–04. Both were drawn into Alick's life through hearing him speak and others speak of him. Our publisher at Aboriginal Studies Press, Gabby Lhuede, made the task of publication a pleasure. We hope we have presented these voices, that of Alick and his contemporaries, in such a way as to reveal his extraordinary nature.

Richard Broome and Corinne Manning
October 2005

1 Growing up Greek

Castellorizo is a small island with a turbulent and colourful history. This Greek Dodecanese island in the Aegean Sea, located approximately two kilometres from the Turkish coast, was for centuries conquered in succession by France, Italy, Russia, Spain and Turkey. Despite being occupied, Castellorizians identified themselves as Greek and maintained Greek values and customs. From the seventeenth to the late nineteenth centuries Castellorizo grew into a dynamic and prosperous trading island, giving many of the 9000 Castellorizians a high standard of living. However, during the late nineteenth and early twentieth centuries the economy floundered due to a downturn in maritime trading. Poor economic conditions encouraged many Castellorizians to migrate to countries such as America and Australia. After the First World War the island was transferred from the control of the defeated Turks to Italian rule. Living conditions on the island worsened and a second wave of migrants left in search of a better life for their families.

The initial members of the Jackomos family to arrive in Australia were part of the first wave of migration. Alick's paternal grandfather Alexios (or Alexi as he was commonly known), and his two great-uncles arrived in Perth in 1912. Between 1914 and 1917 Alexi assisted the migration of his wife Panayota, his two sons, Andreas (Andrew) and Yakomi (Jack), and his daughter Megthalia, and her husband Steve Pallaras. By 1920 all of Alexi's family, his brothers and sisters Areti, Angelo, John, Basil and Mick, and their families migrated to Perth, Adelaide and Melbourne. Coming from a country with a rich tradition of cultural and economic exchange, the Jackomos family embraced the new opportunities offered to them in Australia, although they maintained Greek values and customs within their new homeland.

Postcard scene of Castellorizo, island of Alick's forefathers

Andrew spent his first years travelling and working in Western Australia and the Northern Territory. During this time life was an exciting adventure as he was exposed to new environments and cultures. He worked as a railway worker, helping in the construction of the Darwin to Pine Creek railway line, and then became a sponge diver and also a fish seller. Through his employment Andrew met other migrants, especially Chinese railway workers who taught him to speak a few Chinese words and phrases. He also met many other Castellorizians, mostly young men, who were forging a new life for themselves in Australia. With entrepreneurial vigour Andrew worked alongside his father Alexi in Perth. They started an independent business selling fish door-to-door, a venture reminiscent of traditional Castellorizian enterprises. Before the economic downturn on the island, Castellorizo had been a vibrant fishing and trading port. With baskets of freshly caught fish in their arms, bought from the local fish markets, you could hear Andrew and Alexi's calls 'fisho, fisho' echoing through Perth's streets. After building up a reliable clientele, Andrew and his father earned enough money to purchase a horse and cart. By his mid-twenties Andrew had a steady income and regular work in his adopted homeland.

By this time Andrew craved more than travel and business adventure; he wanted to share his newfound life with a wife and family. It was during this period that he and his parents relocated to Melbourne where a small Greek community flourished. A number of Castellorizians lived in the city including the Mangos, Spartels, Fermanis, Conos, Augustes, Kanis, George and Adgemis families. Andrew became friendly with two Castellorizian brothers, Peter and Manuel Augustes, who owned a fruit shop. The Augustes brothers worked for many years in order to raise enough money to enable their mother, three sisters and younger brother to travel from Port Said, Egypt, to Australia. In 1922 their efforts were successful and after a long and arduous six-week voyage, the family was reunited in Melbourne. It was not long before Andrew and Asimina Augustes were engaged. It is unclear whether their marriage was pre-arranged, as their families were acquainted in Castellorizo, or if they fell in love when Asimina arrived. Shortly after her arrival in Melbourne, on 1 April 1923, they were married in the Greek Orthodox Church 'Evangelismos' in East Melbourne.

Castellorizo family picnic, 1928, including the Jackomos, Fermanis, Conos, Spartels, Mangos and Papalazadou families

On 24 March 1924 an olive-skinned, brown-eyed, baby boy was born in a small private hospital in Canning Street, North Carlton, to excited parents Andrew and Asimina Jackomos. Proud of their Greek heritage, they named their son in the traditional Greek manner, after the paternal grandfather Alexios, although they were aware that some Australians were intolerant of peoples from non-Anglo-Saxon and Celtic backgrounds. Racist attitudes were encapsulated legislatively in the White Australia Policy of 1901 and in the imposition of annual quotas and a landing tax on those from Southern Europe. Andrew would have met abusive and intolerant Australians during his adventures up North and the Augustes family also knew of the social marginalisation of migrants and Aboriginal Australians. Andrew and Asimina were determined to assimilate themselves and their children into mainstream Australian culture and decided to use a more Anglophile version of Alexios — 'Alick'. The willingness of Andrew and Asimina to accommodate Australian mores into their lifestyle signalled the manner in which Alick was raised. His parents ensured that he acquired a combination of Australian and Greek cultural traits, which later equipped Alick with the skills necessary to work and socialise confidently within many sectors of Australian society. As they cradled Alick in their arms, little did they know that their first born child would become a successful entrepreneur, soldier, boxer, wrestler, historian, genealogist and civil rights activist.

Andrew and Asimina worked tirelessly to ensure that their children had opportunities to succeed and live a secure life in Australia. From his early days in Melbourne, Alick's father, like many other Greek immigrants, worked in the food sector. In Andrew's case he worked in a business that he knew well — fish. His first fish and chip shop was situated on the corner of Park and Station streets, North Carlton. His decision to remain in the fish industry was partly due to his expertise, his individualist streak, and because it was difficult for many Southern Europeans to find other employment. The problem was due to language difficulties and to racist attitudes held by those Australians who refused to hire 'Dagos', as Southern Europeans were termed. Alick noted:

> What else could migrants do when they came here in the 20s? It was either a fruit shop, a caffy or a fish and chip

shop...it would be hard to get a job in a factory...as most Southern Europeans, not only the Greeks but the Italians, any dark skin was a Dago.

Alick recognised the economic advantages of running a fish shop: 'You didn't need big capital...a couple of coppers, scales and a counter and an icebox, and that made a fish shop...and you didn't need a lot of skills, you just cooked fish and chips'. From 1922 to 1965 Andrew and Asimina owned fish and chip shops in succession in Collingwood, Balaclava, Northcote and Carlton. The investment in this type of business proved to be a success as it supported the Jackomos family even through harsh economic times, particularly during the 1930s Great Depression.

The fish and chip shop was a central feature of Alick's childhood, as the family home was often perched above it. The long hours needed to support the business meant that Andrew and Asimina were both required to work. Unlike some other migrant families who were able to take advantage of free childcare through living in extended family situations, Andrew and Asimina lived independently. Consequently, from his birth Alick was a regular fixture within the family business, propped in the corner of the shop, strapped into his pram for safety. Perhaps this constant exposure to customers encouraged his gregarious nature. Over the next eighteen years the Jackomos family grew steadily, and Alick was joined by five siblings — Mary, Angelo, Christella, Maisie and Michael. Being the eldest child, Alick held a special position as mentor, provider and protector of his siblings. He took these responsibilities very seriously as he grew, and always endeavoured to support members of his family. This protective influence came from his mother, who was the primary carer in the Jackomos household.

Andrew and Asimina were often torn between their desire to be considered 'good' Australian citizens, while holding on to their Greek culture. The commitment which Andrew and Asimina felt towards their adopted homeland prompted their decision to become Australian citizens in 1928 (about one third of Greek immigrants were naturalised in the interwar years), although Greek culture remained vital to the family's sense of identity, and Greek traditions and customs were manifest in their daily lives. Asimina had very little time to cook

Andrew and Asimina (née Augustes) Jackomos and their children (l. to r.): Mary, Angelo, and Alick, c. 1928

many traditional Greek dinners for her family. Most evening meals consisted of fish and chips — gummy shark and barracuda were most popular. She did, however, make some Greek favourites such as the tender vine leaves stuffed with savoury rice known as *dolmades*, and lamb was a Sunday staple. Greek was the language spoken at home, as Asimina did not have a strong command of English. From a very young age Alick and his siblings were bilingual: speaking Greek at home and English elsewhere. The mixture of Greek and Australian lifestyles helped prepare Alick to live in a culturally pluralistic society.

In 1928, at the age of four, Alick commenced primary school in Faraday Street, Carlton, a strong working-class suburb. It was likely that he was one among forty or fifty students in his class, so opportunities were limited. Alick's education was also interrupted by the family's relocation to Balaclava, Northcote and Collingwood. Between 1929 and 1934 Alick attended Brighton Road, Northcote and Cromwell Street (Collingwood) primary schools. In his recollections there is very little mention of the academic nature of Alick's education, aside from his self-deprecating comment: 'I wasn't really smart'. At Cromwell Street Primary School in Collingwood he learned to print but not to write in copperplate, a method which he preferred to use as an adult.

Deprived of much formal education, Alick possessed a keen intelligence, a photographic memory and a superior level of recall. These intellectual skills were evident throughout his memoirs and oral testimonies in which he gave vivid descriptions of his working-class childhood experiences. For example, Alick fondly recalled the fun of playground games and childhood friends. While the girls were playing hopscotch and using knuckle bones as jacks, the boys were in the corner fighting to be the cherry-bob or Tooleybuck champion. Alick remembered:

> Now a cherry-bob is the stone out of a cherry. In those days you'd walk around the gutters around the streets pickin' up cherry-bobs that people had eaten and spat, isn't it unhygienic?! They'd be white. Or you'd collect the red ones if Mum'd cooked some cherries…Now, you had a little bag made of canvas, like a little money bag, maybe about 4 inches by 3 with a string on the top…[At school] you'd dig a little hole in the ground, about three inches [in circumference]. Then…you'd stand back about six feet and you'd throw your cherry-bob, and if it landed in the hole you got a bonus, you won a cherry-bob. That was the easy way. But then a lot of us made what they called a Tooleybuck. This was a piece of stiff cardboard about 24 inches [in circumference]. You'd put a hole in the middle and a cotton reel where that hole was. Then you'd put a meat skewer in the middle of it and some string around the skewer and the bottom of the cotton reel, so that you could pull that string and it'd turn around…[like a] Roulette [wheel]. Instead of being numbers, we'd have…famous horse cup winners of the '30s, Pharlap, Wotan, Shadow King…Peter Pan, and you'd gamble…you'd say…'Four to one Pharlap, three to one Shadow King' etc. [We] started gambling at the age of six and seven and eight!

Alick would often play these games with his schoolmates: Adams, 'Digger' Whitburne, 'Bubby' Thomas and 'Wally' Gully. Throughout his childhood, there were very few migrant children at Alick's schools, so most of his friends were Anglo-Australian. At the age of eleven Alick transferred to Collingwood Technical School, but before two years had elapsed Alick told his mother that he was no longer required to attend school. This misinformation was unquestioned by Asimina, and Alick ended his formal education before completing eighth grade.

Alick did not evade Greek school so easily. His parents considered Greek school to be vital to his education as it encouraged the maintenance of Greek culture within an Australian context. Therefore, like many Greek parents, Andrew and Asimina were willing to pay for this supplementary education. The Greek school was situated in central Melbourne where Alick was required to attend classes three times a week: on Tuesday and Thursday nights and Saturday mornings. The type of Greek learnt by students was a blend of Greek and Australian. Alick recalled, 'We learned a Greek that included a lot of Aussie words…You know for the tram we'd say "trammie" in Greek…for bank we'd say "banka"; the Greek word is *trapiza*… so we mixed this bit of Greek with Australian and made our own [language]'. While important to parents, Greek school was a trial for children. Alick's cousin, Theo Conos, recalled, 'every young child of that age [was] terrified of being cast as foreigners'. Alick often resisted such an education. According to Theo, 'Alick was a rebel…he used to get into arguments with the teacher and get thrown out [of class]'. His resistance may have been due to the nature of education and teaching at Greek school, his not being academically inclined or simply youthful rebelliousness.

Throughout his childhood, religion was an inherent part of Alick's upbringing, under the influence of his mother who was a deeply religious woman. The importance of religion in Asimina's life can be seen in her claim that Alick was born on 25 March, *Evangelismo* or Annunciation Day — the day that Christ was conceived. It was not until adulthood that Alick obtained his birth certificate that listed his birth date as 24 March. In the family home religious icons were placed in each room, illuminated by the flickering light coming from homemade oil lamps. Every Sunday Asimina marched Alick and his siblings to the Greek Orthodox Church in East Melbourne for the morning service. This church was the spiritual centre for Melbourne's Greek Orthodox community. It was also where Asimina and Andrew were married and their children baptised. Around the age of nine, Alick served at the church as an altar boy, and in later life he chose it for his own children's baptisms. Religion always played an important role in Alick's life, although the focus of his spirituality later moved away from the Greek Orthodox Church and more towards Western Christian groups such as the Church of England. Even as a child, when he lived in Collingwood, Alick attended two churches. In the morning he went to the Greek Orthodox Church, while the afternoon was spent at the non-denominational, Children's Church in Harmsworth Street. It was not the place of worship that mattered to Alick, but the general ethos of religious doctrines and the sense of community it instilled.

Unlike Asimina, Andrew was not an outwardly religious person. In Alick view, 'Dad wasn't so much for religion, his religion was backin' horses and playing cards…and drinking grog, you know! He was a good Dad, but that was his religion'. The behaviour of Alick's father was typical of many Australian men of this era, especially those existing in a working-class culture, who regarded women as responsible for homemaking and the moral upbringing of the children. Despite his reluctance to participate in formal religious ceremonies, Andrew recognised and celebrated Greek religious holidays. Alick noted, 'Easter time was a big thing…on Easter Sunday we'd go visiting families, all the cousins and relatives we'd…have the Greek eggs…and a little Greek cake'. Andrew and the family also celebrated Name Days. In the Orthodox tradition, if a person is named after a saint, a celebration is held on his/her Name Day. Many Greek people consider Name Days to be more important than birthdays and organise open house parties for relatives and friends. Alick recalled, 'you'd always go and visit somebody [on his/her] Name Day. You'd go and visit them and they'd bring a little tray around with first of all some grapefruit or orange boiled in sugar and then a glass of water and a little whiskey or ouzo…that's for the men'. Andrew's willingness to participate in this form of festivity was increased by the location of these gatherings in the homes of family and friends, rather than in a solemn church. Greek Easter and Name Days were also celebratory events with lots of eating, drinking, dancing and frivolity, which the gregarious Andrew enjoyed.

Andrew similarly emphasised involvement in events organised by the Greek community. The Castellorizian migrants established a social club in the city centre, the 'Cassie Club', where members socialised among countrymen. Gambling, drinking and chatting on weeknights and weekends was a popular attraction for many men. The Club also organised more family-centred activities such as an annual picnic, festivals, dances and other social events. Alick recalled:

> We'd go to the 'Cassie Club' and there'd be all these old Cassie songs and dances where you form a ring and hold each others hands…Dad was good at that. He'd take the lead and instead of holding hands with the next person, he'd hold a handkerchief in between…he'd jump over it, do a bit of a somersault or jump and clip his heels.

The Club was an important focal point for migrants as it gave them an opportunity to relax and socialise with fellow 'Cassies'. It also served as a sanctuary where members were protected from the possibility of racially-motivated abuse by people who disliked migrants. The Club sustained familial and social networks within Melbourne's wider Greek community.

At the Jackomos' house, entertainment and hobbies were a mixture of Greek and Australian amusements. Andrew owned a gramophone and a collection of Greek music records that he played regularly. The melodic sounds of traditional music wafted throughout the house accompanied by emotive lyrics about Greece, its people and history. Andrew was a musical man with a penchant for playing the acordion and singing traditional Greek songs. Australian radio programmes and sports broadcasts were also popular with the Jackomos clan. For example, in the evening the quintessentially Australian radio programme, 'Dad and Dave', took over the household. The adventures of Dad, Dave, Mabel and Alf were amusing to these city dwellers and essential listening for many people. When the Jackomoses lived in Collingwood, from 1931 until 1935, they did not

The Jackomos children (l. to r.): Maisie, Mary, Angelo, Alick and Stella, c. 1935

own a radio. So the family gathered with other locals outside a radio shop that broadcast the cricket test matches from England. Through music, song, drama and sports, Alick acquired further knowledge about Greece and Australia, which contributed to his identification as a Greek Australian.

During Alick's early formative years he became an avid collector. At first he collected coins and stamps, venturing to Port Melbourne to meet the passengers of docking ships, begging for foreign and exotic booty. As he grew older, Alick's interest extended into postcards and photos of boxers and wrestlers. Through his early business ventures, which will be considered in more depth in the next chapter, Alick came into contact with many famous local and international sporting figures including Chief Little Wolf, Sliding Billy Hassan, George Saharis, Billy Rainsby, Terry Riley and Mickey Miller. Postcards were often used as a form of advertising for sporting professionals, and many boxers and wrestlers carried copies with them to hand out to interested people. As Alick sold bags of peanuts at sporting events, he mingled with many boxers and wrestlers. He often asked for a copy of their photos or postcards for his collection. Through striking up conversations with boxers, wrestlers, managers and trainers, Alick acquired the personal addresses of other renowned sportsmen. He wrote to these men and asked for their photographs and/or postcards, and received photos from Australian and world champions such as Joe Louis, Jersey Joe Walcott, Gene Tunney, Jack Dempsey and Bob Gommery. Alick was proud of his collection and continued to indulge his passion throughout his adult life.

Alick became passionate about Australian Rules football and going to the 'footy' was an important part of his childhood, particularly as his father was a patron of the local Don Football Club. Alick often accompanied Andrew to local football matches in Carlton and Collingwood. Before long Alick was a dedicated Collingwood fan and would attempt anything to see his team play. During the Depression years, he often tried to convince men who were receiving sustenance benefits from the government to 'adopt' him for the day, as family members received free admission. When this strategy failed, Alick would sneak into games through gaps in the fencing. He recalled: 'In those days, Collingwood Football Ground had a corrugated iron fence and if we couldn't get in the gate we would get in through the loose corrugated fence. Everybody, including adults, knew where all the gaps were'. Alick's ingenuity and bravado indicated a 'streetwise' intellect that proved valuable throughout his life.

While Alick fondly remembered his childhood, he also acknowledged the difficulties that the family faced. Living above the fish shop proved to be challenging in many respects. The house in which Alick spent most of his childhood was above the fish shop at 153 Elgin Street, Carlton. The living space was small and cramped. Downstairs included the shopfront, a small kitchen, and a dining room, less than three metres square, where the family ate their meals. Upstairs there were three compact bedrooms and a spare room which measured less than two square metres. The spare room was also used as a bedroom. With eight people in the house, overcrowding was a problem. There was no area where the family could gather away from the working environment. The ventilation was poor and often the fumes and smoke from the cooking permeated the household. Many Australians in Collingwood and Carlton lived in poor housing exacerbated by a downturn in house building during to the Depression.

Alick found living in a fish shop to be humiliating at times:

> We lived in this stinkin' fish shop...the fish odours and cooking in fat went right through the shop...and throughout the upstairs. So all our clothes [smelt], we all smelt of fish and chips. And when you got on a tram, people would sniff and say 'Ooof! Fisho!' or something like that...It wasn't a comfortable life.

While an antique bath was available in the upstairs part of the house, it was unsatisfactory and Alick and his siblings bathed outside in a big tub. This weekly ritual coincided with his mother's clothes washing duties. Alick recalled:

> We had to have our bath out in the yard, it was a big tub. Now, there was a copper where Mum did her washing in those days, there were no washing machines. So you boil the copper, you boil your clothes, and then you put them into the sink there, the stone sink with some Reckitt's blue or Rennett's blue or whatever they called it. But Sunday, you'd boil the copper and you'd fill the [bath] tub. I got into it first...things were a bit rough those days!

Once a week Andrew and Asimina went to the local city baths where they paid one shilling for a bath. The early battle with smells and grime left Alick with a lifelong emphasis on his personal appearance and a concern with always being well groomed.

Alick's olive, Mediterranean complexion sometimes drew unwarranted attention from onlookers and in the close-minded world of the 1930s exposed him to racist abuse — even attacks. As a young boy, Alick was standing in a queue waiting to enter a football match when a passer-by yelled, 'You little Dago' and smashed a hot meat pie into Alick's face. He was taken to hospital and received treatment for his burns. Alick recalled many other incidents when complete strangers chased and beat him because of his physical features. Alick was a victim of racial intolerance, yet he did not look upon these incidents as evidence of his rejection from Australian society: 'I still felt that I was part of Australian society because I was no different to anyone else. [My treatment was] maybe no different to Aboriginals, they were part of Australian society, but they were barred in many ways'. Racial abuse may have been one reason why he later forged close connections with Aboriginal Australians and fought to eradicate racism in Australian society.

Alick fiercely resisted this exclusion from the wider world: 'I'm an Australian, I'm of Greek descent, but first I'm Australian'. While his Greek heritage was ever present in his upbringing and remained important to his identity, Alick always looked upon himself foremost as an Australian. This was an attitude he carried with him throughout his lifetime. Like many other Australian boys, he embraced Australian Rules football and the Club of his locality. He worshipped Australian sporting heroes and played with Anglo-Australian friends. He shrugged off the occasional abuse. During the Great Depression, his youthful adventures into the world of work, sporting arenas and local community deepened his connection with Australia and its Anglo and Indigenous peoples.

2   Youth and the Great Depression

In October 1929, just as Alick entered school, a financial catastrophe in the United States, the Wall Street crash, reverberated around the globe. The economies of many countries including Australia plummeted into chaos as commodity prices tumbled and overseas debts could not be serviced. Australia slipped into what has been called the Great Depression despite drastic government efforts to maintain social and economic stability through the devaluation of the Australian pound and cuts to award wages. Businesses closed and people were retrenched, resulting in high rates of unemployment and a collapse in the living standards of many Australian families. From his parents, Andrew and Asimina, Alick learnt the importance of thriftiness, charity and kindness towards others. They were fine examples of people who successfully combined family-centred values with a social responsibility to care for those more unfortunate than themselves. As Alick matured he explored his neighbourhood and made new friends. Through his social and work contacts he witnessed the benevolent and altruistic work undertaken by local individuals and organisations, and Alick's memories of his youth were coloured by the unique circumstances and suffering brought about by the Great Depression.

As the Depression deepened, Alick's parents struggled to make ends meet by operating the 'Magpie Fish' in Johnston Street, Collingwood. Andrew hoped to attract custom from football-mad residents by this allusion to the local team's totem. While both parents worked hard it was Asimina's frugality that ensured the family's survival, since Alick's father had a more liberal attitude towards spending money on leisure. After a hard day's work in the shop, Andrew enjoyed a good night out, playing cards, smoking and drinking in the company of male friends, a pastime that cost money. Aware of her husband's inability

Alick Jackomos at Camberwell, c. 1932

to be frugal, Asimina was determined to establish some financial security for her family. She adopted thrifty money management skills and secretly squirrelled away enough money from the business to ensure that her family always had a roof over their heads and food on the table. Alick noted:

> [Mum] always seemed to have a few bob put aside…Dad didn't value anything, as quick as the money come in…he put it on the sure thing and that'd come second! It was Mum, she valued money…she'd nick a little bit of money now and then…to feed us and to pay off the bill in the fish shop…In later years she bought a little house in Station Street, again with the takings from the fish shop. But if Dad had had control, the money would have gone.

Asimina was a shrewd woman who understood the value and security of property ownership revealed by the purchase of their Station Street house. She recognised that if her family was to survive, she needed to be proactive in financial matters.

While his attitude towards spending money may have been somewhat carefree, Andrew worked extremely hard to ensure the success of the family business.

> Dad would wake up at four o'clock in the morning and he had a horse and cart in those days, he never had a motor car...he'd go to the market on the corner of Spencer Street and Flinders Street and get his fish, and then come home and clean the fish.

Alick also praised his mother for her strong work ethic. He recalled, 'Mum'd get us off to school early in the morning and by about eight o'clock we were gone. And then she was cleaning the oven, the stoves... and clean the shop...Dad and Mum'd work all day in that fish shop ...[except] Sunday'. Asimina was often left alone to work the evening shift, often until midnight, while Andrew socialised at the Greek Club. On these occasions Alick's sisters and younger brother helped their mother. Despite his father's absences, Alick's parents generally worked well together. They provided a secure home environment for their family even during this tumultuous economic period. Alick soon adopted his parents' work ethic and his mother's financial acumen.

During the Great Depression Alick learned the value of charity and helping others. The 'Magpie Fish' was located near many industrial factories where people would gather to seek employment or to collect goods being discarded as waste. The availability of cheap meals from the fish and chip shop and its location near these factories meant that Alick and his family were often in contact with unemployed and impoverished people. The cheap price of fish and chips attracted hungry patrons to the shop. For 'thruppence' a person could buy a piece of fish and enough chips for a meal. Although Andrew and Asimina were also under duress, they showed compassion for others less fortunate. Alick recalled:

> During the Depression, many people were in need...at lunch time dad would give me a large newspaper parcel of fish and chips to hand out to the kids at school...that happened nearly every day...Mum was very religious and she'd always help people. She'd never knock [back] anybody that came

to the shop collecting for Red Cross or Legacy or whoever it was. Anyone that'd come to the shop she'd always give to them. And anyone that was hungry and didn't have the money for fish and chips...they'd [both] give them fish and chips.

Alick inherited the benevolent ideals held by his parents. He was always ready and willing to provide material and emotional support to people who were suffering hardship and turmoil in their lives.

Although he had only been a child and young teenager during the Depression years, Alick remembered the struggles that many people endured: 'I always remember the family next door to us...they were struggling! She was a widow with kids there, and I always remember that every time I went in there all they ate was Weetbix, that's all they had...a lot of families were hungry'. On other occasions he witnessed people handing out stale bread, cakes and other goods to destitute people near his home. Alick was privy to the charitable work done by religious bodies to alleviate some people's suffering. At St Mark's in Fitzroy, and St Joseph's in Hoddle Street, the staff showed silent movies and provided soup and a roast dinner, or a roast dinner and dessert, for one penny. Alick and his friends were recipients of this scheme and he recognised the value of such charity for many people at that time.

Hard times bred maturity. From the age of ten, Alick was a regular contributor to the family's income. Until his enlistment in the Army in 1942, all of his earnings were given to his mother and used to support the family. This was of paramount importance during the Depression when money was tight. Alick's first job was selling newspapers before and after school. Come rain or shine at five o'clock in the morning he got out of bed and stood on the corner of Gipps and Hoddle streets in Collingwood selling the *Sun*, *Age* and *Argus* for a penny and half-penny each. When he left school in 1936 Alick continued to sell newspapers in the city centre for a man named Fred Mitty.

Eager to make more money, Alick and his brother Angelo started a lucrative business selling peanuts at local football, boxing and wrestling matches. Alick recalled:

John Augustes (Alick's uncle), ice cream and sweet pie hawker, 1927

My brother and I, we'd buy our peanuts at a ...Chinese place, [Wing Lee's], a wholesale merchant in Franklin Street, opposite the Victoria Market, and also from Drakes [Kingaroy] Peanuts in Elizabeth Street. We'd buy about twenty pounds of peanuts...for about sixpence or sevenpence a pound...and bring them home and bag them, six bags a pound...[we'd] sell them for threepence a bag, so it was good money! And we'd go to the...Collingwood Football Ground...and the West Melbourne Stadium...and sell them.

Always up for adventure, Alick chose to sell his peanuts at the ringside entrance of the West Melbourne Stadium where cars and taxis delivered patrons. 'I'd go and open the door [of the car] and put a bag of peanuts in someone's hand as they were getting out, and say "threepence"'. When all of the spectators had arrived Alick lurked around the boxers' and wrestlers' entrance offering to carry their Gladstone bags. He used this as a ruse to wrangle free admission to

Albert ('Bert') Clarke and Alick (right) spar at the Exhibition Police Boys' Club, c. 1939.

the night's entertainment. Once inside, Alick would wander around the bleachers selling his wares, making sure to elude the attention of the local caterers who would have his head for invading their turf. While he was a convincing and elusive salesman, Alick was sometimes chased from the Stadium grounds by the police: 'There used to be a copper [who] use to hunt me all the time, good copper, his name was Jack Dyer, the footballer!…every Saturday night outside the West Melbourne Stadium he'd hunt me, but [when I was caught] he treated me well'. Even if Alick was evicted from the grounds he always returned to sell his goods by sneaking into the venue by any means possible. As his cousin Theo Conos declared, '…he was the Artful Dodger'.

A savvy entrepreneur, Alick soon recognised further opportunities for business expansion. Before too long he was selling green ribbons and badges at the St Patrick's Day marches, as well as fruit boxes to be used as stands by spectators behind the front rows at the Anzac Day Parade. However, his business endeavours were abruptly interrupted when his family, except for his father, was forced to flee Melbourne for Adelaide. This upheaval was due to a poliomyelitis epidemic which was sweeping through Melbourne in 1936. To escape the risk of infection, Andrew and Asimina decided to temporarily relocate to Adelaide where a number of family members had settled from the 1920s. Andrew was unable to accompany his family as the 'Magpie Fish' had to remain open during the crisis. In Adelaide, Alick started his first 'real' job working for the Blind Society. He was paid fifteen shillings a week to act as a companion to a blind man who travelled around the city teaching other vision- impaired people how to read Braille. When the polio scare receded, the Jackomos family returned to Melbourne and Alick resumed his previous business activities.

Asimina realised that her son needed to acquire vocational skills if he was to secure stable employment. Aware of the growing automobile industry, Asimina understood that Alick's future prospects would be enhanced if he qualified as a motor mechanic. She knew that one of the fish and chip shop's patrons was a cricketer who played alongside Lyle Nagle, a director of the Shields Motor Company, in the state team. In the depths of the Depression, Asimina was prepared to risk rejection and public embarrassment by asking this man if he would approach Nagle about job opportunities for Alick. The patron agreed and Alick at the age of sixteen was employed by Shields as an apprentice motor mechanic. He was content to take this opportunity and worked over forty hours a week, earning fifteen shillings a week in the first year and just over seventeen shillings in the second year. Like most apprenticeships, Alick learned vocational skills in the workplace and attended classes at a technical college. While he worked as a mechanic, Alick continued to reap further financial rewards by maintaining his entrepreneurial sidelines.

In the early 1930s harsh economic conditions in country areas led to a growing number of Aboriginal people moving to the city in search of work. Alick befriended many of these families who took up residence in Fitzroy and Collingwood. He met Aboriginal boys at the Exhibition Youth Club, where he boxed and wrestled, and was invited home to meet family and kin. Without understanding his motivation, Alick felt drawn to this group of people: 'I can't tell you why…I just wanted to be friends with Aboriginal people'. Perhaps

Workmates at Shields Motors, 6 Flinders Street, Melbourne, 1940: (rear l. to r.) first three unknown, Harry Marshall, Harry ---, Fred Galbraith, Bert Palin, Stan Cassidy; (kneeling l. to r.) Alick Jackomos, Frank Walsh, Harry

Alick sympathised with the plight of Aboriginal Australians. Like many dark-skinned migrants, Aboriginal people often suffered social stigmatisation and racial abuse. Or perhaps it was the fun-loving, close-knit nature of Aboriginal community life that appealed to Alick. One of his first Aboriginal friends was Willy Terrick whose mother came from the Wandin family — Coranderrk Mission people. When his family moved back to Carlton, in 1935, Alick maintained these friendships and fostered greater ties with Aboriginal friends, their family and kin. 'When we returned to Carlton, my association with Aboriginal families increased, in particular, the families of Norm and Mary Clarke, Ebenezer Lovett, George Clark, Martha Niven and her sister Jessie Terrick.' He also kept in contact with Jack Clarke, Eric and Winnie Onus.

Alick's early contact with Aboriginal people would prove to be life defining as he became part of a movement aimed at attaining civil rights for Aboriginal Australians. His initial friendships with political activists began when he attended meetings held by the

Australian Aborigines' League, established by leading Aboriginal activists including William Cooper, Doug Nicholls, Kaleb Morgan, Marge Tucker, and Eric and Bill Onus. He was introduced to the League by Ebenezer Lovett. At meetings in the members' homes, Alick came to realise the extent of discrimination for Aboriginal people in Australian society. In the late 1930s Alick often spent his Sunday afternoons on the Yarra Bank at Batman Avenue, an area of approximately one acre, reserved for public speakers who wished to air their grievances and/or promote a specific cause. It was on the Yarra Bank that Alick listened to the inspirational and moving speeches of political activists such as William Cooper and his protégé Doug Nicholls. Through the jeers and taunts hurled by onlookers and the support of others, these leaders spoke of the injustices faced by Aboriginal Australians, and outlined the necessary steps to redress inequality throughout the country. The Yarra Bank was a place where many people went for an afternoon's entertainment. They enjoyed heckling the speakers for sport and fun, similar to the Speaker's Corner in Hyde Park, London. The Yarra Bank forum also provided an opportunity for fundraising. Young Alick was often given the job of rattling the tin — an art he never forgot.

One of the campaigns for which Alick collected was support for the Cummeragunja walk-off. In 1939, Aboriginal residents of Cummeragunja, a mission on the New South Wales side of the Murray, near Echuca, walked off in protest at the harsh conditions they experienced there. This protest received wide public attention in the media and intensified the efforts of Aboriginal rights campaigners. The money collected from the Sunday meetings was used to support the Aboriginal protesters who had moved from the mission and settled in places such as Barmah, Shepparton and Mooroopna. Alick recalled with pride his job 'to shake a collection tin to raise funds for the people who had walked off Cummeragunja'. Alick's interest and involvement in Aboriginal politics was temporarily shelved by the outbreak of the Second World War, but his experiences as an infantry soldier furthered his understanding of the poor treatment of Aboriginal people by Anglo-Australians throughout the country.

Alick's politicisation was a by-product of the relationships that he had previously forged with Aboriginal people. Alick enjoyed socialising with Aboriginal youths his own age. These friendships were based on mutual respect, understanding and common interests, rather than political activism. His association with the Clarke family was particularly rewarding. Norm and Mary Clarke encouraged their sons, Frank, Henry (Banjo), Norman and Albert to take up boxing. Alick became friendly with the Clarke boys and welcomed the opportunity to train and box with them at the Exhibition Youth Club. Alick's attraction to boxing probably stemmed from the influence of his father and other family members who prided themselves on their physical prowess and sporting ability. Alick's father was locally renowned as a physically strong man and a competent fighter. Andrew's nephew, Theo Conos, remarked that he was, 'a hard-working, fighting, tough guy'. Even as a youngster Alick never shied away from a fight. On one occasion his cousin Theo was confronted by some members of a local street gang, known as the Bouverie Mob. Without hesitation Alick came to his cousin's aid and beat the aggressors into submission. Theo recalled, 'He was protecting me. He didn't care…he was very, very athletic, very strong, physically fit'. Alick was around eleven or twelve years of age at the time. His first official fight was a four-rounder at the New Fitzroy Stadium when he was about sixteen. Alick failed to recall whether he was victorious, but fondly remembered the place where he had been introduced to the boxing world.

During his teenage years Alick came to know many Aboriginal people in Melbourne. Laurie Moffatt, a Lake Tyers resident who was visiting Melbourne, invited Alick to stay in his cottage at the Lake Tyers reserve. Alick welcomed the opportunity to follow in the footsteps of his forebears and undertake an exciting travel adventure. Lake Tyers is over two hundred kilometres along the Princes Highway, in East Gippsland, near Nowa Nowa. In the late 1930s Jim McKinnon ran a transport service to Orbost. Many Aboriginal people travelling to Lake Tyers hitched a free lift with Jim McKinnon from Napier Street, Fitzroy, to the Lake Tyers turn-off or on to Orbost. Alick was a passenger on one of these journeys:

> This was my first visit to Gippsland and I travelled on Jim McKinnon's truck to Newmeralla where there was an

> Aboriginal community which included the Thomas, Murray, Ashton and Hudson families. I stayed with Winnie Onus's parents, Herb and Eva Murray, and grandparents, George and Agnes Thomas. After one week, I moved on to Lake Tyers.

At this time visitors to the station were required to carry permits. Alick failed to ask for a permit because he was aware that he would probably be denied entry if he made a formal application. He had no 'real' business at the station, just a desire to meet the residents and experience life at the reserve. So he crept undetected on to the station, located Laurie and Gena Moffatt's cottage, and avoided the reserve's manager for the duration of his visit.

> At that time, there were some 200 people living at Lake Tyers, which included the Moffatt, Harrison, O'Rourke, Wandin, Hayes and Edwards families. There were some 30 cottages in a double row around the cricket ground, these were built in the 1920s, plus a few older brick cottages close to the administrative office and church. Laurie Moffatt lived in one of the weatherboard cottages and Laurie introduced me to his neighbours, Jim and Grace O'Rourke and family. Jim took me into his home where I stayed for about a week, then Ted (Chuck) and Nora Mullett asked me to stay with them. This was the commencement of 40 years regular contact with the Lake Tyers people.

After his visit at the main station area, Alick and his new mate, Ken Hayes, rowed to Cocky Roberts Island in Lake Tyers. Here they stayed with Tom Foster, Nora Mullett's brother, and his wife Ada who were living in a mia-mia. For several nights Alick enjoyed the peace and serenity, sleeping under the stars warmed by the coals of an open fire.

At Lake Tyers Alick was exposed to the voyeuristic nature of relationships between some Anglo-Australians and Aboriginal people. Every Wednesday and Sunday was visitors' day at the station as people came to see how Aboriginal people lived. Alick outlined their itinerary. On arrival they were invited to purchase boomerangs, handmade baskets, shell work and other souvenirs. They were then escorted on a tour of the station, including the church, and finally to the hall where a concert was performed. Members of the Gum Leaf Band played tunes and afterwards Chuck Mullett and others impressed onlookers with a display of boomerang throwing. At the end of the day the visitors re-boarded the launch and returned to Fishermans Landing. The entrepreneurial skills of the residents and the public displays encouraged the residents to continue traditional customs within the reserve environment. In his later role as an advocate for Aboriginal rights, Alick used some of the same techniques to educate others about the value of Aboriginal culture.

It was perhaps not surprising that, on his return home, fourteen-year-old Alick was beaten by his father for his sudden two-week disappearance. Andrew and Asimina were then unaware of Alick's close affiliation with the Aboriginal community. Alick sensed that they would not approve of his choice of friends and companions because, like many others, they held preconceived ideas about Aboriginal people and their culture. These ideas were most likely of a negative nature. Even though he was beaten, the punishment did not deter Alick, and a year later he revisited the people. Alick was excited about returning to the place where he had made so many new friends and enjoyed a freedom from the daily grind. He travelled to Orbost where some of the Lake Tyers residents were picking maize. He spent a few days with Vera Scott and family who were camped under the Snowy River bridge. This second visit served to consolidate ties with Aboriginal people in the region. Alick continued to visit Lake Tyers, and the relationships that he forged with many people during this period continued throughout his lifetime. Alick's social network of friends in the Aboriginal community widened when in 1942 he followed the lead of many of the Lake Tyers men and enlisted in the Army.

3 Off to War

On 3 September 1939 Great Britain declared war against Germany, sparked by Germany's invasion of Poland which broke numerous treaties and promises made with Britain and France. Europe's plunge into war had far-reaching consequences as countries throughout the British dominions joined forces to fight against the German enemy. In a radio broadcast to the Australian nation, Prime Minister Robert Menzies announced that Australia would follow Britain into war. He described Australia as belonging to 'a great family of nations' that were committed to winning the war 'at all costs'. For the next six years war occupied the minds and homes of all Australians.

From the outset of the war many Australians were concerned about homeland security, and some people feared that Australia's alliance with Britain exposed the country to possible attack from its enemies. In 1940 and 1941 tensions were raised when Japan signed a Tripartite Pact with Germany and Italy (September 1940), a Neutrality Pact with the Soviet Union (April 1941) and moved troops into southern Indo-China (July 1941). Homeland security was high on the Australian Government's agenda when, on 7 December 1941, the Japanese bombed Pearl Harbor. This act of aggression signalled Japan's official entry into the war. Fear and apprehension reached fever pitch among Australians. Many were concerned that before too long their beloved country would be in the hands of the Japanese. Australia needed men and women to come to its defence and thousands of people, including an under-aged Alick, answered the call.

As with the First World War, many Australian men were lured into military service through both a sense of patriotic duty and the prospect of overseas travel and adventure. Alick was no exception. From the moment war was declared he was eager to enter the fight. He had listened to Menzies' radio announcement that Australia was at war, and while he had little interest in politics, he felt drawn to military service: 'I tried to get in before Japan came in...I wanted to be in uniform, I just wanted to join up'. From the age of sixteen Alick tried to enlist on several occasions, but was refused on the grounds that he was under age. Army recruiters in a number of centres, such as Carlton and Richmond, informed Alick that he needed parental permission to enlist. Alick felt deflated as he knew that, like many parents of under-age youths who wanted to enlist, his mother and father would never agree. They were by no means unpatriotic, but protective of their son's well-being. War was for adults, not 16-year-old boys.

As time passed and war drew closer to Australia Alick grew restless. For two years he had waited on the sidelines, but on 12 January 1942 Alick and his friend, Otway ('Otty') Atkinson, an Aboriginal man from Cummeragunja, attended a Methodist church service in Fitzroy run by Sister Maude Ellis. After the service Alick and Otty talked about the war and decided to enlist together. The next morning they walked into the Melbourne Town Hall and joined the Army — the Australian Imperial Force (AIF). Otty was old enough to enlist, but Alick was still only seventeen years and nine months old. So Alick falsified his papers: 'I put my age up to nineteen, so that I could enlist because you had to be nineteen to enlist in the AIF. And I made my birthday Christmas Day so I would *remember* it...Christmas Day 1922'. Like many young men of his day, Alick signed off on a 'white lie' on his attestation form, and his boxing and wrestling, combined with his naturally robust frame, meant that he easily passed the physical examination. Alick Jackomos, a 'single', 'motor mechanic' of '19 years 1 month' (only two-thirds of which was true) was accepted. He was assigned to the 2/1st Battalion of the AIF. On 13 January he was taken to the Caulfield Racecourse and kitted out in the uniform that he had so desired. Alick's excitement about his successful enlistment, however, wavered somewhat as he contemplated the difficult task of telling his parents.

Proudly dressed for military service, Alick returned to his parents' fish and chip shop in Carlton. Rather than walking in the front entrance, he chose to slip through the back door; he wanted to break the news gently to his mother and father, but as he walked through the backyard he ran into his mother. She was shocked by Alick's soldierly

In uniform at last, 1942

appearance and upset by her son's actions. His father appeared indifferent, perhaps secretly proud, as he was never one to avoid a fight. Trying to spare his mother from further pain and anguish, Alick told her that he had joined the Militia — he would not be sent overseas. Unfortunately for Alick, a Greek man from the Southern Command was in the shop that evening, and told Alick's parents that Alick was wearing an AIF uniform, which meant overseas service. He offered to get Alick out of the Army for a hundred pound fee — a black market deal. Whether they paid the man is unknown, but Alick was aware that they attempted to have him discharged. Their efforts were in vain and eventually they came to terms with their son's decision.

Soon after Alick's enlistment, Japanese forces launched a devastating psychological blow against Australia. Darwin was bombed on 19 February 1942 killing 243 people. On 31 May 1942 three Japanese midget submarines entered Sydney Harbour torpedoing a Sydney ferry

Alick in uniform flanked by Angelo and Maisie, with siblings in the front row: (l. to r.) Stella, Michael and Mary

With Joey Westcott, a sailor from the USS *Phoenix* at Luna Park, 1942

and causing great alarm. An invasion appeared inevitable and Northern Australia was the most likely entry point for Japanese forces. Personnel and equipment were sent to defend the North. During this period Alick was stationed in and around Melbourne, working in ordnance and motor workshops. His skills as an apprentice mechanic were being put to good use to bolster the Australian war effort. By the end of the year Alick joined thousands of service personnel who were sent further North to maintain Australia's defence lines. He was stationed in Morphett Creek, a hundred kilometres north of Tennant Creek, in the Northern Territory. For nearly a year his unit helped the Civil Construction Corps to build a bitumen road from Alice Springs to Darwin. Army life was not what Alick had expected: 'it was very boring…I mean you enlisted to go overseas and here you are in the middle of central Australia in a Field Workshop'.

While Alick felt that his military work at Morphett Creek was unsatisfying, he later valued the experience as he developed a greater understanding of the inequities which existed in Australian society between Aboriginal and non-Aboriginal people. Before the war Alick had formed relationships with Victorian Aboriginal people, attended their political meetings, visited Lake Tyers and, through sporting and social activities, had become friendly with Aboriginal people living in Fitzroy. He knew instinctively that Aboriginal people were not well off, although those he knew in Fitzroy had housing, work and access to schools. There were many other struggling Australians in the inner suburbs where he grew up, including migrant families like his own. In the Northern Territory, however, where Aboriginal people lived in missions and institutions and under strict government control, Alick became aware of the extent to which inequality and racism permeated parts of Australian society. He wrote, 'It was in the Northern Territory that I realised that Aboriginal people suffered enormous handicaps and were treated inhumanely'. Alick recalled one incident of racism which remained etched in his memory. Shortly after arriving in Morphett Creek, he had a finger tip severed and was hospitalised at nearby Banka Banka. At that time of year, the nights were freezing cold and Alick noticed that the Aboriginal patients were sleeping on the verandah. Concerned for their well-being, Alick asked the nurse why these people were sleeping outside, and was told that Aborigines

In training at Morphett Creek, Northern Territory, 1942: (back row l. to r.) Alec McDonald, Bob Cook, Mick Laughton, Harry Bray, Alec Turner; (front row l. to r.) Alec Kruger, Alick Jackomos, Jimmy Smith

were not allowed on the wards. Alick was appalled that Aboriginal people were being treated as animals.

In the North, Aboriginal people were often regarded by other Australians as second-class citizens. On a trip to Mataranka Army Camp, Alick was exposed to the racist segregation entrenched in the Territory. In his conversations with Aboriginal people who worked at the camp, he discovered that Aboriginal workers were being paid far less by the Army than non-Aboriginal personnel. He wrote, 'At Mataranka Army Camp, Aboriginal servicemen received two shillings per day and non-Aboriginal servicemen received six shillings and sixpence'. He considered the difference in pay to be unjust. Alick's memory is somewhat inaccurate here as their pay was in fact one shilling a day. This may appear even more unjust than he thought, but they were not servicemen as he suggested, but employed by the army for labouring work. Where Aboriginal men of mixed descent were fully enlisted servicemen, their pay and conditions were exactly the same as everyone else. However, Alick was right to be astonished when he discovered that Aboriginal workers in private industry in the Territory were not being paid at all, being given only rations and shelter.

In the Army and through his work in the Territory, Alick became friendly with many Aboriginal people. In his unit there were six Aboriginal enlisted men from Alice Springs whom Alick regarded as friends — Mick Laughton, Alec Turner, Alex Kruger, James Smith, Harry Bray and Alec McDonald. He also socialised with Aboriginal servicemen who were stationed in a nearby Engineers camp at Morphett Creek. These friendships continued throughout his lifetime. Alick's experiences in the Territory revealed the extent to which Aboriginal people were exploited by other Australians and led to his later decision to work in the cause of Aboriginal people across Australia.

After several long months of training in the Northern Territory, Alick was excited to be posted overseas. On 10 December 1943, after a short period of leave in Melbourne, Alick's unit was shipped to Port Moresby in New Guinea. He was anxious to enter the fighting, but he was disappointed to find that his unit was based in Port Moresby away from the front lines. For two months Alick anxiously awaited his orders to go into the field, but they were never issued. When the 2/14th Infantry Battalion needed soldiers to replace those who had been killed or injured in battle, Alick eagerly volunteered. He wanted to face the enemy as a member of the renowned 2/14th, a battalion that had won acclaim in the ferocious battle for Shaggy Ridge in the Markham–Ramu Valley, which had stopped the Japanese push to Port Moresby; but again his hopes were dashed. One month after his transfer — and without seeing much action — the 2/14th were sent back to Australia for recuperation and further training.

On their return home, Alick was once again faced with the racism that pervaded Australian society. His unit was initially stationed at Strathpine, near Brisbane. Alick had become friendly with an Aboriginal serviceman in his battalion, Archie Mullins. When Alick arrived at Strathpine he met 'Otty', with whom he had enlisted. By sheer coincidence, 'Otty' had married Archie's sister Agnes. On the weekends 'Otty' used to take Alick and Archie to Dunwich on North Stradbroke Island to visit Aboriginal families who lived there. Alick recalled: 'Ottto introduced us to the families on Dunwich which included the

Martins, Newfongs, Costellos, Mortons, Closes and Ruskas'. These visits were immensely pleasurable and created networks that lasted fifty years. Alick realised that many of these families were forced to live in segregated communities.

But they were not alone. The Red Cross Recreation Centres for US troops were also racially divided. White servicemen had a club in central Brisbane, whereas the black servicemen had a centre across the river opposite the South Brisbane Railway Station called the Doctor Washington Carver Club. Alick chose to patronise the Carver Club because it was the only place selling Coca Cola and apple pie and cream, but his decision was more likely made on the basis that his companions were Aboriginal. His dark complexion meant that he blended with the other patrons of the club. At the Carver's Club he met an Aboriginal woman named Phyllis (Lily) Savage. When Alick told Lily of his transfer further north to Cairns and Atherton, she gave him the contact details of her family who lived at the Bungalow, a few kilometres south of Cairns. This meeting led to Alick's forging even greater ties with Aboriginal and Torres Strait Islander people in Queensland.

For the next few months Alick was involved in jungle warfare and amphibious training in the Atherton Tablelands and at Trinity Beach in Cairns. He continued to make friends and socialise with Aboriginal servicemen including John Stewart Murray, a Wamba Wamba man from north-west Victoria, who was in the 2/12th. During his leave he sought out Aboriginal and Torres Strait Islanders. He recalled, 'we were camped close to a small community who had been evacuated from Thursday Island. I regularly visited this community'. He also contacted Lily Savage's family. Her uncle and aunt, Pancho and Kappa Cedar, lived in a house with Lily's brothers, sisters and grandmother Maryann Savage. Alick fondly remembered spending time and often staying weekends at the Cedars' house. He wrote: 'Granny Maryann would tell me tales of how as a young girl she would accompany her father and mother, who were missionaries, into the rivers of New Guinea to preach the gospel'. Soon after Alick's arrival Maryann died. He attended her funeral and felt privileged to have witnessed this Torres Strait Islander ceremony.

Through this socialisation Alick began to learn the Malay language. Many people from the Torres Strait and Thursday Island were evacuated to mainland Australia after the Japanese bombardment of the area. Many evacuees were descendants of Malay and Indonesian pearl divers, which meant that they spoke Malay as their first or second language. Alick was able to quickly acquire many words as the vowels were pronounced in a similar way to the Greek language, and he built on his language skills when the Americans provided him with a small book of Indonesian words.

During his service in North Queensland Alick utilised his sporting abilities and business acumen to earn extra money through boxing tournaments. The fighting skills that Alick had acquired at the Exhibition Police Boys Club and in the Fitzroy stadium in 1940 proved profitable. He fought approximately seventy matches sponsored by the Army. He recalled, 'I had a lot of fights with the Army. They had inter-unit fights…we were getting two pound a fight…four pound you could earn in a week'. This was double what he earned weekly in the Army, so he sent most of his prize money home to his mother.

Like most service personnel who were stationed in Australia, Alick received leave to return home only once or twice a year. He missed his family, and just as he had done throughout his pre-war working life, Alick sent money home to support them. While Asimina was grateful for the gesture, she secreted Alick's earnings and presented them to him when he was demobilised. Alick recalled, 'When I joined the Army I was getting six shillings and sixpence [a day], but I made five shillings of that an allotment to my Mum. But, unknowns to me, when I came out of the Army, Mum'd saved all that money for me'. These savings gave Alick a financial stake after the war — perhaps amounting to £300.

In June 1945 Alick's unit returned to active service much to his delight. They landed in Morotai in Indonesia before arriving as part of the invasion force at Balikpapan on the east coast of Borneo in July 1945. Finally Alick was on the front lines. He was fighting in a multinational force, with the Americans, British, Dutch and Indonesians, against a tough and determined Japanese enemy. Alick's uncle, Theo Augustes (RAAF), was also a member of the invasion force. Further north, at Tarakan, his cousin Alec Pallaras (AIF) was serving with

Scenes of devastation, Balikpapan, Borneo, 1945

the Ninth Division. The reality of war soon seared his mind. On his arrival in Balikpapan, Alick was shocked by the scenes of horror and despair before him and, like many other servicemen, said little about it for the remainder of his life. However, in his 'Memoirs' written around fifty years later, he briefly recalled:

> Like all other countries that had been occupied many people died at the hands of the Japanese. The people of Balikpapan had also suffered with malnutrition, Beri Beri and other illnesses. The Japanese had bayoneted many of the Indonesian men in the hamstring...[that] permanently handicapped them while trying to walk and work. Even after 50 years I remember vividly the tragic events.

Danger surrounded Alick as he patrolled and fought in the jungles and streets of Borneo, but he avoided serious injury and, aside from contracting malaria, dengue fever and a variety of tropical skin diseases, he remained relatively unscathed. On one occasion, however, Alick nearly became a casualty of war:

Alick and his uncle, Theo Augustes, had a brief meeting at Balikpapan.

> We was on patrol at Balikpapan, and we were walkin' in single file, there was a bomb crater in this path, so we had to walk to the left, walk around it...but the Japs'd put a mine in this path...I stood on it and realised that I'd stepped on this mine. But what happened was, there'd been heavy rains, the mud'd seeped under the cap of the mine...And it'd hardened the mine. So when I stood on the mine it didn't go off! That's the closest I came to death.

As some of Alick's colleagues and mates suffered injury and death, Alick knew that he was indeed fortunate: 'I'm one of the very lucky ones, no injuries, no bullet wounds...a lot of my young mates, [aged] nineteen and twenty, died you know'.

Less than a month after Alick was sent to Balikpapan, the war was effectively over. On 6 August 1945 America dropped an atomic bomb named 'Little Boy' on the Japanese city of Hiroshima. Three days later another bomb annihilated the town of Nagasaki. It is estimated that nearly a quarter of a million people were killed by these deadly attacks. On 14 August 1945 Japan agreed to an unconditional surrender.

The war was over; yet the Japanese in the Balikpapan region took some time to realise and acknowledge this, and dangerous military clashes continued for days. Alick felt a sense of relief after the bombing of Hiroshima, however:

> [I] felt positive, because we were told that we were eventually going to Japan, that was our next stepping-stone, and we were well aware that...a million or so allied troops would have died in the landing. I feel sad that people died [from the Bomb], and the after-effects, but if they hadn't died we'd have died landing there.

In the 1950s he was again in uniform in the Citizen Military Forces, although in later life Alick became an opponent of all bombing and wars. Yet he was never against the commemoration of war and the public remembrance of the sacrifices of service personnel. He would march each year on Anzac Day with the 2/14th and for weeks before, brave April weather selling badges to raise money for the Returned Services League. But he came to consider 'all wars [to be]...a waste of life!'

Alick had to decide his future now the war had ended. Would he return to Melbourne, his family and his motor mechanic apprenticeship, or continue to taste wider adventure? After Japan's official surrender, Alick and his brother Angelo volunteered for the British Occupation Force in Japan, but Alick contracted a tropical infection in his left foot, requiring a stay in hospital, and the occupation force sailed without him. Alick was transferred from Balikpapan back to Morotai. Disappointed by his failure to reach Japan, Alick decided to 'go home and get discharged'. He later regretted this decision, musing: 'I really liked the army'. This regret was natural as Alick had tasted a life of action, travel and camaraderie in the army. He had narrowly escaped death from a land mine, and through the 'lottery' of his service assignments, had been spared war's worst horrors.

Alick had joined up in January 1942 as a pudgy-faced youth of seventeen with tousled black hair, but returned home tanned, slim and mature in mid- 1946. His Army records stated he was almost 24, but he was actually 22. He was discharged at Bandiana in July 1946 after 1652 days of war service, and headed for the family home in

The joy of homecoming is on all faces, especially Alick's, fourth from the left on the rails with right hand raised, early 1946.

Elgin Street, Carlton. The smell of fish and chips guided his final steps. Although he had seen his family several times during the war years, he had missed them. But he realised he had matured and grown apart from home, like every other young man who faced war and death, and experienced the company of men. As he recalled, 'I'd grown up. Goin' to the war, you grow up, you become a man, you become very independent, even to the point of doing your own washing and cooking meals in your dixie'. This war left a terrible beauty in the mind and made many young men feel strangely alive. Alick remarked fifty years later: 'you'd travelled the world, you'd seen a lot of people, and you were an adult…you had girlfriends. I got a taste of travelling around the world, although it was only the Pacific'.

Many men with or without ties were made restless by war. Some never settled. Alick relinquished his apprenticeship and took a series of short-term jobs as, 'I was unsettled … and in those days after the War you could walk out of one job and go to another the next morning, there was a shortage of labour'. The work routine in industrial Melbourne irked an adventurous young man. 'I worked a little at

Commonwealth Industrial Gases, but that was just repetition work on a lathe, drilling oxy-welding tips. I worked in Port Melbourne, at Johnsons that made fumigation gases. I was very restless'. Within nine months of his discharge, Alick decided to journey back to the East Indies — Indonesia and Java in particular — where intense experiences of war and cultural difference had ignited his imagination. He had heard that managers were needed in the oil industry and he spoke Indonesian. With the name of a contact at the Shell Company in his wallet, he headed for Sydney by train in March 1947, with hopes of a job in the petroleum industry in Java. His parents resigned themselves to a further separation from their first-born.

4 Tent Wrestler

The 'Spirit of Progress' was a slow night train to Sydney with a change of rail gauge at Albury. It was a trip conducive to long conversations and big decisions. Alick 'sat up' on the 'Spirit' to mingle with people and save money. By chance he met Harry Johns on the train: a meeting that was to change his destiny.

Alick knew Harry Johns, as Johns lived at 38 Kerr Street, Fitzroy, not far from Alick's friends, Aunty Mary and Uncle Norman Clarke at number 76. Their sons, Bertie and Henry ('Banjo') had boxed with Alick at the Exhibition Boys' Club. Johns was a boxing tent operator and the boys including Alick had sparred in his backyard ring, and boxed in 'a couple of little tent shows' run by him. Johns was accompanied on the train by Clarence Reeves, an African-American boxer who toured the stadiums as the 'Alabama Kid', under Johns' management before the outbreak of war. Alick only knew the 'Alabama Kid' by his reputation as a formidable lightweight. Reeves had attempted to return to America in June 1940, but his ship, the *Niagara*, was torpedoed off the coast of New Zealand. Reeves survived and returned to Australia where he fought in tents and stadiums for the duration of the war with a special exemption under the Immigration Act. Johns and Clarence Reeves were at this moment bound for the Kempsey Show on the north coast of New South Wales.

By the time Alick alighted at Central Station in Sydney his plans about a job in petroleum in Asia were shifting. He had boxed in the army with lucrative results, why not again? He spent the day with the 'Alabama Kid' in Lawson Street, Redfern. They met Aboriginal people including the dashing Ron Richards, who was a household name, being a former Australian middle- and heavyweight champion and also Empire middleweight champion. By day's end, Alick was star-struck and aboard another train with Johns and the 'Kid', bound for the Kempsey Show and the life of a tent boxer. The boxing tent experience proved to be an intense and exotic one, much like the Army, Asia and Fitzroy all rolled into one. The northern rivers tour with Harry Johns' troupe began a period that Alick once termed 'the best time of my life'.

Harry Johns' 'recruits' lived rough, army-style: fighting by day, working hard erecting and dismantling the tent after each show, before driving to the coming field of 'battle'. They slept in the back of the truck, as it rumbled to the next show, or on the floor of the tent on a bed of sawdust and tarpaulin. They ate stews together out of a camp pot, prepared by a roughhouse cook. They teased, bustled and wrestled each other in boyish fun. They were men together, bound by being part of the troupe, facing local opponents each time they mounted the line-up board, a two-metre wooden bridge outside the tent, ready to take on all comers. Johns' troupe had a boxing uniform called 'combinations' which deepened their camaraderie: long tights with briefs over them and a singlet with the words 'Harry Johns

Alick on Harry Johns' line-up board at the Bombala Show, 1949: (l. to r.). Harry Johns spruiking, Monty Faye his tent boss, Danny Marks of Dimboola, Alick Jackomos, and three unidentified Aboriginal youths

Troupe' across the chest. Dirt was no stranger to these men. Alick recalled of the 'combinations' that

> they stunk, you stunk, everything stunk. You never washed anything. Sometimes when you travelled with boxing troupes there mightn't be any hot water till the next town three or four days later and so you had to sweat. It was a way of life in those days having that odour with you.

Alick entered an exciting world centred on country agricultural showgrounds. Exhibits of farm machinery and produce, together with animal stalls, were cheek by jowl with a sideshow alley where exotic and itinerant show people ('showies') offered entertainments. Sideshow Alley contained thrilling rides, trick riders, knife throwers, contortionists, animal trainers, flea circuses, hypnotists, magicians, sword swallowers, bubble dancers and girls 'encased' in ice. There were Wild West shows, 'leg' shows and 'freak' shows featuring giants, fat ladies, leopard men, 'pin-headed Chinamen', and half-man/half-woman shows. The world's 'tiniest', or 'biggest' horses or dogs were on display. The acts were as endless as human imagination. Alick also rubbed shoulders with people from distant places: Tahitian fire dancers, Indian Swamis, African Pygmies, Chinese acrobats and Native Americans. All were new to him and others in mid-twentieth century Australia, where 90 per cent of the population were Anglo-Australian. 'Showies' without intriguing exotic personas invented them. Danny Marks of Dimboola, an Aboriginal boxer who occasionally wrestled as well, fought as 'Johnny Wilson, a Maori from New Zealand', to make him sound more exotic. When the show opened, the dusty showgrounds bustled and were filled with noise, as cattle bellowed, salesmen called their wares, and spruikers touted for custom. It was the most exotic place in Australia, and Alick was there, revelling in the atmosphere.

Young men of all types flocked to the boxing tents to test their manhood against members of the troupe and earn a day's wages in little more than five minutes. Tent owners employed Aboriginal boxers to ensure dramatic black–white contests in an Australian countryside still imprisoned by racial stereotypes and rivalries. About a quarter of

Alick squatting on the right, with showmen in north Queensland, c. 1947

the troupe were Aboriginal men. Local Aborigines also rolled up to pit themselves against whites on equal terms in the ring, gain pride, some cash and perhaps join the troupe. The boxing tents provided an escape from the humdrum of local life and sometimes a route to the ranks of professional boxing. Ron Richards entered professional boxing through the boxing tents and fought his way to money, fame and an Empire title. Others followed Richards, including Jack Hassen, whom Alick met that touring season.

For Alick, these involvements with Aboriginal people proved to be indelible, forming friendships and memories that lasted a lifetime. When he joined the troupe at Kempsey, he soon met fellow boxers, Percy and George Ritchie, who fought under the name 'Sands'. They were two of six Ritchie brothers, from Burnt Bridge Aboriginal Reserve, who all held state or Australian boxing titles. Alick met their brother Dave, a revered Australian titleholder, who shortly afterwards won the British Empire middleweight title, but whose world title claims were cut short by his death in a road accident in 1952.

Alick went home with these boxers, met their families and experienced their sparse, often deprived, living conditions. He met many other Aboriginal people through the boxing tents and socialised with them, extending his Aboriginal network. He also saw racism at first hand. After the Kempsey Show, Alick attended a picture theatre with Percy, who fought as Ritchie Sands. He recalled: 'to my surprise, Aboriginals had to sit in the front rows…during my tour of northern NSW and Queensland, I was to see many similar situations, where Aboriginals could not enter hotels, were refused service in cafés. In Queensland showgrounds separate toilets were [provided] for Aboriginals'.

The tent boss, Harry Johns, was a hard-nosed penny pincher who even recorded the cost of ice creams consumed by his own children. Most boxers had no great affection for him as he paid less, and was harder on his men than other boxing tent operators. He would pick up swaggies or Aboriginal youths on the road and without any training put them in his troupe. However, he earned grudging respect for his clever business tactics and for operating a skilful tent show, which survived for over thirty years. Johns was a fierce individualist, who was disliked by many showmen, as he refused to join the Showmen's Guild. He was eventually forced to operate at shows not controlled by the Guild until the Guild finally froze him out of most showgrounds, forcing him to sell out in the 1960s. One of his greatest supporters was Johnny Harris, who boxed with Johns for twenty-five years from around 1940, before becoming his tent manager. Harris, whom Alick met in 1947, had a similar sense of humour to Alick, and despite infrequent contact, they remained good mates all their lives. Alick tolerated Harry Johns when many did not, and worked for him on and off over many years.

Johns trusted Alick with his precious and luxurious Packard car, quite a privilege for one of his boxers. When on tour, Johns always stayed in a local hotel with his wife Stella, away from the showgrounds. Alick dropped them there and minded the car overnight, before picking Johns up next morning. Alick slept in its roomy, padded back seat, which was more comfortable than a camp stretcher in the boxing tent. Johns silently condoned this as Alick's presence

With his brother Michael on the showgrounds, c. 1948

prevented the car's theft or damage, especially as he often left his leather bag initialed with 'HJ' in the boot, full of the day's takings in coins. Alick occasionally took the Packard for a spin: 'it came in very handy, a young kid driving around in a Packard. I got all the friends, girlfriends and boyfriends. After the show we'd go back to the mission with some of the Aboriginal men you'd fought that day'. Once when driving back to Purfleet Mission outside Taree, he drove the Packard slowly towards a mission house. Suddenly it erupted with activity, as Aboriginal people dived out of doors and windows, fearing a police raid on their card party.

Alick made a further momentous career change during his 1947 northern rivers tour with Johns' outfit. Alick had developed strong limbs and a powerful frame and chest, making him a middleweight. However, his modest height of 5 feet five inches (165 cms) left him vulnerable in the boxing ring. He recalled that he took 'regular hidings from much taller lads'. At the Grafton Show 'Headlock' Bailey issued a wrestling challenge. Harry Johns did not have a wrestler in his troupe, which was typical, as wrestling required special skills. Indeed, there were dangers of broken limbs and other injuries in wrestling contests between untrained contestants, so tent bosses usually steered clear of such matches. Both Johns and Alick were crazy enough to accept Bailey's challenge. Alick had wrestled a little as a teenager at the Exhibition Boys' Club, so he felt he was not a complete novice. He wrestled Bailey on six occasions at the Grafton Show before packed houses and for the next twenty years, with few exceptions, he stuck to wrestling.

Alick was proud to be a wrestler as it was a traditional Greek sport. His Uncle Jack and grandfather Alexios had both wrestled. Besides, wrestling at a basic level required more skills comparatively than boxing. Alick considered that wrestlers were often a better type of person: 'most wrestlers that I ever wrestled in the boxing troupe were people who were tradesmen, who had skills'. Wrestling was also less violent, which suited Alick who lacked natural aggression. Bernice McLure, a fellow Showie, recalled that Alick once caused a man to bleed and was 'quite despondent about it, saying "I did not aim to do

Alick prepares for a tent wrestle, as his second Johnny Harris, looks on, at the Adelaide Show, early 1950s.

that"'. The man was drunk and had provoked Alick. Whereas boxing aimed at rendering an opponent ineffective to the point of unconsciousness, wrestling was about subduing an opponent by scientific holds and strength. It is physically very challenging. It is also more co-operative than boxing, as wrestlers have to work with each other to a degree for it to be successful as a sport and spectacle. And, unlike boxing, which involved aggressive blows, wrestling allowed much greater scope for humour: one of Alick's fortes.

In May 1947 the 'Alabama Kid' and Alick, both dissatisfied with pay and conditions, hatched a plot to leave Johns and join the rival Sharman troupe. 'Alabama' delayed his departure after Harry Johns threatened to make trouble for him with the Immigration Department, but Alick immediately joined Sharman at the Gympie Show — as a wrestler. From Gympie, Sharman's troupe headed for the Cairns Show on the Queensland show train, comprised of flat-top rail wagons on to which the showmen drove their trucks, alighting at each significant town. A 1500-km train journey with Showies was an intense experience for Alick. He spent long hours yarning as the train travelled north, enjoying the camaraderie and absorbing Showie values. These people were fierce competitors for the audience's coin, but thick as thieves when hardship was experienced or trouble with outsiders arose. Alick recalled: 'whether you was black or white or you was a little pygmy from Africa or a little Chinese, you were all one family on the showgrounds'. Indeed, he once confided to me in some awe: 'they're closer than Aboriginal people'.

Alick soon became a consummate wrestler. His mentor was the 'Russian Strongman', John Sampson, a 110-kg Estonian, who worked for Sharman. 'I wrestled him a lot and he taught me all I knew. By the time I'd finished with John or he had finished with me, I knew all the holds good enough to get me in the stadium. When I first wrestled with Sharman I was just very crude'. The two men wrestled the preliminary match for each boxing tent performance or 'house'. If the tent was slow to fill, they killed time by demonstrating wrestling holds, further consolidating Alick's skills. Alick wrote in his 'Memoirs':

> By September 1947 I had had hundreds of bouts with John Sampson…John weighed 15 stone [110 kg] but he was a

great wrestler and instructor. He was always the bad man and the crown hated him. I could never physically beat him but the conditions of the match were that if John could not beat me with a pin fall or submission I took the decision. I always won and the crowd loved it.

In his dotage Sampson was cared for by the daughter of Roy Bell, a former employer. This became further proof to Alick of the virtue of show people.

Alick, now twenty-three, had developed a powerful build fit for a wrestler. He was also handsome and proud of his physical presence. He purchased his own gown with his name on it, and with a boomerang and the word 'Australia' on the back. He was always proud of his country. His physical awareness was encouraged by the masculine pursuit of wrestling, and competition each day in the tents, as well as the antics up on the line-up board in front of and above the tent. Sharman acknowledged the strength and physique of his boxers or their challengers in his spruiking to draw a crowd, and most young women in the audience did not waste a chance — rare in the 1950s — to see strange men stripped to the waist or in their Bond's singlets. Gail Magdziarz (née Allan), although only a girl in the 1950s, waxed lyrical about the film star looks of Tony Lonos, another wrestler, and thought that Alick was 'not bad either'. Fifty years later she remarked to me, 'Alick's chest was deep, did you notice how big his chest was, like a swimmer's, more of a wrestling physique'.

Alick perfected his wrestling skills with Clive Coram, a boilermaker and returned serviceman from Fitzroy and Camperdown who took up with Johns and then Sharman after the war, while working in transport and demolition. Clive was four years older than Alick and they became great mates after a thousand or more wrestles over several decades. They began wrestling together in Sharman's tent in 1948 and continued into the late 1960s in Sharman's and other troupes. They could have wrestled blindfolded or in their sleep after so many encounters. Clive Coram remembered that Alick was a good wrestler who wrestled fair, fast and strong, which was to Clive's liking: 'it gave you a good work out'. They trained and also practised holds. Clive recalled that one commentator claimed he had never seen a bout with so many different holds applied. 'Young Jimmy' Sharman, Alick's employer now ninety-one, remembered that some visiting American wrestlers were so impressed with their routine that they returned the next day to be coached by Alick. 'Young Jimmy' added that Alick was 'a bit of a psychologist', as he knew how to liven up a crowd. Clive, his co-wrestler, agreed that Alick could get the crowd going. Alick would argue with the audience while he applied a hold on Clive. They might think it was unfair or that Clive had reached the edge of the mat and should be released, but Alick would dispute this to get them excited. The two would also plan to throw one or other near the crowd, or next to some young women, to create a bit more excitement.

Tent boxing and wrestling followed a well-worn formula, which made them more performance than sport. The aim was to draw and please a paying crowd — in the way of country fairs since the oldest at St Bartholomew, which began almost nine hundred years ago in 1123. The boxing tent, like all sideshows, had a 'line-up board' in front of the tent, on which the performers displayed themselves to attract the passing crowd. The tent boss spruiked his patter to the crowd, which stood below on the 'pitch'. Drawings of St Bartholomew's Fair show this to be an ancient technique. The spruiking, which was to attract customers from among the 'mugs' or audience, was in Australia called 'dragging'. Drums, megaphones and later loudspeakers, and even singing, were used to gain attention. Often a paid employee, planted in the crowd, acted as a 'ram', by being the first one to step up and pay, thereby leading other customers or 'sheep' into the tent. Heightened interest could also be created by a paid 'gee' planted in the audience. The 'gee' created added drama to convince onlookers to pay money and step inside. The use of 'gees' was frequent and a trade secret. 'Young Jimmy' Sharman recently refused to acknowledge the existence of 'gees' even at the age of ninety-one, thirty years after the tents have closed.

The spruiking, which introduced the performers, was imaginative and often very funny. When Alick and Johnny Harris met in 1995 they broke into a spontaneous patter. It was rapid fire and funny. Alick, playing the tent boss, sparked it off:

AJ 'You've had a fight or two have you son?'
JH 'Oh I might have done'!
AJ 'You'd better get up on the board if you have done a bit of fighting. How about this fellow down the end? Up here Johnny what do you think of this bloke? Have a go at him. Look I'll give you 2 quid for two rounds'.
JH 'No I want £3 Mr Sharman'.
AJ 'Well if you want £3 up go the pounds up go the rounds. The further you come up the track form, the better fighter you get. You know what you get if you fight him and he beats you?'
JH 'Ah, I don't want nothin' Mr Sharman'.
AJ 'Don't worry about that, you'll get nothin' but a lot of experience'.

The tent owners valued Alick's skills as a 'gee' as well as a wrestler. He used his language skills, his ethnicity, his love of people and his confident humour to great effect. The broad scenarios of the drama may have been premeditated, but the script was spontaneous, and showed Alick's quickness of wit and intelligence. One of his favourite routines, which he dreamed up himself, was to pose as the Greek cook from the local Greek café. By the 1940s most country towns, especially in Queensland, had a Greek café. Alick visited these a few days before show time, to say 'good day mate' to a fellow countryman, and offer to help out, perhaps serving on tables. He received conversation and good food in return. When the show opened a few days later, Alick appeared on the 'pitch' as the local Greek cook, wearing a suit or perhaps even an apron, and challenged the out-of-town troupe wrestler. This created a drama of opposites: local against stranger, migrant against Anglo (the snowy-haired Estonian, John Sampson, could pass as an Anglo-Australian).

Before the 1947 Mackay Show, Alick did this 'Greek-cook' routine, being farewelled afterwards by the proprietor: 'the boss or his daughter or his wife came down with a couple of the staff to the railway station and brought boxes of sandwiches, cakes, fruit and drinks as a matter of good will'. The owner of the Neo Café at Shepparton was always in on the act, and Sharman would even advertise in the press that the local Greek cook was taking time off to challenge his wrestler. One headline stated: 'Greek Wrestling Cham. Will Worry Sharman'. The article continued:

> The wrestling ability of spectacular Greek Alex Jacomos has aroused a great deal of interest among his countrymen. Rated by his many Greek admirers to be the best wrestler in his weight and inches in Australia, Jacomos has an undefeated record in this State. The wily grappler is helping his countrymen out in one of the town's Greek cafes during the city [show] week. He intends working an early shift tomorrow so as to clash with Sharman's wrestlers at the show.

The truth was bent as much as the spelling of Alick's name, all to create excitement. At other shows Alick might be on the line-up board as part of the troupe, billed as the 'Greek champion'.

Alick mastered impromptu performances, especially featuring ethnic identities and prevailing antipathies. While a 'gee' in Sandy Moore's tent at the Ipswich Show, Moore 'disqualified him', and refused to pay Alick £2 for going the distance with his wrestler.

> When I came outside the tent in my broken English I said: 'I'm gonna get the police Mr Sandy Moore. I'm gonna get the police'. I went and dragged a policeman from the other side of the show ground and cried out: 'Mr Police Mana, Mr Police Mana, this man taka my money'.

People rushed to the commotion and when the crowd arrived back at the tent with Alick, he pointed at Moore, claiming, 'this man up there he taka my money'. Moore gave his version of the events, ending: 'He's rough and he's dirty, the Greek, and I don't want him near the tent. I'm disqualifying him. You people don't want him near the tent do you?' But the crowd yelled back 'yes we do, yes we do!' So Moore relented, invited the policeman and Alick up on the board, and arranged another match. The officer held the stake and the crowd spilled inside and paid again to see the return match.

Alick remembered such performances with zest. He was also acknowledged by Showies as one who could tell a good tale. Bernice McLure recalled that Alick was so good that she and other nearby stallholders stopped their activities to watch his 'antics, because honestly it was hilarious'. She recalled an impromptu incident, when Alick knew his fellow troupe wrestler wore only the top of a sock, and he knew why this was so. Alick, acting as a 'gee' in the audience, climbed up the ladder to accept the challenge, and then suddenly jumped up and down, complaining, 'I'm not going to wrestle with you with those big heavy kicking boots on. Take them off'. After a period of banter and 'argument', the troupe wrestler finally said: 'I can't'. Alick then pressed, 'why not?' As McLure recalled, 'Alick pursued it and pursued it and pursued it, and the crowd was really incited the way he went on and everyone from the stalls ran to the tent'. More paying customers were drawn into the tent hoping for a fiery match. Finally the troupe boxer relented and took off his boots to expose only the top of a sock. Alick then applied further pressure, asking why the sock was in such a state. The tent wrestler finally confessed — to the mirth of all — that a dog had eaten the rest. A paying audience was gathered in and another show began.

Alick Jackomos with Australian lightweight champion, Frankie Flannery, at Paulsen's tent in Tasmania, early 1950s

Occasionally the antics backfired. In Tasmania, where Alick often toured at New Year with Harry Paulsen's troupe, he revved up the crowd using regional antipathies. 'I'd always wrestle a local bloke in the crowd. So I was the man from the mainland, the dirty Greek or the dirty mainlander. They hated mainlanders over there you know.' Alick responded to their taunts by calling them 'dirty rotten Tasmanians' and sometimes between rounds spat water from his bottle over the audience in the tent. The antagonism could be intense, and once a woman dragged a nail file down Alick's back, causing a nasty wound. Usually just bottle tops and the like were thrown at him. During one bout with 'Killer' Cole, a local arch rival and a 'gee', they purposely tumbled out of the ring into the crowd (for Paulsen actually had a proper ring, not a mat on sawdust). When they jumped back through the ropes to continue, some of the excited crowd joined them and the ring collapsed, bringing the match to an end. Alick was the consummate performer, for

> the more they hated you the better the show went. Anything the local boy did, even if he couldn't wrestle, you made him look good. You get him on the ground and put a hold on him but then you roll over and he's got you! Then you stick your elbow out and he'd grab it. You had to make them look good, while at the same time you were arguing with the crowd.

Wrestling unknown men could be dangerous. 'Takes' occasionally turned up, men who had no thought of working in with the troupe member and who were out to make a name. Sometimes they might be a bit drunk, as the boxing tent was always near the beer tent. 'Takes' usually sought to participate in boxing matches, but 'takes' in wrestling were more dangerous as non-cooperation could more easily lead to injuries. Alick recalled of 'takes':

> you're trying to put on a bit of a show with him, but at the same time he's trying to break your neck or bend your arm. In wrestling you make a lead, you give him your arm thinking that he'll put on a hold and roll you, but if he leans the wrong way or bends your arm the wrong way and you roll, you'll break your arm. So wrestling with 'takes' [is dangerous]. Sometimes you had to pin them immediately.

The tent boss would try to protect his wrestlers, who were scarcer and thus more valuable to him than a boxer, and whose injuries were more likely to be broken bones and take longer to mend. The tent boss might interrupt such a challenger, saying: 'look there's two people we don't want in the tents. We don't want drunks and we don't want idiots, now you have had too much'. But the boss would add, positively, so as not to offend, 'now you sober up and come back. You're not going to come here and get hurt. We've got to look after your health'.

Alick was always prepared to do extra work on the showgrounds. He washed shirts for other showmen, for 'two shillings a shirt, no ironing'. He worked as a clown or 'on someone's knock-em-down joint before Sharman had lined up at say 1 o'clock, for a couple of hours to give them a break'. He acted as spruiker for Captain Jansen's show, which exhibited snakes and crocodiles. Alick called out: 'we've got snakes and we've got crocodiles from the jungle infested waters of Cummeraaaah — gunjaaah. Watch Captain Jansen step into the pool of death of swishing and turning crocodiles knowing that one false move may mean the loss of life or limb!' Inside, Jansen handled snakes, showed a four-metre stuffed crocodile and waded in a one-metre square pool with a number of 30-cm crocodiles, which he held up to the crowd. It was still scary stuff for his hands were exposed, and so exaggerations instead of lies were being told. Alick had to be careful with such work, for he was employed to be a 'gee' for Sharman's troupe. 'You had to move quick because you always had to be in Sharman's pitch on time. If you ever upset Jim you were finished. But my timing was good because never, never ever once, did I miss being outside Jimmy Sharman's tent'.

Alick also worked as a 'gee' in a 'girlie' show run by Tommy and Shirley Castle, which among song and dance acts included one called 'Kiss the Girl'. Men could earn ten shillings if they could pin a young girl in one minute and plant a kiss on her rosy red lips. Alick of course would have had little trouble achieving that feat but, as a 'gee', he was paid 20 shillings to fail to do it. As he recalled: 'you've practically got her on the ground and just as you are going to kiss her she throws you off, and you come back and try and pin her again'.

Of course the girls sometimes did not face a 'gee;' but a real situation with a customer trying to win the 10-shilling note. Betty Clements (née Atkinson) and her sister Lucy, who lived at Wamba Wamba Aboriginal camp, outside Swan Hill, did showground work for a few months in their mid teens. Betty played the role in 'kiss the girl'. She was tiny, only 152 cm tall, and slim, but she was lithe and quick and when oiled up could evade most big men. Alick met the sisters at the Bendigo Show in 1949 and, as Betty said, became their protector, to make sure they were safe on the showgrounds and in town. Alick was paid to protect her during this act. As she recently recalled:

> Alick used to be there to watch me. So if there was any big man that came in that looked like he was getting a little bit rougher than he should have been, well that's where Alick would step in and he would say: 'That's enough'. So, that would stop.

But Alick did not have to rescue Betty much at all and mostly 'he'd stand back and he'd have his laugh! Well, he'd laugh and laugh that much'.

Alick extended his protection to after hours. As Betty recalled:

> he'd always make sure that he'd take us out, instead of us being stuck around after each show…he'd make sure that he escorted us to a dance, him and the remainin' troupe members who didn't have girlfriends. And if there was a picture-show on he'd take us. So we was never ever alone and afraid, you know in strange towns with him there… Course he got the word around to all the troupes, that he was our carer, he was our protector. Anything funny and they'd have to answer to him. He *was* a big man, you know, he was big-built. And I never ever went to see him wrestlin' in the cities, but I always seen it on the newsreel, you know? And I'd say: 'I know him!'…You could see him on the big screen so his face was well known around Melbourne and Sydney as a wrestler.

Alick encountered many fascinating characters during his experiences in Sideshow Alley during 1947–48. His relations with them were refreshed during casual wrestling in the tents at the big city shows most years until the 1960s. These personalities — Old Jimmy Sharman, Rud Kee, Tiger Williams, Chief Little Wolf and 'Joe Blow', to name a few — captured Alick's imagination and filled his memories for the rest of his life. We cannot understand Alick, this 'man of all tribes', if we fail to see his fascination with these characters. His vivid memories and admiration for them sheds light on his own values and moral universe. For above all else Alick valued honesty, hard work and business acumen, physical skills and prowess, humour and comradeship, a sense of community, and egalitarianism.

Jimmy Sharman, 'Old Jimmy', loomed large in the memories of many people besides Alick. He was Australia's premier boxing showman whose troupe lasted sixty years from 1911. Sharman, a consummate businessman and spruiker, reputably ran the cleanest show and boxers and Showies, including Alick, considered him a 'straight shooter'. Sharman's 'uniform' was a black leather jacket and felt hat, and despite being the wealthiest of all the showmen, he wore glasses for years with frames patched with sticky tape. This conjunction of wealth and frugality amused Alick. During the early 1950s Alick often drove with 'Old Jimmy' and his secretary Flo Carroll from their Melbourne base, the Golden Fleece Hotel in Russell Street, to Saturday night country shows. Alick recalled friendly chit-chat along the way, being shouted meals, and that 'he treated you as an equal on the show and you knew where you stood with Jimmy'. But Alick still addressed him mostly as 'Mr Sharman', occasionally 'Jim' in private, but never by his nickname 'Squizzy'. 'Old Jimmy' Sharman stopped touring in 1955, handing the business entirely to his son, 'Young Jimmy', who had been his tent boss from the early 1940s.

'Old' and 'Young Jimmy' Sharman's right-hand man was Rud Kee, whose real name was Cheong Lee. Rud Kee emigrated from China as a child around 1900. He gravitated to Sharman's boxing tent at Forbes in 1916 where he fought 'Taggie' Young, reputedly for the 'Chinese Boxing Championship'. Their popular whirlwind encounter was followed by rematches. Kee, a compact 65 kg and only 158 cm tall, joined Sharman's troupe. He once told the *Daily Telegraph* in 1976 with customary exaggeration, that

> most days I fought more blokes than I had breakfasts. Four men before lunch was a quiet day. Some of them jokers would be over 16 stone and well over six foot. I used to knock out three or four blokes a day for years. All I ever lost was a few teeth and the shape of my nose.

Rud Kee in later life as Sharman's right-hand man

However, he met his match at Townsville in 1929 when 'Nugget' Frater, a tough dairy farmer, and a much heavier and larger man, broke Kee's collar bone with one punch in the third round. Kee became Sharman's ticket-seller and book-keeper for the next thirty years, with a reputation for never letting anyone in free. Alick admired Kee's loyalty to the Sharmans, his business acumen and his ideas: Rud 'was a lovely bloke, he was a socialist you know. And I was socialist inclined, so we had a lot of talks about China and the socialist movement'. Alick astutely knew that Kee was a focus of power in Sharman's operation, and 'if he didn't like you it made it very awkward'.

Alick formed many friendships with the boxers but talked most about Irwin ('Tiger') Williams, Sharman's drawcard in the 1940s. Williams was born at Woodenbong Aboriginal Mission in the 1920s. He had a ruggedly handsome face, was known as the 'Black Bomber', and also nicknamed the 'Black Clark Gable', after he grew a pencil moustache. He was a sparring partner for top middle- and heavyweights and boxed in the Stadium himself, although an ankle

Alick at the Brisbane Show in the 1950s flanked by Irwin 'Tiger' Williams (the 'Black Bomber') and boxing trainer Archie Bradley (formerly the 'Gympie Tiger'); Bradley brought his fighters to challenge the tent men.

weakness prevented him fighting bouts longer than five rounds. The 'Bomber' had massive upper-body strength and great boxing skills, especially as a counter-puncher. At one Royal Sydney Show he fought 39 bouts over ten days, being undefeated. The 'Bomber' was a gentle person, with a beautiful voice, with which he attracted crowds to the boxing tent from the line-up board. His signature tune was 'Ned Kelly'. The 'Bomber' married Alick's lifelong Aboriginal friend, Iris Lovett from Lake Condah. Alick recalled that he was 'a mild and gentle fellow...outside of the boxing ring. We spent many, many years with the "Bomber", in Sharman's and Paulsen's [tents] and socialising as well'. When his marriage to Iris and his career ended, Williams worked as a labourer before his retirement and death in 1996.

Perhaps his most colourful remembered friend was 'Chief Little Wolf' Tenario, a Navajo Native American from Colorado, who worked on the showgrounds after the war. Alick had carried his bag into the Melbourne Stadium in the late 1930s to gain undetected stagedoor access for his peanut-selling ventures. 'Chief Little Wolf' became a household name by the 1940s. Despite playing the 'bad guy', he stopped traffic in down-town Melbourne. As Alick recalled, 'he was the most lovable bad man of all. *He* was *so* bad that he used to go to the Children's Hospital to see all the sick kids with all his regalia on'. He was a huge man, not tall at only 175 cm, but massive in the chest, being 110 kg. When showman Jack Allan managed the Chief on the showgrounds he was a smash hit. People came just to see him; hear him talk of Navajo culture; and to watch him apply his famous signature hold, the 'Indian Death Lock', with which he invariably won his Stadium bouts. Alick sometimes helped the Chief demonstrate holds. He always cherished photographs given him by the Chief, especially one autographed 'to my pal Alick, the best to you Chief Little Wolf Shepparton 1950'. The Chief suffered a stroke in 1959 from which he never recovered. Alick occasionally visited him in Mount Royal Hospital, Parkville, recalling that his paralysed facial muscles caused his mouth to droop and necessitated his eye to be taped open. The Chief returned to America in 1980 and died in 1990.

Alick's most notable fellow 'gee' was 'Joe Blow', whose real name was Mick Allen. Allen mostly boxed, but wrestled if Alick was short of an opponent. Allen loved to pose as a country man. Alick remembered: 'he'd cock his hat sometimes, he'd have a cow, which he'd grab out of the pens', amble to the 'pitch', raise his hand and say 'I want to fight'. When asked his name he replied, 'John Joe Aloysius Blow'. Johnny Harris, another of Alick's showground mates, recalled that Allen might add in a funny lisp, 'I'm a took'. 'You're crook?' asked the spruiker? 'No, I'm a took. I'm a tearer's took. I took tacon and eggs, boiled eggs, toached egg, big eggs, fried egg, all tinds of egg. I took tea, toffee, and tocao too'. The crowd laughed, the cow was off-loaded, 'Joe Blow' would climb the ladder, and the audience was hooked. Allen worked for all the boxing tents, until most closed in 1971 in the face of the economic burden of new regulations, which required the attendance of a doctor at each show.

Despite both being top 'gees', their lives took different turns, which caused Alick to reflect on life's choices. Allen never married and spent his final days living as a caretaker of a bottle yard in Darebin Road, Fairfield. Alick reflected: 'I stopped travelling when I got married, that was the end of my show, I only continued doing

Clowning around, Alick with paper fangs and Mick Allen ('Joe Blow') shake hands near the beer tent that usually adjoined the boxing tent.

capital cities. Mick still travelled. He knew every showman. You only had to go on to the ground and say "where's Joe Blow?" and they knew. Everybody knew Joe Blow'.

To meet such fabulous characters in 1947 was truly exciting for Alick. In subsequent years he worked for other boxing tent owners Harry Paulsen, Sandy Moore and Bill Leach. In all these troupes he met a host of other characters: Piccolo Peter, Sharman's cook, and Johnny Harris and Monty Fey, Harry John's tent bosses. Alick met rising boxing champions like Jack Hassen and George Bracken, current champions such as the Sands brothers; and also exchampions like Mickey Miller. Many tent boxers were from local Aboriginal communities and missions, and many took Alick home to meet their families. These associations deepened his understanding of Aboriginal culture. George Sibley took Alick to Cecilia Smith's house in Brisbane where many Aboriginal people from out of town gathered. Alick recalled: 'From then onwards every time I came to Brisbane for the Show I would stay at her home. Cecilia always fought for the underdog and played a prominent part in the Brisbane [Aboriginal] advancement movement'.

Alick also met overseas boxers like the Black American, 'Gentleman Gunboat Jack', champion of the Orient, who wore flash suits and had diamonds encrusted on his teeth. He toured with the debonair Rush Milling, a Filipino, who gave Alick his fan photograph, inscribed with a personal message on the back: 'To Alex, Friendship where men's affections are cemented by an especial love of freedom, neither life nor fear nor any private interests can ever dissolve it. But we carry it with us to our graves and lay down our lives for its satisfaction. Rush Milling'. He formed a myriad of friendships among show people, which he renewed at show time for the remainder of his life.

In late 1947 Alick was rejoined by Clarence Reeves, the 'Alabama Kid', who had convinced Alick on the 'Spirit of Progress' to eschew Asia and join the tents. Reeves had finally left John's outfit. However, deportation orders were soon issued against him that were not Johns' doing. Reeves was arrested while performing at the Moss Vale Show and deported under the White Australia Policy, despite public sympathy for him, his white Australian wife, and their two children. Reeves left his family in Australia, thinking they would not fit into an African American ghetto, and never saw them again. His wife faced difficulties forcing the Department of Neglected Children to care for the children for a while. Alick was shocked at his deportation, which he considered similar to the separation of Aboriginal children from their parents. He later gave the children boxing portraits of their father.

After two years of full-time tent wrestling, Alick gave up the roving life, but for the next fifteen years he continued to travel to Brisbane, Sydney, Adelaide and Melbourne to do the week-long shows. His employment in the 1950s allowed such trips to take place. Tent wrestling remained a good source of ongoing income, but it was not his prime motivation, for Alick always reached for deeper things when talking about the boxing tents. He remarked in 1995:

> It was my life. I loved the boxing tents. I never got rich, but it was always pocket money. And in those days it was tax free...just being there wrestling, it lifted you up a little bit. It

made you feel good. Not only that, you travelled around… from one town to another. I met a lot of Aboriginal people who in later years I met in the Aboriginal movement or I met their brothers or sisters.

Alick was never injured in the tents to dampen this enthusiasm, merely suffering a slight 'cauliflower ear'. The tents were an adventure and a place where men were bound to each other as in sport and war. That was the attraction for Alick to this unique phenomenon, causing him to call the boxing tents the 'best time of his life'.

5 Just Like Hollywood

Alick and Merle became lifelong mates and lovers. They first saw each other in a fleeting, teasing, heart-stopping, romantic way like a Hollywood movie and it is a story that Merle still loves to tell.

Alick and Merle's meeting was accidental, but in a sense it was destined. Betty Clements (née Atkinson) of Swan Hill, who met Alick on the showgrounds in 1948, occasionally saw him at gatherings over the years. She recalled that each time they met he would banter with her as was his way with everyone and say:

> 'Remember years ago, mate. Remember, years ago on the showgrounds, when I said to you, 'Oh, I'll be marrying a Koori girl without fail?'. He would then add, 'I did marry a Koori girl, didn't I?' and I would say: 'Yeah, brother!', and Alick added: 'And she did come from Cummera too, aye!' And I'd replied: 'Yeah, brother!'

Others have told a similar story, that Alick 'always wanted to marry a dark girl'.

Merle Roberta Morgan, the fourth of seven children of Mick (Michael) Morgan and Maude (née Ross), was born in 1929 at Cummeragunja, an Aboriginal mission on the northern bank of the Murray River across from Barmah. Her mother died when Merle was six, and Merle and her siblings were raised at Cummerangunja by their great-grandmother, Elizabeth Barber (née Atkinson) and her daughter Bernice Barber (later Charles). Merle was educated at Cummeragunja School to Grade Six level, as was then standard for Aboriginal children in New South Wales. Her first job at the age of sixteen was as a domestic to a hotel owner and his family in Swan Hill. She then moved to the 'Flat' for a year. This was a camping place of makeshift housing beside the river at Mooroopna, where many

Cummeragunja families camped after the walk-off from the Mission in 1939 in protest at the reserve's conditions.

When Merle was nineteen she and her sister Elizabeth shifted to Melbourne to work and experience the city, like many Aboriginal people of her age. They stayed at 'Spring House', a Salvation Army hostel in Spring Street, before moving to North Coburg. Merle worked at Anderson's hosiery mills in North Coburg, one of the new blue-collar industrial jobs for young working women. Sometimes she travelled by train to Echuca and Moorooopna for the weekend to see her family.

In late 1949 Alick was performing with Sharman's troupe in the Wimmera–Mallee and Murray River regions, occasionally returning to Melbourne. He wrestled at the Echuca Show on Boxing Day, in the same week that Merle travelled home to Cummeragunja for Christmas. By coincidence they returned to Melbourne in early January 1950 on the same train. As Merle recalled of her first glimpse of Alick:

> On the train coming back from Echuca, I was sitting in a compartment with sliding doors and looking out the window. There were others in the compartment. He opened the door, I looked up, and he said 'Oh hello! Are you going to Melbourne?' I didn't reply and just turned away and looked out the window like that [turning her head in a haughty manner like a Hollywood star]. I wasn't interested in talking to men, strange men on trains in those days, because that was always instilled into us.

But she did take note of him — quickly — and remembered that he was wearing a suit and a grey one at that. This fleeting moment, and the one-way exchange of a few words, more than intrigued Alick. Merle still believes 'because I did that he was determined he was going to find me! If I said "yes, I am going to Melbourne", he probably wouldn't have been interested'.

Alick watched the vivacious young woman leave the train and was interested, perhaps already smitten at this stage. On fire, he soon wrote to some friends in Shepparton describing this beautiful Koori girl that he had seen on the train, and asking if they knew who she was.

Merle Morgan at Taronga Park Zoo, Sydney, 1949

She had longish dark hair with a fringe, he wrote, a beautiful face, was about twenty and was very thin ('I had a twenty-inch [51-cm] waist then', recalled Merle). The word went around the small Aboriginal community of the day that Alick Jackomos was looking for a young Aboriginal woman whom he had seen on the train. For her part Merle did not give it too much thought, but some time later she was visiting her cousin Melva Day in Melbourne. Merle recalled:

> she had a photo album. I was looking through the album and she had a photograph of Alick. And I said: 'Oh!' I said, 'that's the fella I saw. I saw this fella on the train who spoke to me'. And she replied, 'What! Was that *you* on the train?' And I said 'Yes, he spoke to me on the train'. She must have told him because it wasn't long after that I met him.

Merle and her sister Elizabeth attended the Princess Theatre one Sunday afternoon in August 1950 to see a concert compèred by the actor Alwyn Kurtz.

We were walking up Spring Street near where the Windsor Hotel is and I looked across the street and there was Alick walking up the street. I said to my sister: 'Oh Gosh. Look over there, that's the fella I was tellin' you about!' He was with two of my cousins, Melva Day and May Briggs. And I said [slightly aghast] 'Oh look, that's that man!' I didn't know his name. So we crossed over the road, not to meet him, but to say hello to my cousins. And when he saw me, he clapped his hands and said. 'This is the one! This is the one I was looking for. I was asking about!' And he said to me. 'Oh! Oh! Oh! I've been lookin' for you! I've been lookin' for you'! And he held my hand and he wouldn't let go. And he pulled me a little bit away from the others and he asked me for a date.

Given Alick's ardent reception, Merle agreed to go out with him: besides, her cousins knew Alick. She travelled by tram from Coburg on their first outing and met him at the GPO on the corner of Elizabeth and Bourke streets. Alick looked smart in his suit and, as Merle recalled, 'he was panting' with excitement. They went to dinner and to see a film at the Regent Theatre. More meetings quickly followed. Merle recalled of these first meetings: 'what could I do after all that? He was so handsome! It just took off from there'.

Alick visited about every second day, travelling by tram from Carlton as he did not have a car, and they met on weekends. They went to see films, for meals and walks, attended Doug Nicholls' Gore Street Church, and visited Alick's Aboriginal friends in Fitzroy. Merle was almost twenty-two, but she had been at work since she was sixteen. Alick was just over twenty-six, but had been earning money to help his mother since he was twelve and had been to war. They were mature adults who knew their minds and their relationship developed speedily.

Their whirlwind courtship lasted eight months. There was not a formal proposal between the two, and as Merle recalled, 'we more or less thought all along that we were going to get married, because I couldn't get rid of him [laughter]'. Not that it seemed in any way that she wanted to, for it was a love match, at first sight for Alick, perhaps second sight for Merle. So besotted was Alick with Merle that during their courtship he forgot to pick up his sisters from a dance. His niece, Yvonne Parisi, recalled that Alick went home without them to be confronted by his mother who asked 'where's your sisters?' Fortunately, being the 'golden boy' in his mother's eyes, he probably extricated himself from this predicament — somehow.

This incident may have helped to spill the beans, as their courtship had been secret. Alick was Greek and Merle Aboriginal. Both cultural groups were then noted for their high ethnic in-marriage rates, and strong cultural conservatism when it came to mixing with others. In the 1960s 43 per cent of Australian-born men of Greek descent married Greek women. It might have been higher if more Greek brides had been available, and indeed shiploads of Greek brides were brought to Australia by the community. In the 1960s 53 per cent of Aboriginal women in Melbourne married Aboriginal men. Thus there were strong expectations on both to marry within their groups; and at least half their peers, possibly more than that a decade earlier (around 1950), did so. Merle said that being Aboriginal, 'coming from a cultural background, I sort of understood why they wanted him to marry a Greek', but Alick had already determined that he wanted to marry a Koori girl. Merle also commented that, 'there is no way in the world that Alick would have married a Greek woman, because [by then] he was too involved in the Aboriginal community'. Besides, he was smitten by Merle Morgan.

Once their courting became known Alick came under pressure from his family to abandon any thought of a life with Merle. As Alick recalled of this traumatic moment, when he was being forced to choose between family and Merle:

> Dad again was indifferent, like everything else, Dad just didn't seem to worry. But Mum didn't like it. She was opposed to it, because of the old Kastellorizian tradition that you marry your own. Even for Kastellorizians to marry another Greek, they used to say: "He's married a *foreigner*", even if he married someone from Athens or Rhodes, they were treated as foreigners. But to marry an Australian or an Aboriginal girl, well it just didn't... those things didn't *happen*. But I told Mum that I was going ahead with the wedding and the marriage.

Asimina had fought hard for her family during the economically difficult years during the Depression. She had tried to be a good Greek matriarch by creating a strong household and providing for her family. Alick's own bread-winning efforts as a teenager had assisted her, he was her 'golden' first-born male, and they had been very close. Now that there was a new threat to her family's Greekness, involving her first born, she had to act.

It would have taken a great deal of courage for Asimina to seek out Merle, and argue for her son, but that is what she did. Asimina visited Merle at Anderson's hosiery mills, accompanied by Alick's younger brother Michael, then ten. Merle, who had never met Asimina, recalled in 1997: 'she looked really old', indicating the stress Asimina was under. Asimina told an unlikely story, through Michael, in the vain hope it would prevent the marriage of her son to a non-Greek woman. Young Michael announced boldly to Merle: 'this is my mother and Alick is my brother. My mother said to tell you that Alick is a married man with seven children and a wife living in Egypt'. Merle was taken aback but of course did not believe a word of it. Michael, who later became a great friend of Merle, then added on behalf of his mother: 'I am going to see the priest so that you won't be allowed to get married in the Orthodox Church'. Merle replied respectfully that she doubted the story, and as she was an Anglican they would be marrying in that church. It was a quietly determined meeting, of two strong women, each driven by their love for Alick. Asimina departed, unsuccessful in her quest to uphold tradition, but unexpectedly impressed, as she confessed to Alick later, by the well-spoken and determined young woman.

The family then asked Theo Conos, Alick's slightly younger cousin and childhood friend, 'to talk him out of it'. Theo recalled: 'the family had approached me to speak to Alick, to convince him not to do it, to marry a part-Aboriginal girl'. Theo's recollections suggest that the concern was about Merle's Aboriginality, as much as her being non-Greek, but he admitted that he also later married a non-Greek woman.

> When I got married nobody came to my wedding, because I married an Australian girl! That was resented as well! And

the Australian people resented me! So I spoke to Alick for half an hour and then I said; 'Congratulations! I wish you luck'. He was happy with her. I worked out that's what he wanted.

It was also usual for Aboriginal people of the early 1950s to express some concern over a mixed marriage. They often failed under the racial pressures of the day and, as with Greek Australians, Aboriginal people's preference was that their young should marry into their 'own'; but there was little pressure in this case as Alick was by 1950 very well known to many Aboriginal communities, especially in Shepparton, Fitzroy and Lake Tyers, through his visits and his growing friendship with Doug Nicholls, a prominent leader within the community. Alick had also met and visited many country Aboriginal families during several years of touring with the boxing tents. Indeed, he knew many of Merle's kin before he knew Merle.

> Merle's people all *knew* me after the War. I was up around Shepparton, picking tomatoes on Jamieson's block for a period of time where Mr and Mrs Selwyn Briggs — Aunty Geraldine Briggs, a sister of Aunty Marge Tucker — were living. I even had a little picker's hut with Kenny Briggs. So, they all knew me, and they knew me from the wrestling because I used to go to Shepparton Show in October every year. Everybody knew me there, I was one of the mob, I don't think they considered me as a Greek or an outsider, I was just one of the mob.

As one of Merle's relations, Roma Connors, recalled: 'I used to see Alick around town because he was always with the young dark boys. As a matter of fact I didn't even know he was Greek until we found out his last name, because to my mind Alick was one of us'. However, Merle's aunt in Melbourne did warn her that Fitzroy was rough and that she 'should watch that fella', as Alick associated with Fitzroy's Aboriginal population.

Doubts vanished at their joyous wedding held at St Augustine's Church of England in Shepparton on 31 March 1951. Merle bought her dress — with a beautiful lace train, veil and long lace gloves — from Darrod's in Bourke Street. She looked radiant and was pictured

Alick and Merle on their wedding day, 31 March 1951

in the *Shepparton News*. Her bridesmaids — Elizabeth her sister, Melva a cousin, and Rita Harmes — wore long blue frocks. Alick's best man was to be Merle's brother Des Morgan, but being under twenty-one was unable to sign the register, so Kenny Briggs played that role. Clarrie Higgins was the other man of the official party and of course Merle's father Mick Morgan 'gave her away'. There were about two hundred guests at the wedding all dressed 'to the nines', mostly Merle's relatives who lived at the 'Flat', and in nearby housing in Mooroopna–Shepparton.

After Asimina's attempts to prevent the marriage, Alick and Merle chose not to invite his family to the wedding; but, as Merle recalled,

> in those days they read out marriage banns in the churches and blow me down if his sister didn't hear about it…and when we got to the church his brother was there, and his three sisters and their husbands and his cousin and her husband. One of his sisters was cool, but the others were okay, especially his younger sister, Maisie…That was a surprise 'cos he wasn't expecting any of them there.

Wedding party: (l. to r.): Ken Briggs, Rita Harmes, Des Morgan (Merle's brother), Elizabeth Hoffmann (Merle's sister), Alick Jackomos, Merle Jackomos (née Morgan), Michael Morgan (Merle's father), Melva Johnson (née Day), Clarrie Higgins

At the reception, St Mary's Hall, Mooroopna: (l. to r.) George Aristokelous, Maisie Aristokelous (née Jackomos), Pino Livery, Mary Livery, Alick Jackomos, Merle Jackomos, Mary Christies (née Jackomos), Chris Christies, with daughter Margarita Christies in front

Alick's parents were absent, perhaps their pride preventing them. Merle laughed in retrospect: 'it must have been a great shock for Alick's people. To see all these blackfellas there! But they stayed for the reception [in St Mary's Hall, Mooroopna] and stayed that night in a hotel. And then they came back the next day'. Alick's sisters Mary, Stella and Maisie later married Greek men – Cypriots actually – and Angelo married a Greek girl, but Michael, the youngest, also married 'out', an Australian girl.

The day after their wedding Alick and Merle boarded a bus for their honeymoon up north, which as far as Merle was concerned, lasted for almost fifty years. 'It's just been one long honeymoon!' They travelled north and met up with Harry Johns' boxing tent at the Grafton and Kempsey Shows. Alick confessed 47 years later that 'I don't think my wife knew this was going to happen, but anyhow, it boosted the pocket money for our honeymoon'. It was a working honeymoon, as Alick wrestled his way along the northern rivers route, to Brisbane. They stayed in a boarding house in Fortitude Valley and visited Alick's friends in Brisbane whom he had met during the war. They also visited Stradbroke Island and stayed with Colley and Joan Costello, friends for a lifetime. In Brisbane Alick worked at an engineering company and wrestled at weekend country shows with Sandy and Selby Moore's boxing tent, where he had more adventures with a new group of friends recorded in *Sideshow Alley*.

They had not been long in Brisbane when a letter arrived from his family asking him to come home for Maisie's wedding. They decided not to attend as it was a long way by bus or train and they had little money. 'But then an urgent telegram came: "Mum seriously ill, come home". I don't think they said: "Not expected to live", but "seriously ill"'. They rushed home and booked into the People's Palace, the Salvation Army's cheap accommodation, being unsure of Asimina and Andrew's reception. They braced themselves for their first visit as a couple to an ill and possibly hostile Asimina. But, as Alick recalled, his Mum was 'as fit as a pansy [laugh], it was just to get us home'.

The initial meeting in his parents' Elgin Street lounge room was awkward, but their marriage decision, which was now a *fait accompli*, caused a change in Asimina's attitude towards the new wife of her 'golden boy'. Greeks traditionally give gold to brides and Asimina gave Merle some gold pendants on their return. Merle met her father-in-law for the first time, and 'he seemed okay'. His side of the family seemed more accepting more quickly, whereas Asimina's Augustes kin were cooler to this mixed marriage. At Maisie's wedding, Alick recalled: 'Merle was in the *official* wedding group photo, so they accepted her. Although my mother didn't want the marriage to go ahead, Merle became one of her favourite daughter-in-laws'. Many years later Merle confided to Maisie: 'I've got no animosity towards your Mum because as a mother I understand and I would like to see all of my children married to Aboriginal people, which of course didn't happen'. Merle married outside her community because she loved Alick. 'He was a person; I didn't look on Alick as a Greek'.

6 Entrepreneur and Family Man

Alick left the boxing tents and struck out as an entrepreneur in early 1948, a few years before his marriage. It is not clear why Alick left the tents. It was not through dissatisfaction, as he continued part time with the tents for another twenty years, and the experiences lived vividly and warmly in his imagination for the rest of his days. Perhaps it was the call of Melbourne, his family and his Aboriginal friends, but more likely, as a 24-year-old he was looking to his future. Yet he had no strong career directions and his lack of a formal education was an impediment. As a returned serviceman he could have applied to be funded to study, but he would have needed to make up the secondary schooling he missed. Alick wanted to earn money, not for what it could buy him, but out of a desire for security, urged on by his poor background and Depression experiences. He was well paid for wrestling in the tents, certainly above the basic wage, but that was not sufficient to assuage his desire for a solid financial foundation for his future.

His parents and grandparents on both sides had been in small business so it was natural that he was attracted to that sector. His first job in Melbourne came through the boxing tent network. While on tour he had met Mickey Miller, a former bantam and featherweight champion of Australia in the 1930s. When Alick saw Miller again in Melbourne, he was operating a hamburger 'joint' in Russell Street, on lease from Tommy O'Brien, who had several such shops in Melbourne, leased by ex-boxers, including another in Abbotsford, run by heavyweight fighter Al Moran. Alick, who was always looking for a little extra work, agreed to help Miller in his premises. This was no easy task, because the shop was in Russell Street west, between Bourke and Little Bourke, near Chinatown and some of Melbourne's slums, haunts for colourful types. Alick recalled: 'in those days Russell Street

Russell Street between 1940 and 1960 looking towards the site of Alick's hamburger shop just beyond the intersection on the right (State Library of Victoria)

was a pretty rough district, with prostitutes on the beat, sailors from ships and many of Melbourne's criminal elements hanging around'.

The hamburger joint proved lively at times. *Australian Ring*, a boxing magazine, published an article on Alick's life in 1958 in which it described the hamburger 'joint' run by Mickey Miller and Alick.

> Open all night and every night, Mickey and Alick got all the training they could take in regular later night and early morn battles with Melbourne's street corner tough guys. Miller and Jackomos provided quite a combination — with Mickey providing the skill and Alick the brawn, nobody ever did beat the pair, they'd been known to eject six men in as many minutes.

In October 1948 Alick assumed control of the hamburger shop once Mickey Miller decided to leave for a quieter life. Alick was assisted by his brother Angelo back from service with the Occupation Force in Japan. The business remained lively and full of hard work. The hours were exhausting, as it opened at 6 a.m. until mid-morning, and reopened at 6 p.m. until 3 a.m. the next day. Alick never recorded his work routine, but there is little doubt that he and Angelo purchased supplies, prepared food, served in the shop, handled money and cleaned up, and dampened down any trouble, spending much of their twelve-hour days on their feet. Alick had two cooks, a morning and night shift cook, the former being a distant relative. Alick continued part-time wrestling:

> sometimes on a Saturday I'd go and do a show for Jimmy Sharman. I'd work until three in the morning and then go and do a day show for Sharman...the staff would open the shop at 6 o'clock in the evening and I'd be back after a hard day in the show about eight or nine with Jimmy ['Old Jimmy' Sharman].

The hamburger shop was the haunt of many prostitutes who used its tables, often between three and five times a night, to scrutinise their potential customer in public. Alick remembered:

> I think they must have propositioned someone in Russell Street and to settle the deal they'd come into the hamburger shop and order. She'd order steak and eggs and she'd order it for her partner as well, steak and eggs that was three bob [shillings]. That was a good profit-maker. There's two steak and eggs, neither of them would eat it. I think it was just the proposition. If the steak and eggs weren't touched by the prostitute, we'd just put it under the counter, because we knew she'd be back later on that day. We'd just heat it up and we'd charge again, the client would pay for that.

The joint re-opened each evening, just as the hotels closed at 6 o'clock. Hotel customers headed to the hamburger shop looking for a 'feed'. Homeless men also came in from the cold and for a cheap meal—a hamburger with egg and a cup of coffee for a shilling (about 10 cents). Some of the refugees from the hotels would have bottles of beer with them and the homeless men often carried wine. They would attempt to drink them despite Alick's lack of a liquor licence. As soon as they finished their coffee, the homeless men would

> bring their wine bottle up or put their cup down under the table, and fill it up with wine. So we had a bit of trouble putting them out or telling them to stop. And also if they ran out of wine you had to watch out that they weren't drinkin' your Worcestershire sauce on the table.

Some who had been warned off drinking alcohol caused trouble and had to be ejected. Others, full of beer, were looking for a fight for no reason. One night an Aboriginal woman, ejected for drinking, turned and threw the beer bottle at the shop's window, but fortunately only the bottle smashed. Alick recalled that there were often one or two fights a night. He hired a boxing tent mate, Percy Ritchie, who fought as a middleweight under the name of Ritchie Sands.

> Ritchie would only have to tap you on the jaw and he would break it. One day a bloke was drinking and I told him to stop drinking and he wouldn't. So Ritchie just goes and picks him up and hits him one and broke his jaw and I says to Ritchie: 'look I think this had better be the finish. You can't just keep knocking blokes out you know'.

The business became more and more troublesome. Police who came could also be difficult customers. They would order steak and eggs 'but you couldn't charge them'. To ensure continued free meals, they threatened Alick with arrest for consorting, because of the criminal types who also patronised his 'joint'. Alick was the meat in his steak sandwich, having two opposed categories of clients who were of little business value. Of the criminals he recalled: 'I was frightened to say anything to such criminals because they'd have smashed the joint up'. One night several pulled up in a utility out the front and yelled out, 'Alick, we want to leave a parcel here for a couple of days'. He replied, 'what do you want to leave'? 'A safe!' they replied. 'We knocked it off from Essendon, can we leave it'? 'No', he replied. 'You can't leave it'. The next day the press reported that it had turned up in a paddock — unopened.

The hamburger business did prove lucrative. Alick once termed it 'a gold mine', adding, 'I was earning a hundred pound a week in those days, that's a lot of money'. Indeed it was, being perhaps fifteen times the average wage. His use of the word 'earning', not 'turning over' suggests this was clear profit, which meant he may have saved in a year the tidy sum of £3000–£5000, minus tax and any debts for set up: more than enough to buy a small home outright. So after a year Alick and Angelo decided 'it was time to get out'. The fights, the pressure from criminals and police alike, and the whole atmosphere, caused him to sell the business in September 1949. Alick had to pay £500 to the owner of the premises to enable him to sell his lease. The lease's purchaser, a Polish Jew, paid Alick £2000 for the lease on the business, but within a month it had closed. 'I think it might have got a bit too rough for him. When I was in there I used to have a few boxers doin' casual labour, so the place was always in control, but with someone new to that particular area, I think it just got too much for him'. So Alick left the retail food business after much hard work and in one piece. He had a tidy stake in his pocket, which helped him lay foundations for the rest of his life.

Back in uniform: Alick joined the volunteer Citizens' Military Forces in the 1950s and is pictured on Anzac Day with members of the 21st Infantry Brigade, 2/14th Battalion.

When he first married and moved back to Melbourne, Alick took a job at the APM mills in Fairfield. However, his teenage years and showgrounds experience showed that he was an entrepreneur with the 'gift of the gab'. He had small-business acumen like his father in the 'Magpie Fish' and his grandfather, who sold fish door to door in Perth. His Castellorizian forebears were a powerful and prosperous island-based trading people within the Byzantine Empire. Alick was a little different, a trader not just for the economic reward, although that was important, but also for the romance of the exchange. He was a seller who liked the challenge of the deal, and the interactions with people along the way, as much as the financial outcome. He certainly was not against making money and was clever at making a profit. But it was not his only goal.

Not long after Alick's marriage his brother-in-law Chris Christie (Mary's husband) relinquished his delivery business through ill health. Alick took it over, purchasing his 1937 red Chevrolet truck. The business supplied fruit and vegetables to Greek cafés and hotels in the Lonsdale–Russell Street area. Three mornings a week Alick rose at about 3, drove to the Victoria Markets to purchase supplies and delivered them to his customers. Andrew, his father, had purchased his fish supplies in much the same way over many years, so it was familiar territory. Alick made the very lucrative income of £50–£100 a week, perhaps equal to a professional wage, with fewer hours and far fewer tensions than the hamburger shop.

Men with trucks are valued friends. Alick often used his truck to help people, especially the Aboriginal community which always seemed to be in motion. On Sundays in summer he would pick up a group from Aunty Maude Moyle's house (Eric and Bill Onus's mother) in Fitzroy and take them and his family to the beach on the tray back of his truck. This was perfectly acceptable in safety terms in those days and many Sunday school and social clubs picnickers were conveyed in this way on outings . Alick also helped Aboriginal people move house, which was a frequent occurrence for those in rental accommodation. Merle recalled that he moved families and their possessions from West Melbourne and Fitzroy to Broadmeadows once slum clearance occurred in Fitzroy.

Alick realised that there were no shops in this new area and that he could supply people with fruit and vegetables. He recorded his new venture in his 'Memoirs': 'by about 1960 I gave up supplying cafés and hotels and purchased a Holden panel van and sold potatoes in the new [Housing] Commission areas of Broadmeadows and Glenroy'. He also purchased a trailer to increase his load and travelled further east to Preston and Heidelberg. His son Andrew recalled that 'he would buy big bags of pumpkins, Queensland blues, brown onions and spuds, then bring them home and stack them in the garage on pallets and the next morning put some on the trailer with his set of scales and brown paper bags and went around selling them'. One of Michael's earliest memories of his father is Alick stacking watermelons in the garage. The *Coburg Courier* captured his activities in a front-page article in September 1961, complete with photograph: 'every housewife and child in Coburg and Pascoe Vale has heard of or seen Alick Jackomos and his "spud wagon"'. It detailed his early life and wrestling career, his work for Aboriginal people and commented that 'he did not acquire his comfortable home in Royal Parade, Pascoe Vale, via the easy road of plenty of pocket money and intermediate and leaving certificates'.

Alick at first sold to Aboriginal people, whose addresses he knew, and who had formerly lived in Fitzroy. Mollie Dyer, Marge Tucker's daughter, was one of his early customers. Twenty years later she wrote a reference for Alick:

> Mr Jackomos conducted his own business which involved him in dealing with the general public on a door to door basis. At that time, I lived in an area serviced by Mr. Jackomos. Despite the fact there were stores in the area, people preferred to wait until Mr. Jackomos called to make their purchases because of his honesty in his dealings with them and the quality of his goods…Mr Jackomos, through his honesty, sincerity and warm personality, had the ability to form excellent relationships, not only with the Aboriginal community, but also with the Australian community generally.

Alick on his 'potato run' photographed with his son Andrew by the *Coburg Courier*, c. 1960

As Dyer intimated, Alick also patrolled the streets in this 'spud wagon' alert to the hail of new customers. As the business expanded, the majority of his new customers were non-Aboriginal people. Many thought he produced the potatoes, as he called from his utility: 'From the Grower! From the Grower!' This was not a lie, but a claim more in the showgrounds tradition of good spruiking, that is, to put the best face on things, for they were from the grower in a roundabout way. Richard Barwick, a Canberra friend, attested to his business skills, recalling that Alick once told him that 'it was always essential to have potatoes at more than one price on the truck even though he bought them in at a uniform price, for some women always had to buy "up-market" and would never be satisfied with the cheaper item'.

His skill at detecting a business opportunity was consummate. While travelling near Melton on a summer's day around 1960 Alick spotted a truck, loaded with watermelons, which had broken down. He bought the load and headed for the recreation grounds at Melton Weir, where he sliced the melons. Using his showgrounds spruiking skills, he yelled out: 'something very nice, right off the ice from Surfer's Paradise' or some such rhyming catchphrase, and made a killing by selling the lot. He combined this skill with hard work. As he recalled in 1998:

> I might finish my potato round and I might have a dozen empty boxes in me trailer…I would go up a few side lanes of Coburg and yell out 'Bottle-oh! Bottle-oh! Bottle-oh!' And get a few bottles or batteries. Then still working my way home I would drop them in to the bottle-yard, so there was an extra three or four quid that I'd earned on my way home in a couple of hours…I was earning up to 60, 70, 80 pound a week in those days, on potatoes, three days a week selling potatoes and by doing little odd jobs.

This was in 1953 when the 'basic wage' set by the government at a level to keep a family alive in reasonable circumstances, was £12 a week.

Alick never let money-making dominate, however. He used his rounds to keep in touch with family and friends. Yvonne Parisi, Maisie's daughter and Alick's niece, recalled his visits to their Station Street home. 'We always knew he was coming, because he had his potato rounds. He used to sell watermelons, spuds and pumpkins from his truck or trailer. I loved it when he came around for he always brought us watermelon'. Alick also never failed to help those in need, as had his parents during the Depression. Aboriginal people came in for special treatment. Roma Connors remarked: 'he took fruit and vegies, he used to get it from the Market and take it out to Broadmeadows and sell it to Aboriginal people, cheap, so that'd help them. I don't doubt that more times than not he gave them the vegies because that's how good-hearted he was'. Ronny Johnson recently told Andrew Jackomos, Alick's son, that Alick supplied him at times with vegetables when he was unable to pay for them.

With his savings from the army returned to him by his mother, his stake from the hamburger shop and a continued strong income from his fruit business, Alick and Merle were able to set up house in secure style. After they were married they faced the extreme housing shortage of post-war Melbourne. There was no room upstairs in his parents' Elgin Street premises, but his sister Mary, who lived nearby in Cardigan Street, offered them a 'little room at the top of the stairs that would only be about 4 by 6 feet 9 [1.5 x 2 metres]. We put a mattress in there but when you wanted to open the door you had to lift the mattress off the floor'. When Alick worked at the Paper Mills they rented one room with access to a kitchen in nearby Parkview Road, Fairfield.

Alick and Merle were lucky to acquire their own home by early 1952. Even if a house could be purchased in the face of the housing shortage, there was still the problem of the inevitable tenants. They could stay put under the law, until they or [you as] the owner found them alternative accommodation. Alick and Merle went to see a small bluestone single-fronted cottage, one of a pair at 21 and 23 St Phillip's Street, Abbotsford, three streets east of Collingwood Station. By chance the elderly tenant was a Mr Gully. Alick in his usual way, established a connection by recalling he had gone to school with a Walter Gully, who turned out to be the tenant's grandson. The man said: 'Look son, I'll be moving out in a couple of weeks. You buy these houses and you can have vacant possession. The only condition is that I want you to buy this pedal Singer sewing machine for £15, and something else for a couple of quid'. Alick considered that a cheap deal for vacant possession. They bought both houses for 1000, possibly equivalent to $150 000 today. As Merle said with pride: Alick 'had the money and he bought straight out, he used to do odd jobs and he didn't drink, didn't smoke, didn't gamble'.

Shortly after the move to St Phillip's Street, their daughter Asimina Elizabeth was born. She was named after Alick's mother as was traditional, and after Merle's sister Elizabeth. Alick's mother was no doubt pleased by this acknowledgement, but their daughter was always known as 'Esmai', a unique spelling coined by Merle. Merle was unsure why she did this, and there was possibly some resentment at the time, long since gone and forgotten. Merle recalled recently that she probably thought it 'would be easier for her at school' with a non-Greek name, and observed that most of Alick's family 'have got Greek names and they're called other names, English names'. Their tenants next door, the Smiths, paid 15 shillings rent. They became good friends and minded baby Esmai once Andrew Morgan arrived

Proud parents at the Dandenongs push Esmai in her pram, 1952.

within another year. Their first son was named 'Andrew' after Alick's father, again following tradition, and 'Morgan' was derived from Merle's family name.

Alick and Merle sold the two bluestone cottages in Abbotsford in 1953 for £4000 — a handsome profit — as they were now too small for a growing family. They moved to a three-bedroomed, brick house in Bendigo Street, Prahran, which they shared with a female tenant, who stayed in one bedroom until she found alternative accommodation. They sold the Prahran house for about £6000 in 1956 and paid a similar amount for a two-bedroomed house at 68 Royal Parade, Pascoe Vale South, which became the family home for the next decade. Their third child, Michael Stafford, was born there in 1955. He was named after Merle's father, Michael Stafford Morgan. Hard work, saving and astute property purchases, meant that Alick and Merle owned their comfortable family home outright within a year of their marriage, a very unusual occurrence and one which provided Alick with a security his parents had never enjoyed. This was a process he carefully documented on tape in 1998, and which was to be vital to his later philanthropic work.

Alick and Merle's early domestic life is unrecorded and elusive. Alick spoke little of it in his many writings and interviews, which focused on his public life. Merle is content not to give many details, and, besides, much of the fine grain of everyday life, unless recorded in diaries or photographs, slips from the memory. Their children understandably remember little that happened before the mid- to late 1950s.

Their domestic arrangements in the 1950s paralleled the typical Australian family, for they lived as a nuclear family in suburbia. Pascoe Vale South was close to the city; and Royal Parade was one street east of the Melville Road tram. Their two-bedroomed house had front and back gardens, which afforded sufficient space for domestic bliss. Alick was the breadwinner and Merle managed the home and raised their three children, born within four years. She became the matriarch, which in both Greek and Aboriginal family life was typical, and a role with which both Alick and Merle were happy. Alick mostly moved in the wider world and became a wonderful provider. Their roles matched their temperaments, for Alick was totally gregarious and at ease in the public sphere, while Merle was more private, home-centred and, despite her sense of fun, far less gregarious. Opposites in many ways, they always remained attracted to each other. As Merle's friend and cousin Walda Blow (née Walker) observed, they were 'a perfect match'. Alick helped a little around the home for he was never shy of hard work or thought certain work as a man beneath him. He ran the vacuum cleaner over the floor because of Merle's asthma and maintained the lawns and garden in the manly style of the day. He helped out with their children whom he adored, minding them when needed, and changing a nappy when Merle was busy with other chores.

Number 68 Royal Parade was often full of people. There were many parties, not riotous, for Alick and Merle did not drink, but full of music, noise and fun. Walda and Reg Blow recalled the gatherings they attended at the Jackomos house, filled with laughter and music because guitars would invariably appear and people would sing. Walda recalled: 'the girls would sing and they were very talented

Twenty-first birthday party given by Alick and Merle Jackomos at 68 Royal Parade, Pascoe Vale, for Queensland Aboriginal boxer and Australian lightweight champion, George Bracken, seated on the left; his trainer, Leo White, is by his side with 'Old Jimmy' Sharman standing.

with music. And they'd have stories and cultural things. Most of it had to do with Aboriginal things'. The house always rang with laughter even if just the two of them were there. Alick had a strong sense of humour about life, and Merle is still noted for her laughter. As Roma Connors recalled: 'they had a wonderful relationship, absolutely loved their children and Merle was a wonderful cook. She'd be cooking every night and she laughed all the time'. Alick loved food, especially sweet things, but was never much of a cook, although he could prepare pasta. He was not overly fussy about food and Yvonne his niece and Merle recalled, 'he ate whatever you put in front of him; "Oh, that was lovely Mum"! he'd say'. Indeed, Esmai claimed that if Merle gave him burnt sausages and toast he would still say 'Beautiful breakfast Mum'!

Their household was always open to people, one reason why Alick and Merle added a third bedroom. They accommodated people visiting Melbourne, or those moving from country areas or interstate, who were trying to get established in the city. People stayed a few nights, a few months, and several stayed a year or so. Clare and Roma Connors both stayed several months while they were finding their feet in Melbourne, as did Clive Atkinson and also Walda Walker. One couple stayed for six months in their lounge room after Alick offered to help them out. When asked did she mind that these people stayed, Merle replied instantly, 'no, we both loved it'.

Roma Connors stayed with them for several months in the early 1960s, after she moved to Melbourne. She recalled them as wonderful parents, who 'doted' on their three young children, and remarked that Alick and Merle had a 'wonderful rapport with them'. After bathtime and teatime they would play with the kids, then 'we often sat around and laughed and talked, but at the end of the day, like everyone else, we were all tired'. She added,

> there wasn't a thing they wouldn't do for me, they treated me like I was their own. Alick would take me to work in his little ute when he was on the way to his market, and if he was coming past my work around the time I knocked off he would pick me up and take me home. I never felt uncomfortable with them, they were so wonderful. It was like a home away from home.

The family life that Alick and Merle created was based on generosity of spirit. Roma Connors again: 'Honestly I can't express how wonderful they were. They did so many things out of the goodness of their hearts, they were diamonds'. When Jean Shrimpton, the English model, came out to the Melbourne Cup in 1965 she caused a sensation. Shrimpton wore a slightly above-the-knee shift, then deemed daringly 'short', dubbed a 'mini skirt'. She also wore a pendant on a long gold chain. Roma recalled that all her sisters living in Melbourne had these things, but as she was training as a nurse, she did not have enough money to buy fashion items. So Merle said:

> 'You and I are going out shopping and I'm going to get you one'. She bought me this beautiful aqua-blue one with a gold chain and I was able to go out with them on the Saturday night. She'd just do things for you that she didn't have to, but she would!

Alick and Merle wove their lives into two major networks, his Greek family and the Melbourne Aboriginal community. On Sundays Alick, Merle and the children would go to his parents' place for family gatherings with his siblings and their children. Visits were more convenient when they moved from Carlton to Irymple Street, East Kew. At Elgin Street the adults talked over lunch in the lounge-dining room behind the shop while the children raced around. Alick's children have fond memories of their visits and playing with their cousins. At least once every summer the family picnicked at Rickett's Point. Alick's daughter Esmai recalled that the food would be shared and 'everybody would eat and talk and laugh and then go with their buckets and potato bags and go and get periwinkles and mussels'. Andrew, Alick's father, would lead them like a patriarch on to the rocks 'with his long-johns hanging to gather the periwinkles and mussels', according to another of the grandchildren, Yvonne Parisi. They were boiled up and shared with relish. Esmai remembered that they had 'lots of fun', playing games, swimming: 'That happened over many years'. At Christmas time Asimina the matriarch would pay for presents for all the grandchildren. Maisie would buy them and Alick would play Santa and hand them out. Alick's extended family also gathered at Asimina and Andrew's home for Greek Easter until his parents became too ill and elderly for such gatherings.

Alick and Merle rarely interacted with the wider Greek community at institutions or festivals, although there are photographs in the family album labelled 'Cassy picnics 1955'. The children were baptised in the Greek Orthodox Church and attended name days and other rituals for cousins and family, but otherwise visits to the Orthodox Church were rare. Merle did not speak Greek and all the services were in Greek. Nor did their children learn to speak Greek for they were not sent to Greek school, perhaps because Alick had not enjoyed the experience himself. Merle had the children baptised also in the Anglican Church. So the family's churchgoing was confined to Gore Street Church of Christ overseen by Pastor Doug Nicholls, and the West Coburg Baptist Church in Bell Street, which had a Sunday school and youth club. The reality was that Alick had by his teenage years found friendships within the Melbourne Aboriginal community and thereafter had less contact with the wider Greek community.

The irony was that Alick, a Greek Australian, introduced Merle, an Aboriginal Australian, to the Melbourne Aboriginal community. As Alick recalled:

> Merle didn't bring me into the [Melbourne] Aboriginal community, I brought her…she was always told 'Don't go to Fitzroy' because it had a bit of a bad name in those days… Once I married Merle, I took her to Fitzroy and she met a lot of the families I knew in Fitzroy.

Alick named the Clarke, Onus, Lovett, Nicholls, Green, Hudson, Connelly and Young families. He also brought Merle to Pastor Doug Nicholls' Gore Street church, Fitzroy, where Aboriginal people gathered from the early 1940s. They became particularly close to Eric and Winnie Onus. As Alick remembered, 'they would come to our house and stay at our place, and their daughter Judy would mind our children while we went to functions, and we'd go and stay with them' at their home at Narbethong, just north of Healesville. Alick and Merle also visited Eric's brother Bill, who with his Scottish wife Mary owned a boomerang factory and souvenir shop at Belgrave.

During their early years of marriage, Alick and Merle built rich social networks within Melbourne's Aboriginal community and they maintained Merle's family and kin networks at Mooroopna–Shepparton and the Barmah–Echuca region, by frequent visits and holidays. One family photograph (not included here) depicts a visit to Tom and Rose Dunnolley's house at Barmah Lakes in 1967. They also travelled to Jackson's Track where Aboriginal families lived on land owned by the Jackson brothers, timber-millers, who employed Aboriginal workers. Daryl Jackson married Euphemia Mullett. Doug Nicholls used to hold regular church services at Jackson's Track and Alick and Merle often attended as a photograph from 1958 attests. Daish's Paddock and the 'Flat' at Mooroopna, and camps at Barmah, and Jackson's Track, were dotted with Aboriginal 'humpies', makeshift tin and bagging dwellings. These places, called 'fringe camps' by whites and 'home' by Aboriginal people, schooled the Jackomos children in the knowledge of both Aboriginal material deprivation and kin-based happiness.

The family at Jackson's Track, Drouin, in 1957; Michael is flanked by Esmai and Andrew.

There were trips to the football as all the family were passionate supporters. The boys adopted Alick's passion for the Collingwood 'Magpies', while Esmai struck out on her own, supporting the Essendon 'Bombers'. Merle was passionate about Melbourne, for Eddie Jackson whose mother came for Cummeragunja, was one of the 'Demons' stars. One Saturday afternoon, when the Magpies and the Demons clashed, Alick and the children (or at least the boys) came home crowing over Melbourne's defeat. Merle was serving the evening meal and found the childish gloating insufferable, and they went hungry. Andrew recalled that the dinner finished down the toilet, while a family friend, John Moriarty, heard that it landed on the wall. Merle quietly corrected the family record, explaining that she would never do such a thing, and that it went into the garbage tin to teach those boasting Magpie supporters a lesson in humility.

As the children grew, many summers were spent travelling north to Queensland, to nourish the friendships Alick had formed with Aboriginal people, during the war years. These adventures were all undertaken in the family's Holden panel van, without air conditioning. The children recall these trips with great pleasure. They often visited Archie and Edna Newfong and their children at Wynnum. One of the children, Becky Thomson (née Newfong), recalled that they 'would arrive with watermelons, stone fruit and other goodies…and the house would be full of talking and laughing and it was quite obvious that a special friendship existed between my Father and Alick and in turn this extended to the rest of our families'. The children played party games and Alick and Archie 'always reminisced about their boxing days'. Becky continued, 'Alick would no sooner get here and he'd be off visiting everyone, he didn't leave anyone out, he'd even go over to Stradbroke Island visiting all the families and indulging his love of seafood'. At Dunwich on Stradbroke they visited Margaret and Pat Islam and also Kath Walker. Occasionally they moved on to Cairns to holiday with the Savages. As Becky recalled of these ventures further north:

> we were so intrigued that here was a family of five loaded up to the hilt in an old station wagon (not forgetting the camera, he was always taking photos of everyone and he was articulate about it) and heading to all these places thousands of miles away from Melbourne, they weren't even perturbed they just seemed like they were going for a Sunday drive and Alick was the only driver.

Holiday stopover beside the blue 'EH' Holden outside Joan Hauser's house, Ipswich, Queensland, early 1960s

When Alick travelled to wrestle at the Brisbane Show in September he often stayed with the Newfongs. Becky once saw Alick wrestle in Sharman's tent and 'people showering the floor with money'.

Another January trip was to the Northern Territory, by road to Adelaide, train to Alice Springs, then by road to Darwin. This was a great trek on the Territory's poor roads in the 1960s, and memories of this trip in particular are tinged by exasperation. Esmai recalled, 'it was hot, it was stinkin' hot' and we visited many Aboriginal reserves along the way'. Andrew reminisced: 'I can remember we would sit in the car and we'd cry out, "Not *another* blackfella community"'. We can imagine Alick's optimistic response, telling of the interesting people they would meet and the sights they would see. Esmai recalled similar frustration, and said after visits to Papunya, Hermannsburg and Jay's Creek, to name a few, they cried 'Enough!' Alick was irrepressibly enthusiastic for he was not only 'fact-finding', as Andrew put it, but also educating his children, as Esmai later realised. Alick always followed correct protocol by writing ahead for permission to enter these community places. According to Michael, 'by the time I was thirteen I had visited many communities throughout NSW, South Australia, Queensland and NT and of course Victoria'.

The trips were symbolic of Alick's great drive and enthusiasm, which sometimes left the family struggling to keep up in his wake. Alick led a busy life which, as the children grew, became busier. They all loved their father dearly, and still see him as a role model, Andrew referred to him as 'my hero'. But they all commented that he was a better grandfather than father, because his life became less frenetic in retirement when his grandchildren were present. Andrew said his father's one fault was 'that he didn't spend enough time with us as children'. Michael cannot ever remember being unhappy in his childhood, but recalled that 'as a family our lives were always full on and we didn't spend a lot of time at home'. He added, 'family meant a lot to Dad but I think community was paramount'. Because of the Aboriginal community work that Alick increasingly did, he found little time to attend functions at his children's schools or to watch their sporting activities. They cannot recall many trips to the park or other such activities with their Dad. Perhaps they have forgotten, but their story is consistent. Andrew commented: 'when other kids were riding their bikes down along the creek, we were shaking hands, raising money for the Girls' Hostel. I remember standing outside Victoria Park when I was fifteen years of age in 1966 collecting signatures for the Referendum'.

They were also taken to many Aboriginal meetings partly, Andrew suspects, to quell their complaints of 'not another meeting' by including them. But Alick would also have seen it as an educative experience. All three children later entered Aboriginal affairs and have spent their life's work in that area. Michael recently summed Alick up: 'Dad had a great sense and belief in justice and equality. He abhorred racism in any form and also religious intolerance. Dad also had a work ethic that had him going seven days a week. He never sat still. I would hope I have many of these qualities'.

In 1967 the family moved house again. They were advised that Pascoe Vale was bad for Merle's asthma. They wanted a brick house and searched for one in vain in Northcote, so they ended up at number 22 Lemon Road, North Balwyn, where they stayed until the early 1990s, although it was a disruptive move for the children who lost school friends. This house again became filled with people. Interstate visitors increased after Merle and Alick became involved in the Federal Council for Aboriginal and Torres Strait Islanders (FCAATSI) in the 1960s and established more Australia-wide contacts. Some who came to stay and became close friends included the poets Jack Davis and Oodgeroo Noonuccal (Kath Walker). They held parties so Melbourne people could meet these visitors.

7   The 'Greek Grappler'

Alick continued to wrestle casually in the boxing tents during the first fifteen years of his marriage. He performed with Sharman's troupe at the annual east coast capital city metropolitan shows, namely the Royal Easter Show in Sydney each April, the Brisbane Exhibition in August and the Melbourne Show every September. These ran for a week filled with constant wrestling, excitement and catching up with old mates. Alick also performed at smaller Victorian country shows with Sharman or Harry Johns: 'when I worked at the markets and hawked potatoes around the suburbs it was only a three-day job. So that gave me time if I was doing a Saturday show to finish on Friday morning and then head up to Colac or somewhere and do a Saturday show'.

Wrestling provided added income for Alick's young family. He earned the basic wage in a day from a wrestling program, although this involved a day's travel. It was pay at casual rates and mostly cash in hand. Sharman offered Alick and his partner, Clive Coram, £35 plus airfare for wrestling for ten days at the Sydney Show in 1959. Wrestlers were paid considerably more than most tent boxers, excluding the stars, because they were more skilled and there were fewer of them. Recently 'Young' Jimmy Sharman refused to divulge just how much he paid Alick, and would only say, even when pressed, that 'he was well looked after'.

Alick occasionally was able to combine wrestling and family. They attended when he performed at the Melbourne Show or in weekend country shows near Melbourne. Merle went with the children to look at the exhibitions, but 'she'd rarely ever come into the tents…but she'd go the showgrounds, she'd let the kids loose and they were like homing pigeons, coming back to Jimmy Sharman's. It was safe in those days'. Alick's daughter Esmai recalled:

Wrestling with mates at Castellorizo ('Cassie') picnic in the 1950s; Cousin Theo Conos (left) has an arm bar on Alick.

we'd go and stay all day, we were young, about ten, heaven forbid you'd never let your kids do it now. We'd run around the Show and come back to the tent, then we'd run around again. Dad would be up there or be the 'gee' in the crowd. He was my Dad you know, just good stuff, very impressive.

But there were family sacrifices. Alick was away wrestling in the tents for about six or seven weeks each year in total, but not consecutively, and half of the time just overnight. Alick admitted that the Shepparton Show and the Sports Night the following weekend in early October often coincided with his daughter's birthday: 'there were no arguments, but Merle wasn't happy that I wasn't home for Esmai's birthday'. He once took the family when he wrestled in Tasmania and made the trip a holiday. They stayed with Harry and Sylvia Paulsen, who of all the boxing tent promoters, were the only ones to put up boxers in their own house. However, if a hard choice had to be made between wrestling and family, wrestling mostly lost. As 'Young Jimmy' Sharman wrote to Clive Coram in March 1959:

> Dear Clive,
> A Short note to know if you were coming over for the Sydney Show, starting next Friday March 20th. Alex Jackamos will not be coming owing to his wife's asthma troubles. He told me in his letter that he had to leave the Carnera crowd and come home from Tasmania. It must be awkward for him having nobody to care for his family and children. Still Alex is a great guy and I have a lot of time for the way he has battled on against severe odds at times…and made a 'go' of things.

If it could work out, Alick with his boundless energy would try to do everything as he did on his honeymoon; combining love, wrestling and money in a way that only Alick could do.

Alick's wrestling career reached a new plateau in 1956 when he began wrestling at the Melbourne Stadium. Alick and his partner Clive Coram remember a slightly different version of how this eventuated. Clive remembered that while returning one Saturday evening to Melbourne after wrestling at Kyneton, Alick suggested they duck into the West Melbourne Stadium to see if they might get a bout, which they fortunately scored. Alick recalled that they had complimentary tickets, and were sitting in the audience, when a 'crisis' occurred. All of the preliminary boxing bouts ended quickly, due to a series of early round knock-outs, and there was a gap of half an hour before the main event. One of the Stadiums Ltd staff knew that Alick and Clive wrestled in the tents and asked them to fill in, which they did, quickly borrowing some gear. Whichever version is correct, they were a big hit. Alick recalled that the radio announcer Fred Tupper declared it 'the best demonstration of scientific wrestling we've seen in Festival Hall for years'. The crowd loved it and the two wrestlers were invited back following week.

Alick and Clive wrestled in a more scientific style at the Stadium than in the tents, 'strong and quick' as Clive Coram put it, with less emphasis on a 'showbiz' performance. Indeed, as middle to light heavyweights, they used more skill than the heavyweights at the Stadium, who grunted and 'performed'. Alick described their many holds: 'we did scientific wrestling — referee grip, full nelson, half nelson, short-arm scissors, wrist locks, flying head scissors, step-over-toe hold, and this is what the crowd loved with the light heavyweights'. Alick and Clive wrestled each other as well as numerous other opponents in Melbourne's stadiums on many Saturday nights — Festival Hall, West Melbourne Stadium, Exhibition Building, Collingwood Town Hall, and the Olympic Pool. As usual Alick was proactive.

> Stadiums Ltd had an office in Little Collins Street east. I always made it my business about Tuesday or Monday just to call in on a social visit to see Harold Belf [the matchmaker] just to remind him I was still around...I'd say to Harold: 'well, how about Saturday night?' He'd reply, 'Oh all right, will you wrestle Clive Coram or someone?' I didn't wait for him to tell me, I went in and saw him.

Alick and Clive also wrestled at many local venues for football and especially police boys club fundraisers across the suburbs, and in country towns near Melbourne. *Australian Ring* magazine wrote that Alick, 'a complete teetotaller and non-smoker', gave lectures at boys clubs on 'physical fitness and clean living'. He also demonstrated wrestling holds on television. The magazine added that 'Alick Jackomos is one fellow who lives for his sport. He has helped many youngsters on the way to being clean-living, healthy-minded citizens of the future. Although only a little fellow, he's probably the biggest little ball of fire in the game today'.

In the late 1950s a Greek wrestling boom emerged in Melbourne, featuring overseas imports. Alick was well placed to capitalise on it given his Greek heritage and name, appearing in events at venues not controlled by Stadiums Ltd, including the Melbourne Town Hall and the Olympic Swimming Pool. The *Castellorizian Newsletter* in a profile on Alick (perhaps written by himself), recorded that 'his greatest moment', was when he toured Tasmania in 1959 as a supporting act to Jim Londos, the 'Golden Greek' former world wrestling champion, and Primo Carnera, former world boxing champion turned wrestler. Advertisers continually misspelt Alick's name but he seemed unperturbed by this. He was billed as 'Alec Jackamos', 'Alec Jackomas', 'Alec Jacemos', 'Alex Jacomas', 'Alex Jackomas', and 'Alex Jackoman'. Not one of the many programs and press reports that survive listed his given or family name correctly. If the surname was

At the Stadium Clive Coram applies an arm lock on Alick, who prepares to counter with a throw.

Sometimes called the 'Greek Grappler', Alick poses for a fan photograph.

occasionally correct, his first name never was, but then it *is* an unusual spelling. Clive Coram's name was also often tortured, to the lengths of 'Bruce Corran'.

Programs described Alick as coming 'from Greece', or 'being a Greek-born Victorian'. One report described him as a 'versatile and rugged lightweight, a seasoned professional who has wrestled in all states, a fast and clever mover who gained his early experience with Sharman's troupe'. Another program for a Greek wrestling night held at the Olympic Swimming Pool on 16 May 1959 dubbed him 'perhaps the most colourful of all wrestlers in Victoria. He was born in Australia from Greek parents, and took up wrestling at a very young age. Alex has wrestled with success all over Australia. He is a fast scientific wrestler, and has a wonderful array of holds'. Clive Coram was described as 'Jackomas' greatest rival for many years. 'Whenever these two wrestlers meet you can always expect plenty of fireworks'. An article in *Australian Ring*, which did get his name right, described Alick as a 'person of violent explosive action when he is in the wrestling ring'. It commented that although Alick was only 5 feet 9 inches

(175 cm) — in fact he was really 5 feet 5 inches (165 cms) — and only 12 stone (76 kg), 'Alick combines speed and amazing strength to defeat fifteen stoners'. He certainly wrestled Crusher Webb, Bruce Milne, Ken Furher and others, often heavier, taller men of 15 stone. The programs often billed Alick as a heavier '14 stone', or made him ten centimetres taller than he was, to make the bout appear more equally matched. He had a satisfying win over Crusher Webb in 1957 during a preliminary bout to the world title match between 'Jesse James' and Lou Thez, both Greeks, watched by a large Greek audience. He defeated Webb in 'devastating style'.

Although Stadium wrestling was more scientific, an element of co-operation between opponents was still necessary. This is where Alick and Clive's thousands of routines in the boxing tents gave them a huge advantage. Alick explained: if a wrestler put on an 'arm bar' and you jumped to extricate yourself and put a 'flying scissor' hold on him, he had to support you, otherwise you collapsed when you tried to jump. The 'flying scissors was one of my favourite holds'. So when you jumped and rolled he'd let go of the 'arm bar' and you would have him on the floor in a 'head scissors'. If you rolled the wrong way you could break your neck. 'But Clive and I did that a lot with Jimmy Sharman, it was an easy hold to perform'. You could also get injured picking someone up over your head and throwing them to the mat, 'but I never did a body slam'.

Alick was never injured in the tents, except when cut with a nail file and occasionally thumped from behind with an umbrella, but he received several injuries in the Stadium because the wrestling was more physical and genuine. He regularly suffered displaced vertebrae and occasionally a dislocated knee.

> But every Monday morning after a Saturday night wrestle, I'd go to George Sanders in Victoria Street, he was a masseur for the Australian team at the '48 Olympics and for the Carlton Football Club. He was the world's best! You'd go to him with a vertebrae out, a dislocated knee and he'd put it back, he'd rub you down, and within a few minutes he'd have you right for a wrestle the next day.

During one match with Bruce Arthur, an Olympic bronze medallist, Alick received a body slam and wrestled on, but did not remember the bout.

The Stadium was a world that his family shared far less than when he wrestled in boxing tents. Andrew remembers his father packing his bag for wrestling appearances and the smell of the goanna oil in his clothing. Merle and the children went occasionally, which was a thrill as Andrew recalled, 'every young boy's childhood dream is to have a father who's a boxer or a wrestler', adding, 'it was almost as good as if your father played for Collingwood'. Andrew remembered the excitement of going out to the dressing rooms when he was about ten, where all the wrestlers, the 'Big Caramba', 'Zebra Man' and other 'terrifying guys' with masks were to be found. To his amazement 'Dad would be sitting having a cup of tea with them'. Michael, who was four years younger, was less amazed than confused.

> I remember one time in particular when he wrestled someone who had a mask on. I was really young and I remembered after the bout I went down to the dressing room and Dad and this other wrestler were talking. Then we all went out to Dad's car and we dropped off the other man at his accommodation. I was confused for some time about this; because I couldn't figure out why Dad would be so nice to someone he had just finished fighting.

Alick's big regret was that he missed televised wrestling. He once appeared on a Channel 7 show hosted by a young Ernie Sigley to demonstrate wrestling holds with Clive, and he did a similar thing on 'the Happy Hammond' show. He occasionally appeared on the Cinesound newsreels as well as those that were shown at theatres before the main film. But television mostly eluded him. In 1964 he was wrestling most weeks at Festival Hall when he holidayed in the Northern Territory with the family. While there he developed a tropic ulcer on his knee, a similar infection to the one that prevented him from going to Japan after the war. This time it took six months to heal, preventing any wrestling at the very time Jack Little imported Mario Milano and others to take on the locals. Televised wrestling became extremely popular. Kids in backyards all over the country were trying out holds and routines to emulate the stars. Bruce Milne, one of Alick's long-term opponents, became popular. Alick, with his showground 'gee' skills, his athleticism and his billing as a 'foreigner', would have offered a lot to televised wrestling. This form was far more theatrical than stadium wrestling, and closely resembled the performances given in the boxing tents.

Alick continued wrestling with Clive in the tents after 1965 but less frequently, and it ended when Sharman's (and other tents) were closed by new health and safety regulations, requiring a doctor to be in attendance at each bout. The cost was prohibitive. Jimmy Sharman's tent, which had given sixty years of uninterrupted performances, operated for the last time at the Shepparton Show in 1971. Alick continued to appear at football club sports days in the late 1960s and occasionally in mud wrestling contests. He recalled mud wrestling the footballer Doug Bigelow in aid of the Pascoe Vale Returned Services League. He also mud wrestled at Tom Wittingslow's Christmas–New Year carnival at Lakes Entrance for $10 a bout, but Alick did not particularly like mud wrestling, for it was more dangerous and unpredictable than wrestling on terra firma. 'In the mud he's liable to stick your head underneath the mud, it can get in your eyes and mouth, anything can happen'. Johnny Davis, one of Alick's Lakes Entrance wrestling partners, once broke a leg. However, it was still wrestling, a performance and paid, so he accepted engagements: 'as soon as we'd have our wrestle, it would only go for five or ten minutes, we'd go over to the Tower Hotel at Lakes Entrance, have a shower and clean up and everything was right again. It was clean mud'.

By the early 1970s Alick had virtually retired from wrestling after 25 years of activity. His last wrestling match was at the age of fifty-nine during the official opening of the Fitzroy All Stars Gymnasium during the July 1983 National Aboriginal Day Organising Committee (NADOC later NAIDOC) celebrations. He was invited to wrestle by Jock Austin on behalf of the Sports Sub-committee of NADOC Victoria. Austin tried hard to find a suitable time, writing to Alick, 'a wrestling exhibition by you would be a real crowd pleaser and we are keen to include you in the programme'. A former Aboriginal boxer

Alick shows no mercy to this opponent at Festival Hall, Melbourne.

living in Melbourne, Bindi Williams, agreed to partner Alick. They trained for six weeks and Alick recalled that 'by the time we wrestled, Bindi knew all the tricks. We wrestled to a packed house at the new Gym. Bindi was given the decision and this was his first and last wrestle. He retired undefeated'. It was not so amazing that Alick was able to do this at fifty-nine, for he kept fit all his life. In his early seventies he was still 'working-out' at the All Stars Gym.

Alick's effective retirement from regular wrestling by 1971 did not end his involvement with the showgrounds. He worked casually for Kitch and Bernice McLure, who ran carnival games and 'knock'–em–downs'. He travelled to the Lilydale, Dandenong and other shows near to home, and sometimes helped out at the Melbourne and Adelaide Shows as well. He worked for the McLure's in this casual fashion throughout the 1970s on some weekends and in between his other commitments. He did not need the money. He just wanted to be around the showgrounds for a while to relive the old memories and practise his ability to sell. Bernice McLure said he caused people to stop. 'Somehow or other, without people knowing, Alick'd manipulate them into what he wanted them to do, as he had a lovely, happy manner'.

He also sold boomerangs that he sourced from Bill Onus' factory in Belgrave. This venture began while he was still wrestling around Victoria. He used to buy 30-cm boomerangs for three shillings and sell them for six and the half-metre ones for six and sell them for twelve shillings. Alick recalled that Bill's boomerangs — he was a one-time Australian champion — would 'always come back'. Onus made them from marine ply, as he needed to mass-produce them, and this material worked perfectly. After Bill's death in 1968, his son Lin took over the business until he began landscape painting, for which he became celebrated until his early death in 1996. Alick then bought boomerangs from non-Aboriginal people, including a supplier in Heathcote, who learned the art from Bill Onus. Eventually Asian imports put them out of business.

His boomerang sales were assisted by his 'showie' friends. Sharman permitted Alick to set up his wares between the ropes of the boxing tent, saving Alick the cost of becoming a Showmen's Guild member and hiring a site at three shillings a foot frontage. The Showmen's Guild controlled the shows and permission for membership, and a site had to be sought through them. Alick was eligible to become a member of the Showmen's Guild, because he fulfilled many times over the three-year eligibility rule of working on the showgrounds. But it was not worth it if he wanted to sell at only a few shows each year. Bernice McLure later helped him to obtain his own ground at the Lilydale and Dandenong Shows, in the 'arts and industries' area, as he was not a Guild member.

Alick's family also helped sometimes: 'I'd put a couple of little card tables there while I'm there with Jimmy Sharman or Harry Johns or Roy Bell, my little daughter Esmai would be sitting at the card tables selling boomerangs. I'd be there for a while, until the show started'. Once his tent wrestling ended and Alick could give his full attention to selling, he recalled, 'I had a sandwich board with a lot of nails [on which to hang them]. I used to sell thousand and thousands of boomerangs and this continued for about twenty years'. He demonstrated their returning ability when space allowed, and as Bernice McLure stated, he 'put on an interesting tale'.

Boomerang sales over twenty years never made Alick rich. But it was a good comfortable sideline, with its 100 per cent profit on small amounts. This was important once he was in paid work, not small business, in later life. He liked the thrill of the sale and the thought that he had turned a profit. But he was not there for the money: as his investments would have done much better for him. Bernice McLure, who saw him in action, declared: 'he loved the involvement, he really loved it. He'd been on the showgrounds for years and he knew everyone, and he was very well liked everywhere he went'. Gail Magdziarz was definite that Alick was just like her father, Jack Allan, a showman for over seventy years: 'they were extroverts, they liked the challenge, of meeting harsh conditions and getting over it, they loved the camaraderie'. However, around 1990, after twenty years of selling boomerangs, Alick said, 'I just got tired of it and stopped'. Yet he continued to sell other things until his final year, in order to engage with people.

8 Teaming with Doug Nicholls

When Alick returned from the war in 1946 and was reunited with family, he soon made a bee-line for Fitzroy. The attraction was his many pre-war friends, and one in particular, Doug Nicholls. Alick had shaken a tin on the Yarra bank as a youth just before the war, watching as Nicholls and others spoke on Aboriginal issues. After he met Merle in late 1950, Doug Nicholls' church in Fitzroy was one of the first places Alick took her. As his connections with Nicholls grew in the post-war years, Alick teamed with 'Uncle Doug', first as an 'apprentice' then more as a partner, in a relationship that lasted a generation. Their association focused upon the Fitzroy Church, developed through welfare and community work, but later became more involved in politics and activism through various community and political organisations.

Alick, like many others, found Doug Nicholls to be a magnetic character. Nicholls was originally from Cummeragunja, the Mission on the Murray River just over the border from Echuca, where Merle Jackomos had been born. Nicholls was moved off the Mission as a teenager under the policy of the New South Wales Aboriginal Protection Board and worked on irrigation works, playing country football as well. He came to Melbourne in the late 1920s to further his football career. During the 1930s Nicholls became a noted player for Northcote's VFL side and Fitzroy's AFL team, and represented Victoria in interstate football. He developed a reputation as a speedy winger — dubbed the 'flying Abo' by a sympathetic crowd — and he eventually became immensely respected and popular. Nicholls won the Warracknabeal and Nyah Gifts in 1929, and also fought for a season in Jimmy Sharman's boxing tent in 1931, which added to his magnetism in Alick's eyes.

Alick and his mentor, Pastor Doug Nicholls

After the death of his mother, Nicholls revisited the Church of Christ in Northcote, where they had worshipped together. On 17 July 1932 he committed his life to Christ and was baptised in this church on 31 July. Nicholls' football career continued alongside his Christian profession, and his increasing political involvement with William Cooper's Australian Aborigines League, the first Aboriginal political organisation in Victoria. Nicholls enlisted in the AIF, but was demobilised in 1941 at the request of the Fitzroy police and Aboriginal people, to work among the poverty-stricken Fitzroy Aboriginal community. Nicholls tackled welfare and social problems among Aboriginal residents, who were attracted to the city by work in Melbourne's war industries. Most were crammed into unsuitable rental housing, made worse by the severe accommodation crisis created by years of Depression and now war.

In 1942 Nicholls married Gladys Bux. Doug and Gladys forged a successful marriage, and a great spiritual and welfare partnership, because in 1943 Doug Nicholls began an Aboriginal ministry. It was located in a building donated by the Church of Christ at

258 Gore Street, Fitzroy. Nicholls made the Gore Street church a focus of community, creating an 'Aboriginal Sunday' each Sunday before Australia Day. He invited footballers or well-known sportsmen to attend. The day was later moved to July and evolved into NAIDOC week by the 1960s.

Nicholls' church at first survived through donations, the efforts of Gladys who in the early 1950s ran a small mixed business in the emerging Housing Commission suburb of Broadmeadows from a one-roomed shed, until Nicholls was made coach and then curator at the Northcote Football Ground. Alick became a member of the Gore Street church in 1946 but his involvement was interrupted by his tours with the boxing tents in 1947–48, and his ownership of the time-consuming hamburger shop. However, once Alick married Merle, and bought a truck for the three-day-a-week market run, Doug Nicholls increasingly found good works for him and his truck to do. Alick of course jumped at the chance to do voluntary welfare work among the Melbourne Aboriginal community.

It was an amalgam of people from different areas and cultural groups, Yorta Yorta from the north-west, Gunditjmara from the south-west and Gunai people from Gippsland, to name a few of the groups, members of which had moved to Melbourne to take advantage of city work. They were mutually suspicious and generally married within their own cultural groups. Indeed, research by Diane Barwick, a Canadian anthropologist, revealed that Aboriginal people in the 1950s were more inclined to marry into the white community than into other Victorian Aboriginal communities. This has since changed and one reason for that was the social intermixing that occurred in Melbourne in the immediate post-war decades. Alick played a key role in that intermixing of Aboriginal groups from diverse parts of the state.

During the late 1950s Alick teamed up with Eric Onus, a Yorta Yorta man, to provide community entertainment. As Alick recalled, 'there were no social activities around Fitzroy for the people. A lot of them were living two or three families in one house, with a toilet down the back, shared kitchen, they were horrible conditions... houses were hard to get in those days'. They decided to run dances in the Manchester Unity Hall on the corner of Vere and Hoddle streets, Collingwood.

On the road with Doug Nicholls, 1960s

They operated regular dances at that venue until 1965, when they moved to Northcote. The rent of the hall was £4 a night, and they charged three shillings a family. About a hundred people came most Friday nights. Harry Williams played guitar and was accompanied by Alice Thomas (née Young) on the piano. The music was 'Old Time', perfect for such dances as the Barn Dance, Gypsy Tap, Pride of Erin and so forth. They provided tea and coffee and a biscuit. Most nights 'we made a little bit of profit, not much, maybe three, four, five or six quid, some nights we lost money…it went to someone with a hospital bill, because in those days public hospitals you still had to pay…to a funeral fund, or someone in distress'.

The Jackomos children retain pleasant memories of those dances. Esmai, the eldest, remembers the presence of lots of children. 'We'd tear around on the floor in between the people dancing. We were terrors. In fact Bruce McGuiness always used to say to the parents, [jokingly] "you've got rotten kids." I just remember it so clearly, I can just see it'. Andrew recalled of these monthly Friday night events: 'I just loved them. We used to slide down the stairs and shoot through the room. I was only young, about eight years old…it was the high-

Alick and Merle Jackomos with their close friends Winnie and Eric Onus at George Bracken's twenty-first birthday party, 1956

light of my childhood going to those community dances'. Andrew can still remember 'when I was about nine doing the old time dances like the Pride of Erin and the Barn Dance at the MU Hall'. They felt so much a part of the action as their father was organiser, Master of Ceremonies and bouncer. Esmai recalled that despite the no-alcohol rule, one woman often secretly carried in a little bottle of grog and stayed until Alick saw her play up and then he would say 'Out you go!'. Some others hid rum in Coca Cola bottles, purchased from a vendor outside, until Alick finally woke up as to why people took so long over a small drink.

An Aboriginal Youth Club operated out of the Gore Street church; it was run by Bindi Jack, an interstate Aboriginal boxer, who married Gladys Bryant from Lake Tyers and stayed on in Victoria. Bindi Jack imparted his boxing and fitness skills and Alick did the same. The *Coburg Courier* in 1961 wrote of Alick's voluntary work in many boys clubs, commenting that: 'he also aids the Aboriginal youth club with its activities'. The *Courier* added:

> Whenever he is free there is nothing surer that that he will wend his way towards one of the police boys' clubs where he gives exhibitions on the importance of physical fitness and clean living. Alick stoutly believes as a sport for boys wrestling is superior to boxing, because it teaches the art of self defence and at the same time develops the body. Neither, he maintains, is the incidence of injury as high as in boxing.

Each Christmas Alick also became involved in the community's Aboriginal Christmas tree, where the money raised bought presents for the children. He always saw this work as important because of his belief in providing a good life for children wherever possible. He was often the organiser of these activities and sometimes played Santa. In later life he was still raising funds for the Aboriginal Christmas tree and donating part of his royalties to this cause.

Alick also assisted Doug and Gladys Nicholls to raise money for other causes. The Nicholls dreamt of providing a hostel for Aboriginal youth coming to work in Melbourne to assist them to make right choices in life. Nicholls raised funds through his football contacts and reputation, which brought forth donations of land, materials and money. A Hostel for Girls opened at 56 Cunningham Street, Northcote, in 1956, which under Doug and Gladys Nicholls' supervision, eventually accommodated nine girls who worked in Melbourne factories and retail outlets. Myra Grinter (née Atkinson), now a social worker, lived there for four years and she pointed out that many of the girls 'went on to better things' because of the influence of the Nicholls. 'They gave us kids a vision', she asserted. Doug and Gladys Nicholls guided them to church each Sunday and encouraged them to attend meetings as well as Aboriginal socials. A Boys Hostel, later named the Bill T. Onus Hostel, began a few doors away in 1963. 'Tanderra', a holiday house at Queenscliff, opened in 1963, following a private gift of land and donations of money, material and time to convert a donated building that was moved to the site.

The hostels provided opportunities for Alick and Merle to play a further role in the community. For instance, the young residents were encouraged to form a social committee and plan activities. Myra Grinter recalls that Doug and Gladys Nicholls and Alick and Merle

Alick and Merle Jackomos with Andrew and Michael pictured with Rose and Tom Dunnolley, Barmah Lakes, 1958

Jackomos chaperoned these activities, which included trips to the country or beach weekends at 'Tanderra'.

> Aunty Merle used to stop with us girls and Uncle Alick used to stop with the boys just to make sure we were fed. We spent a lot of time down on the beaches. At night we'd sit down and talk, they were such great times. They took the place of our parents while we were away from home, along with Uncle Doug and Aunty Gladys.

The Jackomos children came along, which added to the fun. As Myra Grinter recalled, 'they were always joking and of course Aunty Merle has got this unbelievable laugh. Everything was fun, all the time'. The Nicholls and Jackomos teams managed this fun within a firm control. Myra stated: 'I can't remember anytime where they had to chastise us. Everything was set out and you were told what to expect and what they expected from you and that was it'.

Aboriginal picnic at Jackson's Track, Drouin, in the late 1950s

In 1962 Alick became a member of the revived Australian Aborigines' League, which had been formed in the mid-1930s by William Cooper. Alick was the only non-Aboriginal member since Arthur Burdeau, who was President in the 1930s. Alick was on the Executive, first as 'Social Organiser' in July 1962, when Stewart Murray was President, Doug Nicholls Vice-President, Margaret Burns the Secretary, and Bruce McGuiness the Public Relations Officer. Alick headed the Social Sub-committee, which organised an Aboriginal Ball in September 1962, an event that began in 1961 (although Alick always maintained that one run by Aunty Margaret Tucker in 1949 was the first). The Sub-committee deliberated on the entertainment, catering and crockery, photographers, publicity and ticket sales. It was to be like any other ball of its day to demonstrate Aboriginal equality to the world: with a mayoral opening, a dance band, dinner suits and gowns, and a 'Belle of the Ball' contest, with a prize of a sash, tiara and a modelling course. The winner of the fundraising contest

— the 'Most Popular Girl of the Year' — won a £100 wardrobe plus sash, and there were minor prizes of a modelling course. Alick was in his element in all these arrangements. Bill Onus reported at the sub-committee's October meeting that the Ball was a great success, except for a long speech, which included reading out a list of donations to the ball, which Alick no doubt solicited. There was also an incident during the judging of the 'Belle of the Ball' contest. Apparently several white girls were asked to leave the floor during the adjudication because Onus had understood that the committee, during an earlier meeting, had given him 'the impression that the Belle was to be an Aborigine girl'. The following year the contest was 'open to everyone'. The profits from the Ball were handed to the recently formed Aboriginal Advancement League.

The annual balls begun in 1961 continued and Alick remained chief organiser and compère for 21 years from 1964 to 1984. Esmai, his daughter, took over in 1985 for several years. No papers survive to document Alick's organisational efforts, but there were many memorable ball nights in the Northcote Town Hall. These balls were extremely popular and full of fun. Myra Grinter recalled, 'us young ones used to go and dress up to the "tees" and catch up with people that you hadn't seen for a while...it created good relationships too'. These balls revealed to the world that Aboriginal people in Victoria were able to match any activity that the white community could mount. It demonstrated to the wider community, in language it understood, that scores of Aboriginal people were sufficiently successful to be able to buy a £1 single ball ticket with a scalloped gold edge, and could also afford to make, hire or buy ball gowns and dinner suits. Surviving pictures reveal that the sophistication they created matched any suburban ball around Melbourne.

Some, including Albert Maori-kiki, a New Guinean guest at the Ball in the late 1960s, misinterpreted these events as assimilative gestures. He allegedly walked out, saying 'these guys just want to be Whities'. The balls were distinctly Aboriginal affairs, however, aimed at building greater cohesion among a Melbourne Aboriginal community, still in the process of coalescing and intermarrying from diverse regional communities. Myra Grinter recalled: 'some Aboriginal people from the country would come to Melbourne and they

The Jackomos family at the Aboriginal Ball, Northcote Town Hall, 1970

would be isolated, so the ball actually brought us together'. Critics also overlooked the fundraising aspects, moneys going towards the Advancement League's building fund. The Annual Aboriginal Balls in Melbourne have survived to this day. Indeed, they became stronger because they were eventually linked to NAIDOC week each July. Alick recalled that there was resistance at first to this change, as NAIDOC was initially run by white 'religious people' from the Advancement League, who thought a ball 'unbefitting' the solemnity of NAIDOC.

Alick played other community-building roles. He instituted and personally wrote 'Aboriginal News', subtitled, 'A Monthly Bulletin of the Australian Aborigines' League, Victoria'. It was a typed and roneoed two-page bulletin produced on foolscap paper, which was a bit blurred at times because of the cheap production. Fourteen numbers were issued between August 1963 and November 1966. They reveal Alick's lesser interest in politics and his greater instinct for community relations. Apart from the Aboriginal congresses, little political news appeared in the news sheets. 'Aboriginal News' was almost silent for instance on the fight to prevent Lake Tyers' closure in the mid-1960s, despite Doug Nicholls resigning from the Aboriginal Welfare Board over the matter in March 1963 and widespread agitation. Nicholls led a march on Parliament in 1965, which caused a government backdown and the gazetting of Lake Tyers as a permanent reserve.

'Aboriginal News' reveals Alick's great interest in people, family and the events that create and sustain a community, its history rather than its politics. The 'Gleanings' column provided news of people's movements, illnesses, anniversaries, sporting successes and appointments to positions on the Welfare Board or as matron to the Aboriginal hostels. It contained information on the annual Aboriginal Ball, the annual Christmas tree, fundraising days and forthcoming social events — dances, talent quests and boomerang field days. 'Aboriginal News' also followed the movements of Doug Nicholls as he stumped the country on Advancement League fundraising ventures and branch openings. It occasionally contained job placement information from companies willing to employ Aboriginal workers.

The bulletins also reflected Alick's growing interest in genealogy and history, as it had sections on births, deaths and marriages, and a 'Down Memory Lane' column. The latter made brief reference to William Cooper and the Day of Mourning; Sister Ellis who ran the 'Bethesda Aboriginal Mission' in Fitzroy from the late 1930s; Margaret Tucker's concerts and her running of the first Aboriginal Ball in 1949; and other moments in recent Aboriginal history — that is, events that Alick had experienced. 'Aboriginal News' quickly changed from monthly to one every second month for the first year and to a quarterly bulletin thereafter. It also altered its subtitle to 'A Newsletter for the Aboriginal People of Victoria', which indicated that the venerable Australian Aborigines' League was fading, and also that the bulletin was seeking a wider appeal.

9 Political Activism

Alick, who had a fleeting experience of Aboriginal politics at Yarra Bank meetings in 1938–39 was drawn more fully and inevitably into the Aboriginal political world through his contacts with Doug Nicholls and others from the late 1940s, despite Alick's natural inclination of not being a political person. As he recalled in 1998, through Doug Nicholls' Gore Street church 'I got involved with some of his political meetings' although, as Alick quickly added, 'politics were never mentioned in church'. The 1950s became particularly lively at the state level as Aboriginal people challenged the assimilation policy, and this continued in the 1960s as the Aboriginal political scene across Australia 'heated up', taking Alick along with it.

With the death in 1942 of William Cooper, Doug Nicholls, along with Bill Onus, Margaret Tucker and others, became prominent political leaders and spokespersons for the Victorian Aboriginal community. By the 1940s, Victoria's Aboriginal Protection Board, then over seventy years old, was moribund. It did not meet or report to parliament; its management of Aboriginal affairs, such as it was, was handled by a few public servants. Children were continually removed from their parents and reserve lands were continually being whittled away and sold off to white farmers. Little wonder that Aboriginal people termed it the 'Aboriginal Destruction Board'. The Board also pursued an outdated policy of refusing to recognise Aboriginal people of 'mixed descent', who formed the vast majority of the 2000 Aborigines in the state, as being 'Aboriginal'. By the 1940s it came under sustained criticism from all quarters, especially Aboriginal people led by Nicholls, Onus, Tucker and others. In particular they challenged the Board's failure to provide adequate housing, health and educational services to Aboriginal people, to bring them to the standards enjoyed by other Victorians.

In a set of 'Objectives and Demands' issued in the early 1950s the Australian Aborigines' League also called for the Victorian government to end its policy of denying that Aboriginal people of 'mixed descent' were Aborigines or that they had special needs. It demanded the government take 'concrete responsibility' for the needs of 'Castes' (that is, Aboriginal people of 'mixed descent') outside the Lake Tyers reserve, without 'policing, interfering or overseeing' them. In particular, the statement called for urgent attention to their health, housing and educational needs. The 'Objectives and Demands' wanted the Lake Tyers reserve's title and property returned to Aboriginal people, and an end to the control of the residents' lives and movements, especially specific food rationing and their sterilisation, 'unless under the terms of their own free request, and not then until they have been examined by at least three independent doctors'. The claim of sterilisation is alarming, but little evidence has emerged about its incidence in Victoria. The League also wanted Aboriginal participation in the reserve's management and future. The statement also called for changes to the Protection Board, including the provision of elected Aboriginal representation.

Alick's political skills were heightened by association with Nicholls, the Secretary of the Aborigines' League. In his 'spare time' Alick toured with Doug Nicholls: 'Doug had a little Ford Escort in those days and we'd go to country towns pushing the political movement on Aboriginal people'. As awareness of the Aboriginal situation grew among the white community in the 1950s, Nicholls was in much demand as a speaker at Rotary and Apex clubs and church groups. Alick accompanied him to these meetings too, acting as his companion and driver. Alick wrote in 1993: 'I went along with him to these meetings. Doug did most of the talking'. But in 1997 Alick added, 'we'd go into the country and he'd give talks and eventually I learned to talk from him. [I would] give a few more little talks, but mostly I was his apprentice'. They also visited such places as the Ballarat Orphanage to check on Aboriginal children who had been removed from their families by the Aboriginal Protection Board. Alick once remarked that there were about a dozen living there most times they visited.

Alick knew Bill Onus, President of the Australian Aborigines' League, well although he was closer to his brother Eric. Bill Onus often promoted the Aboriginal political cause through cultural performances, boomerang throwing and social activities, which was attuned to Alick's community-building penchant. There was a strong vaudeville music tradition at Lake Tyers from the 1930s, and Margaret Tucker and others gave musical performances during wartime to raise money. Tucker organised the first Aboriginal Debutante Ball in August 1949, nineteen debutantes being presented to the Governor, Sir George Knox, and Lady Knox. Alick was to partner a debutante, the only non-Aboriginal person to do so, but that was the night he had to close the sale of his hamburger 'joint' and he missed out.

In April 1949 Onus organised a 'Corroboree Season 1949' at Wirth's Olympia on Easter Saturday, prefacing the program with the words: 'the object of this presentation of an all-Aboriginal entertainment is to show Australia that, given an opportunity, the Aborigine is quite capable of development along cultural lines'. Onus' preface also referred to the decimation of Aboriginal people since colonisation, and the need for a 'new deal' where, if given 'an equal chance', Aborigines would shine. He signed off the program, 'Bill Onus, Organizer and Producer (President of Australian Aborigines League)'. This 'Corroboree Season 1949' presented Aboriginal singers; including Margaret Tucker ('Princess Lilardia'), Edgar Bux, May Lovett and Joyce McKinnon; musicians such as Ted ('Chook') Mullett and his Gum Leaf Band; whip cracker and rodeo star Billy Bargo; and a comedy by Jacky (Eric Onus) and Jemmy (James Scott) 'the Brown Boys of Mirth and Melody'. It is unclear whether Alick saw this particular show although the program was in his archives. He certainly saw other such Corroborees on a smaller scale that Onus organised over the years.

Bill Onus operated a boomerang factory and art shop at Belgrave in the Dandenongs, which became another focus for Aboriginal people or those sympathetic to the cause. As Alick recalled: 'Bill was a great boomerang thrower, he would stand outside his shop a couple of feet from the glass windows, throw the boomerang and it would come back into his hands'. It was Bill Onus who taught Alick to throw,

Bill Onus shows his wares at Belgrave to 'Young Jimmy' Sharman and Alick around 1960.

a skill that later became important to Alick in many ways. Alick, Eric Onus, Bruce McGuinness and Stewart Murray ran the annual boomerang contest at Northcote Oval to raise money for Aboriginal welfare. Alick was often a judge, and later remarked, 'the trouble was that the white blokes used to win the championships' and eventually whites took over the event.

Bill Onus' shop and factory also provided a political education for Alick and others, for Bill was a deep thinker and a frequent speaker on public platforms in the Aboriginal cause. ASIO kept a file on him and this prevented him from making money in the USA throwing boomerangs. In these Cold War times Onus was claimed to be a 'Communist', simply because he had spoken to Communist (and Christian) meetings about the Aboriginal cause. A number of Aboriginal people worked for Onus in his factory, including his brother Eric and his wife Winnie, John, Joe and Bruce McGuinness, Harry, Mervyn and Iris Williams. Alick and Merle became very close to Eric and Winnie, and visited them frequently at Belgrave. It was perhaps at such gatherings that Alick learned to play the gum leaf, possibly from Herb Patten, another skill Alick later used to good effect.

The Australian Aborigines' League remained the only Aboriginal body into the 1950s, but in May 1957 it was joined by a dynamic new organisation, the Victorian Aboriginal Advancement League (the League). It emerged from a controversy in 1956 about the appalling conditions of Aborigines at the Warburton Ranges Mission, Western Australia, who had been displaced from their Maralinga lands during atomic testing after 1947. Doug Nicholls travelled to the West with a West Australian Senator, Bill Grayden, and filmed their living conditions backed by the Melbourne-based 'Save the Aborigines Committee'. Some committee members — Nicholls, Gordon Bryant MLA, women's and peace activist Doris Blackburn, and Church of Christ Pastor Stan Davey — formed the Aborigines Advancement League, to promote Aboriginal welfare and rights in Victoria and across Australia. Alick was there from the outset although he took a back seat to such prominent people. As he remarked in 1996: 'we [Merle and I] were involved right from its inception. I'm not a foundation member but I was there when it first started — with my wife and family...we were the Indians...Nicholls, Davey and Bryant were the chiefs'.

The League focused on welfare, but was not shy of criticising Aboriginal policy in Victoria, or elsewhere in Australia. It certainly attacked the assimilation policy of the newly formed Aborigines Welfare Board in Victoria, which superseded the Protection Board in 1958. The League defined its role in 1959: 'to work towards the complete integration of people of Aboriginal descent with the Australian community with full recognition of the contribution they are able to make'. It defined 'integration' as the ability of a minority to retain its identity. Aboriginal self-reliance, and self-respect, were other key aims.

The League created a unique infrastructure and provided further opportunities for many people, including Alick and Merle, to assist the Aboriginal community. It raised sufficient money to employ Doug Nicholls as a full-time field officer, which freed him from his paid work at the Northcote Football ground. He was to organise practical help for Aboriginal people, such as emergency assistance, employment and legal advice. Nicholls also increased his public addresses to churches and service club meetings. Stan Davey, honorary full-time League secretary, and other voluntary white workers, operated out of 46 Russell Street, Melbourne, and then 336 Victoria Parade, East Melbourne. These offices provided a centre for those living in and visiting the city and complemented Nicholls' Gore Street church. These premises also became a focus for Alick's life as he continued his part-time voluntary work for the community. In 1993 he described his role as 'voluntary welfare and field officer'. He was also a member of the League's Management Committee and on the Executive of Aboriginal hostels, which ran the Girls and Boys hostels in Cunningham Street. Merle was there beside him in most activities, leading some herself.

The women were the prime fundraisers. Gladys Nicholls commenced an Aboriginal Children's Christmas Tree Appeal in the mid-1940s which she organised for the next thirty years. To raise funds she established three opportunity shops in Brunswick Road and St Georges Road, Fitzroy, and held regular street stalls in High Street, Northcote. Merle and other Aboriginal women assisted. They were the driving force behind the push for a children's centre in Northcote,

Alick as Santa at the Aboriginal Children's Christmas tree run by the Advancement League

which failed to materialise due to a lack of a government permit. The building became a boys hostel instead, run by Aboriginal hostels Ltd. Gladys Nicholls, Merle, Geraldine Briggs and her daughters Margaret Wirrpunda and Hyllus Maris, and others, formed the National Council of Aboriginal and Torres Strait Islander Women.

By the early 1960s the Advancement League was supported by 36 branches across Melbourne and Victoria, which were also busy fundraising for clothing, bursaries, holiday programs and building projects. By 1965 the League boasted 2000 members. A survey identified that 88 per cent were professionals or white collar workers, and Protestant Christians and Jewish people were also over-represented. It published its own magazine called *Smoke Signals* in 1957 which ran till the 1970s. The League finally opened its own offices in Northcote, named the 'Doug Nicholls Centre' in 1966, raising 80 per cent of the capital itself. Alick was a key person involved in the fundraising. The League's new building soon became a focus for Aboriginal community and political life. Bill Onus donated a boomerang-shaped plaque, which read: 'This centre is erected to honour humble Australians and to provide a meeting place for those who believe that all human beings are born free and equal in dignity and rights and should act towards one another in a spirit of brotherhood'.

Alick became more overtly political working alongside Doug Nicholls. Alick was a social and welfare organiser by nature, a role he never gave up, but one now complemented by greater political activity in the Aboriginal cause. He also developed a greater awareness of politics in general. He was a Labor man by instinct — being the son of a Greek migrant who associated with Aboriginal people from Fitzroy — and also one by background, having a poor Depression boyhood in Collingwood and Carlton. Alick recalled in 1998 of pre-war politics: 'I didn't take *very* much interest, but even then, I was a Labor man, although I wasn't *voting*'. While in Sharman's boxing tent he often talked Socialism with Rud Kee, Sharman's tent manager, and he recalled in 1995 that 'I was socialist inclined'. Alick greatly admired Gordon Bryant, the federal Labor member for the seat of Wills in Coburg from 1955 to 1979. Besides being a founder of the League, and its first President, Bryant was Minister for Aboriginal Affairs in the Whitlam Government in 1972. Labor's 'It's Time' slogan in its

1972 election victory always appealed to Alick who applied it particularly to a new deal in Aboriginal affairs.

Knowledge of 'over-policing' also politicised Alick. He recalled several incidents for the Royal Commission into Aboriginal Deaths in Custody in the early 1990s. In the early 1960s Merle and Alick visited her aunt who lived in the transitional Aboriginal housing settlement of Rumbalara at Mooroopna. They spent the night there and the next day the police arrived and threatened to arrest them for staying without permission. Fortunately, someone brought in Charlie Huggard, who worked for the Welfare Board as the settlement's manager and rent collector. Huggard identified Alick and Merle, and 'we were allowed to stay'. A few months afterwards Alick was with Sharman's boxing tent at the Shepparton Show and while on the line-up board noticed the police arresting an Aboriginal friend, who was in the audience: 'After the show I went to the police station and said I was a friend…I asked why he was arrested. They said "Drunk and Disorderly". I said he wasn't. The police said "he doesn't have to be drunk for us to arrest him"'. Alick also related another story about having breakfast at the Builders' Arms Hotel in Fitzroy, an 'Aboriginal pub', during an Aboriginal Congress meeting in the mid-1960s. 'Charlie Carter from Lake Tyers was at a separate table. The police came in, grabbed Charlie and others and put them in the panel van and took them to Fitzroy Police Station and charged them with drunk and disorderly. It was about 9 a.m. [and he hadn't been drinking]'.

The Australian Aborigines' League's activities continued to foster Alick's political education. It survived into the 1960s and became the all-Aboriginal branch of the Aborigines Advancement League. In August 1962 the Australian Aborigines' League Executive (but not Alick), met with Ray Meagher MLA, Acting Chief Secretary, to call for more Aboriginal housing, education scholarships, and to discuss yet again the future of Lake Tyers. At the Annual General Meeting in May 1963 Bill Onus reported on a visit to Lake Tyers, and the 'Save the Lake Tyers Campaign' Committee sent a vote of thanks to the League for its financial and moral support. It reported that a list of nine demands had been sent to the government. The meeting also heard a report from Rex Harcourt of the Batman Re-enactment Committee of the proposed celebrations for late May. 'Batman' was to be flown in a helicopter to the Yarra. There was to be a presentation of a boomerang by eight prominent Aborigines to the 'Aborigines Friend of the Year', a boomerang- throwing contest, an essay prize, and several other competitions with proceeds going to the boys hostel. These re-enactments did not appear political, but they were. Aboriginal people admired Batman as the one person who had dealt with them over land, but by the late 1960s Doug Nicholls wanted to give the treaty back as the promised ongoing payments had not been made. By 1972 he was asking for a trust fund of half a million dollars by way of reparation.

In May 1963 Alick was unanimously elected as President of the Australian Aborigines' League. He was, with Arthur Burdeu (President 1936–42) the only other non-Aboriginal member ever allowed into this political organisation. Significantly, Alick was nominated by Bruce McGuinness, who was one of the more radical members, indicating widespread acceptance of Alick's role in the Aboriginal community. Alick remained President for three years.

Little is known of the Aborigines' League's day-to-day activities in this period, as the minutes of the group are missing, even from Alick's personal papers. There is no evidence of any controversy or trouble about his presidency. Indeed Colin Tatz, a lecturer in Politics and Economics at Monash University, and later the Aboriginal Advancement's League's nomination on the Aboriginal Welfare Board in 1965, recalled that Alick was

> a born mediator. He was the born referee given his wrestling career, the referee or the guy in the corner who knew when enough was enough and when to break up the fight and when to let things continue. He had a wonderful sensitivity for when things were about to go wrong in a room and he would try and defuse it before it got to that kind of situation.

While President, Alick stimulated community sentiment and a pan-Aboriginal feeling by editing 'Aboriginal News' and organising annual Aboriginal balls. He also organised three Aboriginal Congresses.

The first was over two days in June 1964 at the Fitzroy High School. Alick stated in his 'Memoirs' that Gordon Bryant gave him the idea. The Congress was attended by 70 Aboriginal people from Gippsland, the Western District, the Murray region and central Victoria. Lynch Cooper, son of William Cooper, drove virtually from Shepparton Hospital to be there. Non-indigenous speakers presented talks: Gordon Bryant, as Advancement League President; Ray Adams on the Cummeragunja farm project; Philip Felton, as Superintendent of the Welfare Board, and Shirley Andrews and Barry Christophers of the Council for Aboriginal Rights, who spoke on Aboriginal wages and conditions in the Northern Territory. A dinner dance run by Alick was held on the Saturday night, with entertainment by Aboriginal performers.

The Conference was a key moment in pan-Aboriginal action, with four 'Aborigines only' separate sessions, although Alick as President was present. The aim was 'the organisation of Aboriginals in Victoria and the forming of regional branches'. The Congress resolved that the Aboriginal Branch of the Aborigines Advancement League (that is, the Australian Aborigines' League) would be the central 'all-Aboriginal' body in Melbourne, with five regional branches at Warrnambool,

With Merle at an Advancement League dinner dance, c. 1970

Cummeragunja, Orbost, Lake Tyers and the Goulburn Valley. Alick was reaffirmed as President of this 'all-Aboriginal' branch, to which there was no objection, confirming once again his unique status in the Victorian Aboriginal community. The Congress urged in particular the rehousing of Aboriginal people within three years and the provision of more social workers.

Alick organised a Second Aboriginal Congress in July 1965. He aimed for 'wide publicity' and informed delegates: 'if you attend with your friends this will demonstrate the determination of the Aboriginal people to press their claims for social justice'. He added, typically: 'bring your Harmony and Musical instruments to the Social evening'. Papers were presented by non-Aboriginal speakers, including Frank Edmonds on the 'Save the Lake Tyers Campaign'; Colin Tatz on Aboriginal health; and Philip Felton on the Welfare Board's housing policy, which was condemned by voices from the floor. The minutes recorded that Alick 'reminded them of the government promise 3 years ago that within 3 years all Aborigines would be housed. This month that time is up. He urged Congress to create urgent and renewed pressure for housing'. The Congress called for the return of all reserves to Aboriginal people, the provision of proper housing, and the election of five Aboriginal members to the Welfare Board. At the end of the Congress, Alick was re-elected President of the Aboriginal Branch of the Advancement League, and a third Congress was planned for June 1966.

The Second Congress decided on half-yearly regional meetings, although in December 1965 Alick confided to Paul Pickford of the Council for Aboriginal Rights (an Anglo-Australian support group) that, 'it is so hard, the committee is so weak, it looks big on paper, but after being elected at Congress, you don't hear from them again, although I write to so many'. Forging unity was also a problem, as Gunai from Gippsland, Gunditjmara from the Western District, Yorta Yorta and Bangerang from the Murray and the Wurundjeri and Boowurrung from Melbourne had to be united. Non-traditional splits also operated. One Aboriginal man in 1964 made a most extraordinary claim to Fran Russell, a white activist: 'Bill Onus is a commo' and 'Doug Nicholls is a red'. It was the Cold War era after all.

A Third Aboriginal Congress presided over by Alick was held in June 1966, at the newly completed 'Doug Nicholls Centre' of the Advancement League in Cunningham Street, Northcote. Forty delegates attended but there were no representatives from the Western District, Mallee or Wimmera. Reports were given on Lake Tyers, by Margaret Tucker on the Welfare Board, and Stan Davey spoke about the Advancement League and FCAATSI. Elections were held, although Alick for an unknown reason did not stand for a fourth term. There is no evidence that his candidature was unwelcome or that he was unhappy; three years was a sufficient term, an Aboriginal person was preferable in Alick's opinion, and perhaps new work commitments shaped his decision.

Bill Onus was elected as incoming President, but Alick remained on the Social Committee to run the Aboriginal balls. The Congress pressed to have two of the five Aboriginal representatives on the Welfare Board recently promised by the government. Stewart Murray and Lynch Cooper were elected, although Murray soon resigned in protest at government policy, much to Onus' annoyance. Two hundred attended the Congress social, testing the capacity of the Doug Nicholls Centre. The report of the social, with its historical illusions, smacks of Alick:

> Many former members of the Cummeroogunga [sic] concert party that toured Victoria prior to the Second World War, when Cumeroogunga was a thriving settlement, entertained with items and were enthusiastically applauded. Former Lake Tyers people gave various items on the Gum Leaves and were also loudly applauded. The Bracken sisters from Geelong, Miss Rosalin Atkinson, the Briggs sisters, were among the artists who performed to the delight of the audience, as also did Mr. Cyril Fisher of Cherbourg Settlement, Queensland, who is now a student at the Lady Nell Seeing-Eye-Dog Centre. He sang and entertained with the gum leaf.

In the early 1960s Doug Nicholls drew Alick into another important organisation. The Federal Council for the Advancement of Aborigines (FCAA, soon changed to FCAATSI to include Torres

Strait Islanders after 1964), was established in Adelaide in 1958 to agitate for Aboriginal rights and justice. In 1962 Alick accompanied Doug Nicholls to an FCAA meeting in Adelaide. Alick recorded in his 'Memoirs': 'there were about 60 delegates from all over Australia including some 10–12 Aborigines, including Kath Walker, Faith Bandler, Chairman Joe McGinness from Cairns and Wynnie Bransen. Many national issues had been raised and discussed and from that day I became more politically minded'. Alick already knew from experience that Aboriginal people were denied access to swimming pools, hotels, toilets in some showgrounds, and confined to the front seats in some country theatres, but at FCAATSI he realised that this situation could be changed. Alick drove Doug Nicholls to several more FCAATSI annual conferences, which were now held each Easter in Canberra. They stopped at Wangaratta to pick up Lynch Cooper. Merle also attended: 'we got to know many people through these conferences. The children stayed with my sister [Elizabeth] or my Aunty. When they were older they used to come'. The three children remember these trips vividly as fun and an education. Esmai recalled that when she was about sixteen 'I went to the meetings and was involved in every aspect of it. I just loved it'.

At the 1964 Conference Doug Nicholls announced that he was stepping down as Victorian FCAATSI State Secretary, and that Alick was his 'preferred successor'. As Jack Horner recalled the incident in a letter to Alick and Merle in 1989, 'there was little formal democratic machinery for election to office, so this was accepted at once, on the personal say-so of Doug. We thought, "if Doug says that Alick is the man for us, that's good enough"'. The Jackomos family made the annual trek to Canberra at Easter many more times. Alick was still Victorian State Secretary of FCAATSI in 1976.

He was certainly 'the man', for Alick was a good organiser and a calming influence in meetings. His daughter Esmai, who saw him at many meetings, said Alick 'played a supportive role, an organising role, but not a dominating role'. John Moriarty, a young Aboriginal delegate from South Australia, who rose to head the Department of Aboriginal Affairs in Victoria before pursuing a successful business career, recalled that Alick 'would not embroil himself in any arguments. He'd try and reason his way out, he was a highly intelligent person…he was very rational, he was very calm…and he was very logical in his approach'. He added that he was 'dignified' and had 'respect' for all peoples.

> He had a funny way of looking at people. He'd look you in the face, but when you started saying something he'd look to the side of the person, and up and wouldn't look them in the eye at that particular time. But then he'd say something and then he'd come back to look at you. And that settled a lot of Aboriginals' minds at ease and they never, ever, felt threatened by him.

Alick also ran the FCAATSI socials held after two days of discussions and before the elections. These were extremely important events, because the differences on the floor of the meetings could be fierce, and things were said in anger that needed to be resolved. Alick recalled: 'we had our little barneys during the conference…well you can't get 400 people in a hall and everyone's going to agree…but all those people that came to Canberra were sincere people'. Alick used his showgrounds skills, which were honed running dances with Eric Onus at the Manchester Unity Hall and the Advancement League Balls. Alick recalled that he struck a 'gold mine amongst Aboriginal people because everybody's a born artist'. Acting as talent scout, Alick discovered that Joe and Amy McGuinness could dance Thursday-Island style, Laurie Moffat would play the gum leaf; and Eleanor Harding and other Thursday Island women could sing. Others played instruments, so a concert was organised: 'everybody got up and was united there'. Then everyone in the hall formed a circle and sang 'We Shall Overcome'. At the end of the conference 'everybody would kiss everybody goodbye, and yell "see you next year"'.

From its inception in 1958 FCAATSI lobbied for citizens rights for Aborigines including equal education, health, employment, and wages, and an end to discriminatory legislation. In 1967 FCAATSI added indigenous rights issues to its platform, including the right to retain language and culture, and the right to control land. Although Victoria had few discriminatory practices by the 1960s, Alick and other Victorian delegates vigorously supported an end to legislative discrimination in the northern states and the Northern Territory.

Gathering mussels at Dunwich, Stradbroke Island, c. 1960

FCAATSI's push to change the Australian Constitution was fought as strongly in Victoria as elsewhere and Alick as State Secretary threw himself into the fight. The aim was to change two clauses: one that did not allow Aboriginal people to be counted in the Australian census (along with other Australians), and a clause forbidding federal involvement in Aboriginal affairs then controlled by the states.

A referendum on the Constitution could only be initiated by government or if sufficient signatures from the public backed a private member's bill to bring pressure to bear on Parliament. Alick was in his element and took to it with gusto — for he was selling something as he always had done since his peanut-selling days in the Depression and life on the showgrounds. As usual he teamed with Doug Nicholls in the work. In 1998 he recalled:

> we'd go along to Smith Street outside Foy & Gibsons on the Collingwood side and put a card table up on Saturday morning. We'd get people to sign the petition giving Aboriginal citizenship rights. ...because the shops closed at 12 o'clock we'd pack up and go to the Collingwood Football Ground grandstand entrance...Collingwood supporters are

all black and white or one-eyed [as Alick would know], they'd go straight into the ground, nothing would hold them, but Doug Nicholls would stop them going in, they all knew Doug because he was a great footballer in the 30s with Fitzroy and Northcote. They formed a queue and signed the petition. I sat at the card table while Doug was draggin them, he was the figurehead.

In 1965 Alick's working life took a dramatic but not unexpected turn. He was offered a paid job with the Aborigines' Advancement League, following a decade as Doug Nicholls' voluntary offsider. The League, now with a permanent home at Northcote, felt sufficiently buoyant to offer Alick a position as its second field officer alongside Nicholls. It was a momentous economic decision for Alick, Merle and their three children — aged ten to fourteen — as Merle was in unpaid work as wife and mother. Their income would drop from a very comfortable £100 [$200] a week to a basic £25 [$50] per week. Most people if asked to cut their income by 75 per cent would laugh first and then refuse. But Alick and Merle had owned their own home for a decade and no doubt had savings given their frugality. Alick also admitted that the potato business 'was hard and I worked in the open all day. This was alright when the weather was fine, but when it rained I got wet through'. Alick leapt at the offer with Merle's full support, despite the financial sacrifice. In his 'Memoirs' of 1987 he wrote: '[I] handed over the business to my brother-in-law' and never regretted the decision for 'this was the work I wanted to do'. In 1997 he again stated: 'Merle used to get $50 [£25] a week as house money, and that's all I was going to get there, less tax. So it was a big drop, but I wanted to do it'. If there is one thing never to be forgotten about Alick, it is that his commitment to Aboriginal people and the ability to work in with them meant far more to him than money.

There is little record of the daily welfare work he did for the League for the next two years. In general he was involved helping those in household and domestic crises concerning food, clothing, schooling and rent; assisting those before the courts; and driving people to and fro. He wrote briefly in his 'Memoirs':

> Much of our time was taken in fundraising by attending service groups, churches telling them of the situation and depending on donations. There were no government grants in those days. Although there was a need all over the state of Victoria, the Gippsland situation seemed worse off and most of my welfare work took me to Gippsland.

Alick worked among the bean pickers, who travelled from as far as southern New South Wales to pick at Lindenow. 'My role was to encourage families to send their children to school, but the families depended on the children's earnings and very few, if any, went to school during the picking season'. Alick also visited the isolated mill towns of Cabbage Tree, Club Terrace and Bonang where there were no community services.

Alick was outspoken on some issues for the League, especially the transitional housing settlement of Rumbalara that he knew so well, because Merle had relatives living there. Ten prefabricated concrete houses were built in 1958 on 'Blue Moon Estate', behind the Ardmona cannery, a kilometre from Mooroopna. The settlement was part of the Welfare Board's 'New Deal' for Aboriginal people. The houses were tiny, only four squares, and were built at half the cost of other Housing Commission homes. They had running water, a fuel copper for hot water, electricity operated by a coin slot machine, but no laundry, and no internal doors. They were an advance on riverbank 'humpies', but smaller and cheaper than the usual Housing Commission home, and inadequate for the size of most Aboriginal families. Design faults and building defects were soon evident, including internal doorways that were too narrow to admit standard furniture. They were also ill suited to extremes of temperature. A Mrs Hyland wrote to the *Age* in February 1967, saying that the Aborigines should not complain of their housing, and should be thankful for what they had. Her letter drew an angry response from Alick who claimed that the houses were 'hot houses', and that the Aboriginal women who 'complained' were widows with large families. They had no other choice but Rumbalara, yet were entitled to live in 'normal society' the same as Hyland. A lucky few were given standard Housing Commission homes in town but, as Alick remarked later, they were all workers employed in Don Howe's packing-case business or his tomato farm. Howe was a member of the Welfare Board and secured preference for his workers, despite some of those at Rumbalara with much larger families being left with smaller and poorer housing.

Alick was also outspoken in 1965 over the proposal by the Welfare Board to build a transit housing settlement at Morwell in Gippsland to assimilate Aboriginal people into the community and allow the Board to close Lake Tyers reserve. Alick along with Doug Nicholls was interviewed in September on a television current affairs program 'Watch This Space'. Alick reminded the audience that this proposal had been howled down by 47 Aboriginal delegates at the Second Aboriginal Congress headed by Alick in July. He claimed the $35 000 to be spent on creating housing at Morwell would be better used on refurbishment at Lake Tyers, which some Aboriginal called home, and others wished to visit. He appealed for Aboriginal self-determination over Lake Tyers:

> While they were at Lake Tyers they had all this hand-out system, but they've left all this, they don't want it, they've left Lake Tyers, they've got their independence and now they feel that Lake Tyers is there if they want to go back, retain the land, develop it and be independent.

His outspokenness meant that Alick inevitably represented the Advancement League on an inquiry into Lake Tyers that Colin Tatz engineered to stave off the Welfare Board's attempts to close the reserve and sell the land for tourism development. Tatz was the Advancement League's representative on the Welfare Board, placed there in 1965 as a reform move by the Government in the face of Aboriginal pressure for a voice. Tatz became a thorn in the Board's side through acute manoeuvring: in February 1966 he proposed an inquiry as a response to the Government's March 1965 statement that it would consider 'any reasonable and sound proposals for future control and administration' of Lake Tyers. Tatz assembled a committee of ten, Alick being an Advancement League nominee. The Committee held eleven meetings over eight months, visited Lake Tyers several times, consulted with 47 Aboriginal people, took eighteen verbal submissions and sixteen written submissions and called for specialist reports on the farming, timber and employment potential of Lake Tyers. Alick was an invaluable member of the Committee as a trusted friend of the Lake Tyers community over almost thirty years. 'He vouched for me', recalled Tatz; 'I couldn't have done it without Alick's advice on a number of issues'.

Tatz, the consummate politician, predetermined the Board's favourable response to the report on its submission in November 1966. He released the report to the press with a date embargo — the very day the Board was to consider the report — but with no time of the day embargo on it. So journalists read it before the Board and reported on it favourably the morning of the day the Board met at 3 p.m. The Board was confronted with widespread press support for Lake Tyers becoming an agricultural and training centre; a site for reafforestation and cattle fattening projects; a refuge for the aged and a rehabilitation centre for 'those families experiencing difficulty in adjusting to an urban, European environment'. The road to ownership of Lake Tyers was now clearer.

Alick believed in and assisted the move to Aboriginal control of Aboriginal affairs, but the momentum towards this was to have ironic consequences for him. By aiding the formation of pan-Aboriginal loyalties across the state, by running Aboriginal congresses and being State Secretary of FCAATSI, he was eroding regional differences and helping to form new identities. People who stressed their regional Aboriginal affiliations called themselves the 'dark people', eschewing the words 'black' in the 1950s; and even a minority who attempted to merge into the general population by the late 1960s took greater pride in their Aboriginality. For instance, the word 'Koori (e)' emerged as a pan-Aboriginal name by this time. This search for a more defined identity and a heightened sense of a pan-Aboriginal identity placed new emphasis in people's thinking on the binary terms: indigenous/non-indigenous. This binary view of people placed Alick apart from the Aboriginal community in the minds of some, and it became evident in a number of unpleasant situations from about 1965.

Adventures at Pine Creek, Northern Territory, early 1960s

Colin Tatz, who came to live in Melbourne in 1964, actually witnessed one of these episodes, which shocked him, not only due to its nastiness, but it was the moment when he realised Alick was not Aboriginal.

> He spoke Aboriginal, he thought Aboriginal, he looked Aboriginal, he was married to an Aboriginal woman, his children were Aboriginal, and I just assumed he was Aboriginal...not that he *ever* posed as an Aboriginal. I just assumed that he was. Because his *idiom* — and I mean not just his speech idiom, his mental idiom, was totally attuned to Aboriginality.

Many others outside the Aboriginal community thought the same. Even some Aboriginal people thought he was Aboriginal. Almost all from the community who knew his origins still warmly included him. Myra Grinter (née Atkinson), who came from the Murray region to work in Melbourne as a young woman in the 1960s, recalled, 'even though it was explained to us that he was Greek, we never ever thought of him that way, as far as we were concerned he was Aboriginal, because he fitted in so well. He was very accepting of everything, and was a very caring, gentle man'.

The episode happened at the Advancement League some time in the late 1960s (Tatz left the state at the end of 1970). Tatz recalled that, during a meeting, Stewart Murray 'stood up and said "Blacks only" would be sitting in on this session. Alick just sat there and Murray looked up and said: "And that means you, Buddy". Alick stood up and had to leave the room almost in tears'. The blow was perhaps harder to bear as Stewart Murray was a son-in-law of Doug Nicholls. If Nicholls were there he would also have been pained.

Until the 1960s the Aboriginal /non-Aboriginal divide was not important for most Aboriginal people, including Doug Nicholls. The question for them was your attitude and willingness to work with Aboriginal people. As Alick recalled in 1996:

> I started following Doug in 1936 with the Australian Aborigines League as a young boy going down to the Yarra Bank. And you might say that I became Doug's apprentice because I was with Doug for just on fifty years. But we were friends too. We were very close friends.

He was not boasting here but reiterating his credentials, which included marriage into the community when racism against Aboriginal people was rife and his own family disapproved of the match. Also the people he most admired included other Aboriginal community leaders besides Nicholls, such as William Cooper, Eric and Bill Onus, Margaret Tucker and others from a younger generation. He had also chosen to associate his life and work with the Aboriginal community and its history. And never for a moment did Alick ever claim he was Aboriginal. But from the 1960s for some people this was not enough: this minority wanted him out of their organisations once they developed a sense of their Aboriginality that excluded non-Aboriginality.

A similar moment happened at a FCAATSI meeting around 1966. John Moriarty recalled that Alick was excluded. His family threatened to walk out, but a vote was taken and he was allowed to remain.

Merle remembers on one occasion at FCAATSI when Alick and some other non-Aboriginal people were asked to leave. The Aboriginal poet and activist 'Kath Walker jumped to her feet and yelled "if that man walks out of the room I go with him"'. Alick was then asked to stay and as noted above was still State Secretary in 1976. John Moriarty believed that Alick 'was very hurt when he was ejected from those discussions. And many of us felt for him. We felt it was unjust because of the amount of work that he did'. Alick's son Andrew reflected:

> Dad understood, but I think that he still would have been hurt. Dad never once said he was Koori…I know a lot of people who have questioned the income that the Jackomos family earns in Koori issues. My father, my family would have been so much better off financially if my father didn't go to work for the Advancement League and kept his business and bought into fish shops and properties, like other members in his family.

Alick himself said little of these painful incidents at the time or later. Such incidents were not included in his many autobiographical writings. In 1997, however, in an interview he remarked: 'I was always accepted in the Aboriginal community. There was never any thought of being non-Aboriginal, you were just a person, you were just one of them'. He added:

> Not only with me, but with a lot of white people or non-Aboriginals who mixed with Aboriginals in those days, who married them, the thought [among Aboriginal people] never came that you're not one of us…It has only come in the last ten or fifteen years where people seem to have an animosity against non-Aboriginal people. But the dinky-di Aboriginal people that I knew in those days, any white person that was involved, friends or that; race or colour never came into it.

This was the attitude Alick himself adopted, for he said in an interview in 1981, 'all I preach is that you don't look at a person's skin. I don't consider whether he's Chinese, Greek or any kind of race — he's a person. That's all I care about'.

Others who had not married into the Aboriginal community, or who were without a long history of involvement with the community, suffered more. In August 1969 Roosevelt Brown, a Bermudan MP and representative of the Latin American Black Power movement, visited Melbourne on the invitation of some Aboriginal officers of the Advancement League. Brown fostered their interest in indigenous rights and identity and sparked a public debate. A power struggle for control of the League ensued, which is outlined in *Victims or Victors?* (1985). Doug Nicholls resigned, finding that 'Black power' was a 'bitter word', but soon re-joined as patron. Indeed, in 1960 he had pioneered an 'Aboriginal only' session before each FCAATSI conference. The League issued a statement rejecting violence and black supremacy, defining 'Black Power as the empowerment of black people to make their own decisions'. Bob Maza, Harry Penrith (Burnum Burnum), and Geraldine Briggs from the League's Aboriginal branch and the Victorian Tribal Council, asked all white paid workers and committee members to step down. Stan Davey, a co-founder of the League, was spared this humiliation, having left to work with Aboriginal people in the Kimberley in 1968.

Bob Maza took over as Director assisted by Bruce McGuinness. Myra Atkinson (now Grinter) who was nineteen became a secretary. She recalled of the change:

> there was sadness at that happening, but it was also self-determination for us to start handling our own affairs and helping our people to make changes. I got the feeling that they understood and that they were very, very supportive of us... they were people who were really dedicated to seeing big changes, for our part we felt sad because they were like family to us.

FCAATSI experienced a similar split in 1970, but managed to retain white members by keeping FCAATSI and forming a National Tribal Council to which whites could belong and speak, but not vote.

Alick understood these moves but bemoaned the loss of strength as all 28 white branches of the Advancement League folded almost overnight. In 1981 Alick reflected that it was done 'badly' and instead of telling people to get out, 'maybe we could have patted the white people on the back and said, "thanks very much", because they did work hard'. He added in 1996:

> you might say some of them were paternalistic or do-gooders. But a lot of them were sincere in helping Aboriginal people …we lost a lot of that white support. Maybe I'm biased because I'm not Aboriginal. But I think we could have said, "look this is self-determination. Let us do it. But we still need you. You've helped us in the past". [But the support] it just disappeared.

Alick was not pushed out and he continued to work for the League and the community for another thirty years. He was on the League's Committee of Management during the 1970s. Once he was made a Life Member of the League in 1978, on the nomination of Doug Nicholls, he automatically remained on that Committee. Bruce McGuinness, one of the 'radicals' in the takeover, remained a firm friend and supporter. All of Alick's children worked for the League. Esmai was secretary to Bruce McGuinness for two years during the 'troubles' (1969–71) and found it 'extremely challenging' and 'exciting'. Michael also worked as a field officer (1975–77) and as a treasurer and a committee member in the 1980s. Merle was a member of the Management Committee of the League 1970–95, Vice-President 1976–86, and President in 1986. Alick's Life Membership made him the only non-Aboriginal person to have that distinction. Over the years he became 'Uncle Alick' to many of the community, the respected title of elder. So he remained 'in', but the spectre of rejection was ever present, and made him thereafter a little wary and always keen to prove his credentials.

10 Welfare Board Officer

In 1966 Alick applied unsuccessfully for a job with the Welfare Board. He was not unhappy at the Advancement League, but he knew how precarious its finances were. While content with $50 a week, he did not relish the prospect of no pay at all. There would be no question if the League's finances faltered that it would be Alick and not Doug Nicholls who went, and Alick would have not wanted to supplant his much-admired mentor in any case. In his autobiographical 'Memories' Alick wrote:

> In 1966 the Victorian Aborigines (*sic*) Welfare Board advertised for welfare officers and I applied but was unsuccessful, but I knew that with all my previous practical involvement with the Advancement League, FCAATSI…and working with Doug Nicholls, I had more experience than some of the successful applicants who had never met an Aborigine.

Alick felt rightly aggrieved that his limited education had meant that his wealth of experience and commitment had been cast aside, in favour of a new and perhaps even uncommitted graduate, to whom the position was just a job. To Alick it was his life.

The Aborigines Welfare Board, which succeeded the Aboriginal Protection Board in 1958, enjoyed a two-year honeymoon of general support; but its inability to solve the housing problem, and its strong assimilationist policy, soon alienated Aboriginal people. Trouble centred around the issue of Lake Tyers, the Board wishing to phase it out and shift Aboriginal people into the general population, whereas the people saw its retention as a key element in the struggle for land. The Advancement League through its black branch, the Australian Aborigines' League, lobbied for more representation on the Board and its current representatives Colin Tatz, Margaret Tucker and Con Edwards, together with Donald Thomson, the anthropologist, pushed for change within the Board. A powerful coterie of three — J. H. Davey, the Chairman and a Ministry of Housing bureaucrat; Don Howe, a Mooroopna employer of Aboriginal people; and Arthur Holden, a Morwell accountant involved in Apex — dominated the Board, its policy and the staff.

In 1966 a crisis developed. Colin Tatz and his supporters forced the creation of a policy sub-committee assisted by Superintendent Philip Felton, to reassess the Welfare Board's aims and operation. It issued a lengthy and revolutionary report in 1967 which redefined 'assimilation' from the former view that Aboriginal people 'will attain the same manner of living', to read, Aboriginal people 'will choose to attain a similar manner of living to that of other Australians'. The report undermined the tyrannical rule of the coterie, arguing that Board members, staff and Aboriginal clients must work together. It declared the need for minimum rights and standards for Aboriginal people and included policy statements on education, health, employment and training, housing and the retention of Lake Tyers and Framlingham reserves.

Charlie Huggard collects the rent from Joyce Atkinson at Rumbalara, 1960s.

In March 1967 debate raged over the Board's future and the Government promised reforms. Colin Tatz declared that relations between the Board and its staff were 'at bedrock'. He added — later claiming to have been misquoted — that too many who worked in Aboriginal affairs were 'dead-beat, no-hopers [who] did not make the grade in the white community', whereas people in Aboriginal affairs have to be twice as qualified due to the 'extreme complexity of the problems'.

It was perhaps with some satisfaction that Alick learnt that the Welfare Board was in a staff crisis early in 1967 and that social and welfare workers were leaving. The Mallee region was left without any staff at all after its field officer, Frank White, was transferred to Lake Tyers to fill a vacancy there. Alick recalled:

> in March 1967 the Aborigines Welfare Board (AWB) was experiencing many problems and members of the staff had resigned. The Swan Hill office was unmanned and to demonstrate that an Aboriginal organisation could do the job as good as government departments, the Aboriginal Advancement League offered my secondment to help out. The AWB had no option but to accept my services.

Despite the fact that Alick had been refused a position with the Board the previous year, probably on educational grounds, the Board urged on by Tatz, Tucker and Edwards, accepted the League's offer. On 10 March 1967 the Welfare Board appointed Alick to a temporary position at Swan Hill until White's return. It agreed to make an ex gratia payment to the League to cover Alick's salary and expenses. He reported to the Board and drove to Swan Hill the same day, with 'no orientation, no training, no nothing'.

Alick arrived at the Swan Hill Court House and was given a key to an office in the building. The room was about three metres square and 'dirty and dusty and [with] piles of blankets, clothes, toothpaste and brushes which were to be issued to families. There was an old typewriter, but no typist'. Alick was it! And his area of responsibility stretched for over two hundred kilometres from Swan Hill to Mildura, taking in Robinvale and its transitional housing settlement of Manatunga — an area with some of the heaviest concentrations of Aboriginal people in the state.

Aboriginal people in the Murray region were less fortunate than those in Melbourne. Aboriginal city dwellers, even those least well off in Fitzroy, had stronger work opportunities, better housing and more educational opportunities than rural dwellers. From 1957 they also had the Advancement League to assist them. Most rural dwellers, however, survived on seasonal picking work, and were accommodated in makeshift and over-crowded huts. The end of the season usually brought further unemployment. Their lack of income forced them to live in 'humpy' housing on vacant land adjoining river banks. Many at Swan Hill lived across the river at Wamba Wamba, a fringe settlement formed in the 1930s. They were isolated from community services, and dependent on walking to town or taking expensive taxis, as few people had cars. Alick found that most were not on social services, as 'many Aboriginals were not familiar with the Government policies, and due to a lack of interest by many public servants they were not aware, or receiving the social services and other entitlements'. A small minority were better off, housed at Manatunga or better still in Housing Commission homes with rental assistance. A few had permanent jobs in local councils or with utilities such as the forestry or railway departments.

Alick recalled that his work at Swan Hill was

> mostly bandaid work, just helping people to get houses, education grants, taking them to doctors, helping them to solve a few problems, food orders…people were always coming to ask you for food orders for help. In those days we had a book, an order book, and it was at my discretion when someone came and needed help whether to give him $10 or a $10 food order. And you were always giving food orders. People were really hungry. And nobody had cars in those days and there were family problems and debts. Families would come to you from Swan Hill and say we can't get to such and such and so I'd run them there. I went over the border to Balranald and elsewhere.

The work was constant and people 'used to queue at the door at Swan Hill'.

Alick's daily work sheets, which survive for this period at Swan Hill, confirm his statement in much richer detail. The first recorded week, beginning Monday 3 April 1967, was a busy one and marked by long working hours. On Monday he held thirteen interviews, nine of them in the field as few people had telephones, concerning welfare payments, a rail pass, applications for furniture, property inspections with the housing officer, a court matter and the organisation of a Melbourne dental appointment for a client. He collected a washing machine for a woman at the railway station and met with the Citizens' Aboriginal Welfare Committee at 8.00 p.m. On Tuesday he held six interviews, four in the field, two being at Woorinen fifteen kilometres from Swan Hill, wrote several letters and attended a meeting. On Wednesday morning he wrote several letters, attended court, and then drove 140 kilometres to Robinvale, stopping at three Aboriginal households en route. Alick visited twelve households in Robinvale that afternoon delivering and explaining housing applications, the last being at 8.15 p.m. Many no doubt involved cups of tea and a chat, bringing him closer to many families. He saw nine people in Robinvale on Thursday morning regarding welfare payments, food, clothing and bedding assistance, met with Ray Hicks the manager of Manatunga, drove back to Swan Hill that afternoon, visiting a client at 6 p.m. He was called to the police station at 10.15 p.m. concerning a woman charged at Balranald with 'needing care'. On Friday he held nine interviews in his office, and wrote letters and made telephone calls regarding the Balranald woman.

Alick stayed working in Swan Hill over his first weekend, but left for Melbourne after lunch on his second Thursday, spent time with the family then visited the Welfare Board Office on Monday for a briefing with the Superintendent, Philip Felton. After obtaining a new tyre for his car Alick returned to Swan Hill. He did not always return home for weekend leave in such good time; he recalled in his 'Memoirs',

> most crises occurred on Friday afternoons which would keep me in the office until late Friday night. On some occasions I would be called to Robinvale and as a result I would not depart for home (Melbourne) until late Friday or Saturday morning. I would only spend a few hours with my family before returning on Sunday afternoon.

Manatunga Housing settlement, Robinvale, 1960 (Aborigines Welfare Board, *Annual Report*, 1963)

His memory is quite accurate. His work sheets reveal that he went home most weekends and a third of the time he left for Melbourne out of office hours late on Friday, and several times on Saturday, but usually he left by 2 p.m. on Fridays, which still landed him at home in Melbourne after 8 p.m. — three hours past work time. Yet on two thirds of his weekends at home, Alick attended the Welfare Board office first thing on Monday morning before travelling back to Swan Hill, so most return trips were in work time. Alick was not told of his travel entitlements, or that he was to return home in work time. Some Board employees were hostile to Alick, because he had worked for the Advancement League, which had often criticised the Board.

Alick also met hostility from some country residents, who disliked the Welfare Board's assimilation policy, which aimed at dispersing Aboriginal people in housing through the community. Many Victorians preferred that Aborigines remain separated and hidden away in fringe camps by river banks and not potentially living next door. Alick recalled in his 'Memoirs' that Robinvale was the worst for such prejudice.

> By working and associating with Aboriginal people you were shunned by the non-Aboriginal community. The

whites would argue with you or completely ignore you. At the guesthouse that I boarded at, I got on well with the landlady, but at dinner time her husband would always sit at my table and raise some Aboriginal issue. Eventually I moved out. At that time I was a member of the RSL and found the same situation when I visited the Robinvale RSL. There was so much hostility towards Aboriginals.

If he had occasion to go to the Robinvale police station 'the police would totally ignore you and make you wait sometime before attending you'. However, the police at Swan Hill were the opposite. Alan Anderson, a detective, 'would regularly visit my office to discuss local issues of concern'. Even doctors discriminated against Aboriginal people. Alick one evening took a woman and her sick child to a doctor's clinic at Robinvale, but was told to come back the next day. Alick doubted he would 'have treated a non-Aboriginal in the same way'.

After four months the workload was relentless and his last week in July was typical. Monday was spent driving for seven hours back from Melbourne, attending the Swan Hill Court and visiting households at Robinvale until 8 p.m. He visited nineteen households in Robinvale over eleven hours on Tuesday, delivering garden plants he brought from Melbourne, and discussing social welfare issues and domestic disputes. He met with Ray Hicks about Manatunga, and with Mrs Stroll from the Save the Children Fund, whose work Alick greatly admired. He spent twelve hours on Wednesday visiting more Aboriginal households, noting domestic disputes, reconciliations, house applications, births, unemployment and the movements of people. On Thursday he held interviews, sat with several who appeared in court and then drove back to Swan Hill, stopping to see people at Happy Valley, a place called 'Pumps', and Koraleigh en route. One woman at 'Pumps' had 'just returned from seeing children at Ballarat', probably in the orphanage. On Friday he wrote ten letters, made seven telephone calls, and had fifteen interviews with people both in and out of the Swan Hill office about social service and housing entitlements, and heard several air their domestic problems.

All these interviews and visits were carried out in a context of great love and respect for the people. It is certain that Alick was more generous than most other public servants in administering food vouchers and monetary assistance. He was also keen to ensure that Aboriginal people gained their proper entitlements. They were denied them for decades after other Australians received them and, once eligible, they were rarely accessed due to the distrust that Aboriginal people felt for governments and welfare officers, and due to their itinerancy as seasonal workers. Most public servants were loath to chase up Aboriginal people to extend benefits to them, but not Alick. During sessions in which he helped people complete social welfare forms, Alick built a wealth of information that gave him unparalleled knowledge about the Victorian Aboriginal community.

From 2.30 p.m. on Friday 28 July 1967 Alick's work sheet reveals that he met with Philip Felton and Welfare Board members, Colin Tatz, E. Thorpe and Bill Onus. Meetings followed until 11.30 p.m. with Councillors and members of the Swan Hill Aboriginal Welfare Committee at the Council Chambers, and afterwards on the dry-docked tourist riverboat, the Gem. Something was afoot. The meetings arose because Frank White, the welfare officer at Lake Tyers, had been seriously injured in a car accident. The Board decided on 21 July to transfer Alick to White's position, but the Swan Hill Aboriginal Welfare Committee, which included local Aboriginal spokesperson Hilton Walsh, objected because of local needs. After hard bargaining, the Board arranged for a vacant State Rivers Department building adjoining the court house to be released to the Welfare Committee for renovation as an Aboriginal community centre. Jim Hullick, the Headmaster of Woorinen Central Primary School, was also to be seconded to assist the welfare work in Swan Hill until Alick's return. The Committee reluctantly agreed, but Alick never did return. His last week at Swan Hill was spent in the normal way, but on Friday he handed over to Pat Fraser of the Aborigines Welfare Committee, conducted one last interview, gave himself a 35-minute lunch break, the first one recorded in eighteen weeks at Swan Hill, and left for Melbourne.

Alick had performed well at Swan Hill. He worked much overtime, whether paid or unpaid is unclear, contacted many Aboriginal people, and attended to their needs. The people were very loath to lose him. The Welfare Board also seemed satisfied. Indeed as early as 21 April, the Board's minutes recorded that Alick, acting welfare officer at Swan Hill, may be interested in applying for a position as a welfare officer. The minutes added, that the Board 'would be happy to have him as a staff member'. On Friday 4 June 1967 Alick travelled to Melbourne and at 4 p.m. lodged his application to be appointed as a 'welfare officer' with the Aborigines Welfare Board. His acceptance to the position came through in August just after his posting to Lake Tyers. His life as a fully-fledged public servant had begun.

Len Rule, a former manager of Lake Tyers and now a neighbouring farmer, stepped in until Alick's arrival on Monday 7 August. He was mystified when word spread among the Aboriginal residents that 'Alick was back', for Rule had worked at Lake Tyers since the 1930s, but could not remember Alick Jackomos. Alick soon told Rule that he visited Tyers as a youth in the late 1930s, but stayed clear of the manager, lying low in the peoples' houses.

Lake Tyers was in poor shape when Alick arrived. The Protection Board had moved light-skinned residents off the reserve from the 1930s. During the war period others were encouraged to move to Melbourne for employment, causing the population to spiral downwards from 250 to fewer than a hundred. The Board's successor, the Welfare Board, had increased efforts to move the remaining families off the reserve in order to close it completely. When families left, their house was demolished. Some, like Charlie and Phyllis Carter and their eight children, had refused to move. Indeed, eleven families applied to return in early 1966, finding life outside too tough or too alienating; but the Board deferred their applications, forcing seven families to return without permission. By mid-1966 there were seventy residents crammed into five houses. Another seven houses were unoccupied, vandalised and unfit for use. Rationing of food and clothing ended that year.

In 1967 some rebuilding commenced at Lake Tyers, as a consequence of the Tatz Committee report of November 1966, referred to in the previous chapter; but morale was still very low. There was minimal employment on the 320-hectare farm operation which was unsupervised in 1967. There was no store, and purchases were made only after arduous trips on foot to Lakes Entrance or during visits by a Nowa Nowa storekeeper with basic supplies. As most adults were

Alick and Reg Worthy flank Chaplain Arthur Malcolm outside Lake Tyers church during Alick's tenure as manager in 1967.

unemployed, or on social welfare, there was little money to spend in any case. There was a school, and weekly church services run by Captain Arthur Malcolm of the Church of England Church Army, attached to the Nowa Nowa parish. Malcolm, an Aboriginal man born at the Yarrabah Mission in North Queensland, later became an Anglican bishop. There was no organised social life at Lake Tyers; the community was very isolated, being twelve kilometres off the highway, and a further five from Nowa Nowa and eighteen from Lakes Entrance.

Alick thus found a demoralised community at Lake Tyers that was 'isolated and depressed'. He observed that 'on pay day or pension days some would phone a taxi from Lakes Entrance to go shopping, get a drink and socialise, then catch a taxi back. They would use up all their pension and they were now broke till next pension day'. They were criticised for such expenditure, but what choices did they have? Alick soon found that

> on any visit to Lakes Entrance or Bairnsdale there would always be someone waiting for a ride or [to] ask you to do

some messages and shopping in particular, nearly everybody would ask you to get two bobs worth of pieces from the butcher in Lakes Entrance. Pieces included mutton flaps which were a special treat even to this day.

Only Alick, and Philip Felton when he visited, would give people a ride. Most Board employees stuck to the rules and drove past. Many people hitch-hiked to and fro or walked, leading — Alick believed — to a significant number of road deaths.

Alick's work at Lake Tyers was constant. He was the only resident staff member for some months, before a farm supervisor was appointed and Sister Hildebrand, the nurse, returned after suffering a broken ankle. He had to supervise the four or five farm workers and attend to other reserve matters during the day, including driving people to medical appointments in town, some of which inevitably occurred after hours and in the middle of the night. A community of sixty people with depression and social problems also created numerous incidents. There was trouble from some bored youths, three of whom were sentenced at Lakes Entrance in September, for breaking and entering into the school and community hall.

Alick was isolated too, for he only went home every second weekend, but he became close friends with Mary and Dick Harrison who lived nearby at Lakes Entrance. 'Their house was always open to me and I regularly visited them and dined there'. Alick witnessed their efforts at assimilation and the costs of the policy. The Harrisons and their six children became celebrities in 1961 after they saved to build a home with the help of a land grant from a Lakes Entrance farmer, Joe Rickman, and top-up money from a community appeal. Their house was furnished with carpets and cut-glass cabinets. The Harrisons had a difficult transition into a middle-class home, because some local residents and some Aboriginal people were jealous and resentful. They were a showpiece in the town, a sign declaring: 'To the Harrisons'. They also appeared in feature articles in the Melbourne press. Indeed, Mary Harrison told the *Herald* that

> It hurts. You have no idea how it hurts. A lot of aboriginal friends visit me and I am happy to entertain them. But never once will I allow any of them to spend the night here. If I

weaken once, this home we built could easily be ruined and I can't do that to my children. Not after coming so far.

The couple continued to visit Lake Tyers regularly, however.

The lack of social life at the reserve meant that 'morale was low, [there was] a lot of drinking and plenty of illness'. People felt alienated so Alick formed a committee to run a dance, including as members Charlie and Phyllis Carter, Ivy Marks, Thelma Carter and Sister Hildebrand, and some ex-residents living in Nowa Nowa and Lakes Entrance. Bob and Nora Cockerill played the accordion and piano and Dick Harrison the gum leaf. There was a small donation to support the children's Christmas tree appeal. Up to three hundred people attended from the reserve, nearby towns, as well as Bairnsdale, Orbost and as far as Lake Wallaga Mission in New South Wales. Alick wrote years later: 'After the dance most would go home, but many would stay, and the population would double. It would take nearly a week before households got back to normal. Although people were living in country towns, they always referred to Lake Tyers as home'.

The Board remained nervous about these dances. Alick testified to the Royal Commission into Aboriginal Deaths in Custody around 1990 that 'on many occasions [Head Office] white Welfare Board staff would try to force me to ring the police to have these people evicted. On no occasion did I ever ring the police'. A Board property inspector discovered there were extra people staying in Charlie Carter's house and threatened him with expulsion. Alick reminisced, 'Charlie was the last person to threaten, and he chased the Property officer around Lake Tyers, and eventually he jumped into his car and drove away'. Alick greatly admired Charlie, a former fellow tent boxer with Harry Johns, but the Board considered him a troublemaker. Alick reflected: 'any Aboriginal who stands up to the bureaucracy and fights for a cause is called a trouble-maker and (allegedly) has communistic connections'.

Even for Alick, however, Lake Tyers must have seemed like the hamburger 'joint' all over again. At times the atmosphere was lively, which led to trouble. Alick was now twenty years older, had no boxer's muscle to back him up, and was compromised by his relations with the community. He was both manager and friend and it was difficult to marry both roles when trouble arose. Colin Tatz, a supporter of both Alick and the community, told a Welfare Board meeting in late October that drinking parties and fighting were too much for Alick. He held a community meeting and threatened action if the residents did not support Alick and control the situation. Tatz later reported to the Board that behaviour had improved.

On 3 January 1968 Alick filed a report on Lake Tyers, which revealed much understanding and compassion. One woman had left the station and her children for seven days, but Alick avoided notifying the police, as the children were cared for by grandparents and she returned having spent most of her pension cheque on clothes and food for the children. Alick wrote that involving the police 'would probably have meant the children being placed in an institution'. There was drinking on the reserve, 'but no more than others in Gippsland, and there is very little drinking during the week days'. The men and boys had played two-up openly when he arrived, but 'this has ceased after a short while', and organised gambling nights had shifted to Nowa Nowa. There was now 'much less fighting, although there is friction with the Carters, Edwards and Wandins'. There had been minimal vandalism, and while his house had been broken into by children, only food and not valuables were taken. The only real crime was some cases of 'drunk and disorderly' at Lakes Entrance. All but one person paid rent, Alick remarked: 'I presume there is no other centre in Victoria where everybody pays rent'. He concluded by putting Aboriginal behaviour into perspective: 'Lake Tyers had many problems, but in my 4½ months stay the conduct of the residents on the whole is much better than in some other Gippsland towns'.

Frank White, who severely damaged his neck in a car accident, never returned as welfare officer at Lake Tyers and eventually he resigned; but Alick's stint at Lake Tyers was ended by a broad change in policy. In November 1967 the Victorian Government passed the *Aboriginal Affairs Act* (1967), which abolished the Board and created a Ministry of Aboriginal Affairs from 1 January 1968. On 10 November Alick was told by the Chair of the Board that he would be needed at Lake Tyers only until Christmas. In the New Year he would return to normal duties as a welfare officer, in the newly formed Ministry of Aboriginal Affairs.

11   Public Servant

Alick worked in Aboriginal Affairs as a public servant from 1968 until 1989, first with the Victorian Ministry of Aboriginal Affairs and then from 1974 with the federal Department of Aboriginal Affairs. His work was fulfilling but two things created difficulties. From outside the public service Aboriginal militancy created tensions as a small minority of Aboriginal activists sought to exclude all non-Aboriginal people from Aboriginal affairs. Alick understood their views, but his heart was saddened and a little aggrieved because of his long commitment to their cause. On the inside of the public service he felt unappreciated and excluded at times, not because of his birth, but because of his education — or rather lack of it. He usually shrugged off these abrasions and remained a happy, indeed a chirpy, personality. Those who experienced Alick's warm and extroverted nature would have found such doubts quite astonishing. When certificates of appreciation and recognition for his efforts flowed towards the end of his career, Alick displayed these in his entrance hall at home, not to boast, but to reassure himself that he was valued.

Alick entered a department that was attempting to make breaks with the past. The Ministry of Aboriginal Affairs headed by Reg Worthy broke new ground in Aboriginal policy, but these gains were often unacknowledged due to growing Aboriginal militancy. Worthy was an experienced youth social worker, with a background of four years service in Aboriginal administration in the Northern Territory, where a proactive policy of change operated. The Bolte Government devoted significant resources to the Ministry, some funds coming from the Commonwealth, which after the 1967 Referendum had a role in state Aboriginal affairs. The Ministry grew to about eighty staff. About thirty were Aboriginal people, some employed at Lake Tyers, others in administration and several, including Frank Stewart, were field officers. Worthy was assisted by an Aboriginal Affairs Advisory Council of twelve nominated members, at least three of whom were Aboriginal. The Advancement League pushed for changes. In November 1968 the Government allowed six members to be elected by Aboriginal people, which together with the two appointed by government, created an Aboriginal majority on the Advisory Council. Stewart Murray soon resigned, however, demanding that all Advisory members be elected, and be Aboriginal.

Worthy introduced significant initiatives that broke with 100-year-old Aboriginal policy. He urged Aboriginal people to become independent and responsible citizens, a goal no doubt shared by Aboriginal elders. The Ministry's first annual report stated: 'The Ministry has rejected policies of paternalism and expediency and espouses a programme which will lead ultimately to self-determination by Aborigines'. Handouts should cease, as they 'have taken away their initiative, responsibility, and even the desire for anything better'. Under this new approach, people would pay their own rent, medical bills, and fulfil their own hire purchase agreements. Aboriginal rent subsidies were phased out, the needy coming under general Housing Commission subsidy schemes. Those moving into new homes no longer received furniture selected and paid for by government, but chose and paid for their own, the Government acting as guarantor. An Aboriginal scholarship scheme provided support at all levels of schooling. Rental arrear debts accumulated over fifteen years were written off by Worthy and regular payers were rewarded with a $500 bonus towards rent reduction or a housing deposit. Deposits of $1500 were offered to all and $9000 was extended to those leaving Lake Tyers. Those who stayed at Lake Tyers were given award wages.

In 1968 Reg Worthy dropped a bombshell while addressing the Aboriginal branch of the Advancement League: 'we do not believe in taking children from so-called "sub-standard" conditions and putting them in with a middle class white family. This will stop dead. No home is better than the one provided by your own mother'. A fortnight later, he claimed there were three hundred Aboriginal children (not all Victorians) in foster homes in the state, mostly with white foster parents. While many foster parents were excellent, some were not, and a few made private arrangements to take children and even passed them on to others. One set of Aboriginal twins was passed on and separated by the decision of the second set of foster parents. Another foster parent had fifteen Aboriginal children and six of her own. Many were well intentioned, but Worthy said some people fostered Aboriginal children as a status symbol, and treated them as 'pets'. Some who took children under holiday schemes to give them a taste of a white lifestyle were loath to hand them back. The Government promised legislation, if necessary, to end these practices.

Alick was soon involved in the Ministry's new child welfare policy. He recalled that

> in many cases foster families would not return the children to their Aboriginal parents and as a Field Officer with the M.A.A., I would accompany the natural parents in attempting to get the children back. In some cases we were successful but in other cases they just wouldn't let the children go. Many excuses were given.

One family claimed that the foster mother had a prior mental illness and the taking of the child would cause a relapse. Sometimes Alick and another field officer employed more proactive tactics: 'the natural parents would remain in the car, with either John or myself at the steering wheel ready to drive off while the other officer would go into the house, grab the child, and run to the car'.

Those who wished to foster children were driven by a variety of motives: some altruistic, some indulgent, and some plainly bizarre. Alick remarked that 'there were successful long term foster and adoption placements with white families'. He cited Jack Chester, a returned serviceman carpenter and his wife, who lived at Newmerella in Gippsland, successfully fostering fifteen Aboriginal children who otherwise would have grown up in institutions, but 'there were just as many, if not more failures'. He once received a call from a country woman who wanted an Aboriginal child for a holiday stay, 'a very black child, not a fair one, so she could show her friends'. Another woman 'was bathing her foster child in White King [bleach] to make it fairer'. Problems often arose at puberty, as cuteness waned, and the child began to search for its identity. Alick remembered, 'adoptive parents would phone the Department saying that they could not handle the teenager and now they did not want the child. In many cases the child left the family and would head for Fitzroy seeking to identify with the Aboriginal community'.

Alick worked as a field officer in the Gippsland region, his work diary revealing a pattern of considerable travel in alternate weeks. In his second week he travelled as far as Cann River in East Gippsland covering well over a thousand kilometres in four days, during which time he made 62 household visits, contacting over a hundred people. Most days he worked until 10 p.m. He returned to Melbourne on a Friday for the funeral of Bill Onus and spent the next week in the office writing reports from his field notes and dealing with 38 cases. He returned to the field the following week driving 1200 kilometres to Club Terrace, near Cann River. He made 97 household visits in five days, working until after six on two days, and after eight, nine and eleven o'clock on the others. Whether he was paid overtime is unknown, but he did note the times of visits in his field notes.

The nature of his work was hands on welfare assistance. He helped Aboriginal people (all of whose names are withheld here) access the system: through delivering, demystifying and helping them to complete a range of forms concerned with social welfare, housing applications, tenancy agreements, rental subsidies, furniture applications, secondary education assistance, child endowment and adoption papers. Alick also helped them complete tax forms and those concerning wills and divorces. Alick made hospital and dental appointments for people, visited gaols, attended funerals and organised travellers' aid accommodation for people on the move. He helped some find work. Alick also issued railway travel vouchers and grocery orders for those in strife. He listed who was on holidays or not there when he called because of seasonal work, who was visiting whom, and who had just built new accommodation on vacant crown land. He met people on the road seeking picking work and noted their names. He was not checking or prying, but making notes so that he knew these people in the future. He was mapping the Victorian Aboriginal community in order to be involved in their lives. Not infrequently he simply noted in this field sheet, 'contact', that is, he called in to say 'G'day'.

This pattern of long hours and fortnightly field trips continued for the six months for which the records survive, but he found it immensely satisfying. While at Bonang in March 1968 Alick met Bob and Cora Farnham. Bob was a white mill worker married to Cora (née Stevens) from Lake Tyers Aboriginal reserve. They had eight children, one of whom named Sandra was born with an abnormality of her hands and feet. Alick organised for 8-year-old Sandra to attend the Royal Children's Hospital in Melbourne where she had corrective surgery. In 2003 Sandra Neilson (née Farnham) was delighted to talk about this and Alick, and to demonstrate the free movement she has to this day in her hands and feet because of the surgery. She also recalled that Alick met her when she was an adult and instantly recalled her face and the visit to the Children's Hospital.

His work diary reveals his incredible energy while in Gippsland as each day involved numerous visits and several hundred kilometres of travel. In early April he had one particularly memorable day. At Nowa Nowa he was awakened at 5.45 a.m. to drive a pregnant Aboriginal woman to the Bairnsdale Hospital. Within minutes Alick stopped the car and helped to deliver a baby boy in the back seat. He diverted to Lakes Entrance where a doctor attended the woman at 6.10 a.m. Alick then headed for Bairnsdale Hospital with mother and baby arriving at 7 a.m., where the woman also gave birth to a baby girl. By 9.10 a.m. he had cleaned the car and travelled a hundred kilometres back to Orbost, before visiting Newmerella, Nowa Nowa and Bruthen. He arrived at Lake Tyers reserve after twelve calls in a long and exhausting day, passing the 'evening in [the] Hall with some teenagers and children, record player etc'. That week in April he travelled 1500 kilometres, made about 80 house calls, hospital and gaol visits and played midwife.

All his East Gippsland trips in 1968 involved Lake Tyers, where he had been a full-time officer the previous year. In 1969 the Ministry sponsored a week-long adventure camp at Lake Tyers for fifty teenage boys, half of them non-Aboriginal. They were divided into teams of five, each with a leader responsible for planning their water-based adventure activities, which included sailing, water-skiing, scuba diving and canoeing. Reg Worthy and his wife were the hosts and Victoria's Governor and his wife also visited. Alick was in charge of 'transport and visitors' and his son Andrew was one of the participants. Alick appeared as 'Jaw Jarring Jackomos' during one night's entertainment, wrestling another supervisor, 'Hulk Heaving Hullick'. The Lake Tyers school teacher, Keith Lovell, believed the camp boosted the confidence and enthusiasm of the residents and increased the participation level of the children in sporting activities.

Alick played an important role in the Ministry. He orientated the Ministry's social workers, many of whom were pro-Aboriginal in theory, but knew little about the people. Peter Renkin, who joined the Ministry in 1970 as a social worker at Lake Tyers, knew Alick well, due to his frequent overnight stays there. Renkin recently observed:

> As a non-Aboriginal person you are already a stranger and an outsider. And to establish your trustworthiness, your credibility, you have to start working on things, and part of it is of course acknowledging and recognising the importance of their family and their kin and their origins... Alick would be tremendous, letting you know who those people were and who their relatives were and where they'd been...Alick helped to break down this whole problem of us [social workers] being outsiders...for Alick to be around and to say 'he/she's okay' to people, gave you a foot in the door...gave you a chance of communicating.

Alick was invaluable to the Director, Reg Worthy, who at times genuinely sought community opinion, although at others, as John Moriarty believed, 'ruled with an iron fist'. Alick knew the community intimately, who should be invited to meetings and how to contact them. He also organised the events and no doubt ensured a better roll up. Alick remembered:

> one of my jobs was organising 'consultations' as Reg Worthy called 'em. It was my job to go the various towns, be it Bairnsdale or Swan Hill or Mildura, book the local hall, get the local band, organise the caterers...organise buses to bring the people from other towns...I'd run a social at night, [be] MC at the social'.

Renkin recalled that Alick 'would organise the whole event. ...he was calming waters and feeding in information so that people understood what was going on'.

Peter Renkin and Alick discuss a point as Ralph Henger and Sister McCrae look on, Ministry of Aboriginal Affairs, c. 1970

Despite some Aboriginal antagonism towards Reg Worthy and the Ministry, Worthy was more progressive and more open by far than the regime under the former Welfare Board. He believed for instance that 'unless they [Aboriginal people] are able to stand on their own feet they will never be independent', although his strongly directive efforts were criticised by Aboriginal leaders, who thought he moved too fast and still consulted too little. In 1969 Bob Maza, Queensland Aboriginal entertainer, activist, actor and the first Aboriginal Director of Victorian Aborigines' Advancement League cautioned against 'forcing them to take immediate responsibilities in matters which have so far overwhelmed them'. Aboriginal people should not be pushed too quickly into 'the ruck of our aggressive competitive society', for to force them from one extreme to another causes 'despair'. David Anderson, a member of the Ministry's Advisory Council, accused Worthy in 1972 of being 'arrogant, perhaps racist' when he said that if Aborigines wanted to be treated equally they had to measure up to equal responsibility. Anderson said, 'we are still reeling under the blow of white man's invasion, so it's absurd for Mr Worthy to talk about taking off the kid gloves and giving the Aborigine equality'.

Alick played a practical grass-roots role in mediating this growing antagonism between the community and the Ministry, personified by Worthy. Renkin called Alick a genuine 'Gubbah-iginal' in understanding, that is a homogenised blend of Gubbah (a non-Aboriginal) and Aboriginal, and a man who was not competitive or overtly political. He was a communicator and mediator, recalled Renkin, and one on whom Worthy relied (as he did Doug Nicholls), as another source of feedback from the community. If policy was not understood, Worthy would send Alick to investigate and report back. Renkin believes Alick and Worthy had a good working relationship. Trudi Miteff, who also worked in the Ministry for a while, and who described Worthy 'as a very difficult man', thought Worthy 'appreciated Alick' and his local knowledge. Philip Felton, the Ministry's Senior Research Officer, intimated that they did not get on so well, but Worthy supported Alick's Aboriginal football involvements. Also, probably with Worthy's permission, Alick attended a short course run by Diane Barwick in January–February 1971 at the Australian National University on the 'Culture, Identity and Future of the Aborigines'. Alick was the only non-Aboriginal present and he passed 'with distinction'. Whatever their relationship, Worthy and Alick were able to work professionally with each other. Peter Renkin recalled that Alick was always 'loyal' and professional towards Worthy and the Ministry, when out in the field.

Alick exhibited amazing patience, tolerance and self-control in difficult meetings, according to his colleague Peter Renkin. Given Aboriginal assertiveness, Alick was sometimes abused, as were all public servants. Philip Felton recalled that, despite Alick's physical skills, 'I have never seen him rely on his strength to break up a situation. He was able with his personality and his verbal skills, to quieten it down to deal with the situation'. Renkin added that while Alick tried to mediate between the Ministry and the people, he was not a chameleon, nor one who tried being all things to all men. Renkin is still amazed how Alick managed to belong to Aboriginal organisations and to the Ministry at a time, when there was considerable tension between community members and public servants. Renkin

Alick in front of the man on the rail with fellow 'students' at the Aboriginal Studies short course, Australian National University, 1971

believed Alick survived because 'he was there, he was relating, he was genuine and people trusted him'. Also, Alick always remained true to himself and thus 'was not false to any man'.

Alick who collected signatures for the Referendum, in Smith Street and outside the Collingwood Football Ground, unconsciously helped to change his workplace that he found so satisfying, and to which he made such a worthwhile contribution. He said in a 1998 interview with Barry York: 'I really enjoyed the years that the Ministry was there'. In December 1974, however, the Victorian Ministry of Aboriginal Affairs transferred its functions to the Commonwealth Department of Aboriginal Affairs (DAA). This was made possible by the Referendum victory in 1967, as well as by the determination of the Whitlam Federal Government to administer the whole of Aboriginal Affairs in the country. Alick and some of the Ministry's staff transferred over to the new Department, as a few had moved from the Welfare Board to the Ministry seven years earlier. Worthy transferred to the DAA's Brisbane office before returning to the Melbourne office. Upon his return he reportedly directed former Ministry staff in

Alick with work mates, Lyn Hawkins and Harry Popjoy, Ministry of Aboriginal Affairs, early 1970s

the late 1970s to destroy many of the Ministry's files of Aboriginal people. This caused Alick great distress at the thought of the loss of much personal history.

At the age of fifty-one Alick began a new career in 1975 with the Department of Aboriginal Affairs (DAA); his work with the Department was very different from his previous experience, and the transformation was personally hard for him. He recalled in his 'Memoirs':

> our role [in the Department] had now completely changed from welfare and social work to a funding and coordinating department. The community programs were now being done by the many Aboriginal organisations which had been established in the communities. Organisations which had managed on a shoe string and depended mostly on donations were now funded by the DAA.

He believed this was right and that such funding was 'well overdue'. Organisations could now provide the services 'by Aboriginals for Aboriginals', but this left him out of welfare work. He might have returned to community organisations but, being a non-Aboriginal person, his offer would most likely have been challenged by some and probably refused. Alick lamented in a 1998 interview, 'the personal contact with Aboriginal people in private homes was finished once the Ministry of Aboriginal Affairs was abolished'. Peter Renkin, who later became Regional Director of the new Department, agreed. He said for all the criticism of the Ministry, it had worked at a grassroots level, 'it had people out in the regional offices who knew the families, went to the local events and knew the local scene', whereas the Department was 'into projects and programs, but not into relationships'.

Alick missed the continual personal human contact of welfare work, although his growing interest in photographic and genealogical work was to compensate for this. Not that human contact ended completely, for he worked with Aboriginal people in the organisations which the Department funded; and his experience was still valued by his co-workers and others in the wider society. Eleanor Bourke, a Wergia/Wamba Wamba woman from Swan Hill, who joined the Department in the late 1970s to work with Aboriginal organisations in Melbourne, was greatly assisted by Alick's encyclopaedic knowledge of Aboriginal Victorians, which he willingly shared. John Moriarty, an Aboriginal man from the Northern Territory, who succeeded Peter Renkin as Regional DAA Director, and David Kidney, who became Moriarty's deputy, both relied on Alick's local knowledge. Moriarty likened Alick to an Eastern trader, like his Castellorizian forebears, 'with precise minds and very mathematical. The family structures of Aborigines just fitted into that totally'. Indeed, most people who worked in local Aboriginal affairs, even Aboriginal people like Bourke and Moriarty, found his knowledge, which was generously shared, indispensable.

Alick's experience saved Eleanor Bourke soon after she became adviser to Brian Dixon, the Victorian Minister responsible for Aboriginal Affairs. In 1982 the Victorian Premier's Department created an Aboriginal unit to liaise between the Victorian Government and Aboriginal Victorians, and to work with Aboriginal units established by the ministries of Housing, Health and Education. Dixon was to visit Lake Tyers, but Bourke admitted she did not know much about it, so she suggested they take Alick along. Eleanor Bourke knew Alick well by then, and he was later to 'give her away' at her marriage. She told Dixon, 'Alick Jackomos could drive us because he can tell the stories and he'll give you an absolute insight into some of the issues and its history'. Dixon agreed and was regaled with much information for over three hours. On their approach to Lake Tyers, Alick suddenly hit the brakes because of something on the road, crying out to an alarmed Dixon: 'Óh God! I can't kill Magpies'. (Both Alick and Eleanor were Collingwood supporters, while Dixon had played for Melbourne.) Alick then 'crossed himself the Greek way and Brian Dixon just looked at him'. While at Lake Tyers, Bourke noticed a dapper man in a grey suit and, when they left, she asked Alick who he was. Alick replied, revealing his rare genealogical knowledge about a whole community, 'that's a relative of yours on your grandmother's side. He was your mother's cousin's son...I should have introduced you'.

Alick left virtually no record or comment in his numerous biographical fragments about his day-to-day work with the Department. He did state that some DAA officers gossiped about Aboriginal people, which caused trouble, and he was sent to the local area to 'cool down' the community. He also commented that some 'departmental officers played a part in dividing Aboriginal communities and organisations, by favouring one community against another...the officer would tell the [unsuccessful] organisation, "we can't fund your new item this year as the x organisation has received most of the additional funding"'. A few staff had shifted from the Ministry, but others were 'BINGS', meaning 'been in New Guinea', and some were not particularly committed to Victorian Aboriginal people. It was just a job to some officers, which saddened Alick. His son Andrew said, 'Dad didn't like particularly working for those organisations [the Department and later Aboriginal Development Commission], but he saw them as a vehicle to work with the community'. He added, 'Dad's heart was with people and working with individuals and families rather than program management'.

The work stressed Alick at times, report writing and project work were not his forte, but he managed to remain happy and still made an energetic contribution. Trudi Miteff, a refugee from Cyclone Tracey, became an information officer in the Department and often worked closely with Alick because of his great knowledge of the community. She arrived early each day to check the paper for Aboriginal news, and recalled that Alick was always at work early. 'You knew he was there because he either whistled or he sang and his favourite song which is so cute, was: "Don't Cry For Me Argentina". I knew the words but I could never figure out the melody!' She often pondered correcting his tunefulness, but thought, 'No! Let him sing it as he does'.

Others noted his early starts. Peter Renkin recalled: 'Alick always got to work early' about 8 a.m.

> If Alick had been out on a country trip…I would get a bit annoyed, 'cos I barely got into my office to unpack, and Alick would be in with his 2A form or whatever, to sign for his travel allowance. I must admit I used to think 'Wait! Alick, Wait! Let me get my collar and tie right'…He was always meticulous about getting his entitlements. Alick was always making sure he got all those things right. He was very organised. He was in control. And he was very committed.

David Kidney, another of his bosses in the Department, stated that 'Alick worked for indigenous affairs 24 hours a day. His house was everybody's…He was a worker, no doubt about that'. Kidney added that 'Alick was a fair ground muck-about in public service clothes. He never changed. He never said, "I'm a public servant now, because he never was a public servant, that's where he worked. Indigenous Affairs was his *total* occupation'. Peter Renkin also commented of Alick: 'he never sold his soul. He never sold out the people, and that's the strength of Alick. I mean there are a lot of people who could have moved and enjoyed being with the Canberra bods. But Alick was always part of the grass-roots'.

His commitment to Aboriginal people and his grass-roots style antagonised some in the Department. He also lacked respect for petty public service rules, or processes, when they got in the way of human interactions. Alick's son Andrew recalled one officer who, on trips to Lake Tyers with Alick, ordered him not to pick up Aboriginal hitch-hikers along the highway, which Alick had been doing for years. This hurt Alick and might have affected his relations to Gunai people. This

Alick and Senator Neville Bonner

same officer threatened Alick over his favourite pastime of trading in boomerangs. Andrew recalled that 'Dad used to deal in boomerangs. He'd go down to Lake Tyers or anywhere and he'd buy them [from Aboriginal people] and sell them. He had a couple of places where he would sell the boomerangs on the way home'. But this officer said he would report Alick for dealing in work time. However, most of his relations with work colleagues were smooth, because of his amiable and generous nature. Trudi Miteff recalled Alick placing a chocolate on every desk in the office or bringing in Greek Easter bread for all.

Difficulties at work caused Alick to take several secondments. In the early 1980s he worked for the Aboriginal Development Commission, but little is known of his work there, as he left no personal record of his involvement. In 1986 he applied for a secondment to the Australian Bureau of Statistics to work with the Aboriginal community during the 1986 Census. The position was a Clerical Assistant, Class 6, with the possibility of a temporary transfer/higher duties allowance. The successful applicant had to prepare census awareness materials, visit and liaise with communities and supervise the collection of the census. It was advertised as a 'challenging' position which will 'involve extensive contact with Aboriginal communities'. Alick was tailor made for this position and was appointed in February 1986 with a secondment from March to July.

The Bureau had decided that because of problems with the 1981 Census that a liaison officer was needed. The 1971 Census recorded the Aboriginal and Torres Strait Islander population of Victoria as 6371 and in 1976 as 14 760. However, in 1981 the Census had only recorded 6057, a drop of 59 per cent. There was of course uproar from the community as the count was clearly wrong. Numbers affected budgets, planning, political power and the very psyche of the community. The Bureau had no explanation for the drop and could only point to a change in the census question, although it is unclear how this could have caused such a marked difference. Instead of asking, as did the 1976 Census, 'what is each person's racial origin?' and presenting boxes to be ticked, including 'Aboriginal' or 'Torres Strait Islander'; the 1981 question had simply asked 'is the person of Aboriginal or Torres Strait Islander origin?' The Department of Aboriginal Affairs used its own estimate of 15 339 for 1981 when deciding policy issues, as a census cannot be changed, but clearly the Bureau had to adopt a more rigorous approach in 1986.

Alick set to work with a will from day one. His final report suggests he enjoyed the fourteen-week secondment, as it put him in close contact with Aboriginal people across the state, and was not unlike his welfare officer work with the League, Board and Ministry. He did it well, for as his report stated: 'it was fortunate that I was familiar with all Aboriginal organisations, Departments and communities in Victoria and knew who to contact from my first day of employment'. The work was demanding. In seventy working days he visited 54 bodies and other community gatherings. He twice visited 23 Aboriginal organisations and five DAA district field officers in country areas from Cann River to Heywood and north to Mildura, Robinvale and Swan Hill and over to the northern bank of the Murray; sixteen organisations in the city; and ten Government departments in city and country. He organised photographs of community leaders for posters, which were then placed in all community organisations. Alick also attended many seminars, conferences and meetings where

Aboriginal leaders gathered to convey the census message. The East Gippsland Cooperative was the most responsive and the Framlingham Aboriginal Trust the least. Geoff Clark, Framlingham's Administrator, refused to participate in the census as a land rights protest. Alick found the work pleasurable: 'during my visits to country towns, I socially visited many families and discussed the Census'.

Alick's report assessed the problems of the task. First, those people living in Melbourne were difficult to reach, as not all were members of Aboriginal organisations. Second, even when organisations were contacted, Alick was unsure how much was passed on, as many did not have newsletters, and relied on word of mouth and notice boards. Third, people found the census form too difficult to understand. Fourth, others chose not to complete it, because of a deep-seated fear of government. He reported:

> the CFO [census field officer] is not an easy job, in most cases he is well known to his/her community and he must convince the pensioner who is working, the widow living with a de facto and the Housing Commission tenant who has unauthorised tenants living in the house, that the information will not be passed on to another Government Department.

He recommended the appointment of two officers at the next census as the job was too big for one, or at least the hiring of a liaison officer for three weeks to work with a dozen major Aboriginal organisations.

Alick reported in July 1986 that 'the Aboriginal Community of Victoria is much more aware of the Census in 1986 than in previous collections'. The tabulation of the 1986 Census proved him correct. The total number of Aboriginal and Torres Strait Islander people counted in 1986 in Victoria was 12 611, up by 6057 on the 1981 count, but still below the 14 760 counted in 1976. Alick again worked as a Census Field Officer for eight weeks before the 1991 Census and used much the same techniques: visits to organisations, posters and also badges this time, although he said they were 'bland' and should have been in the 'Aboriginal colours'. He addressed gatherings of leaders and made personal visits. Alick reported that 'during the evenings while on country visits, I took the opportunity to socially visit many families in each town'. The same impediments existed as before, including Geoff Clark, who again opposed participation. Alick addressed an Aboriginal and Torres Strait Islander Commission (ATSIC) State Conference at Moama, where Clark again opposed the Census, but added that he had nothing personally against Alick. Alick recommended that, before the 1996 Census, the Bureau hold a meeting with Aboriginal leaders and administrators, 'seeking their views and suggestions and their cooperation'. The Census count of 1991 was 16 570.

Alick returned to the Department in July 1986. He had felt undervalued and excluded in recent years — as he had at times in his earlier public service placements — mainly because he lacked that piece of paper. Some of his work colleagues alluded to that in interviews. Trudi Miteff referred vaguely to problems and to conversations with Alick where he voiced frustration and disappointment. She always told him: 'you know everybody enjoyed being with you, we know what skills you have, and look what you're doing now [referring to his genealogical work], it's going to be there *forever*'.

Alick left little written record of his own thoughts about such dissatisfactions, although in a letter written on 10 October 1977 declining to accept an Aboriginal Arts Board grant to write a history of Lake Tyers, he commented:

> I am currently employed as a Community Adviser by the Dept of Aboriginal Affairs, South Eastern Region. Recently I was awarded a Churchill Fellowship to study Ethnic Communities in the U.S.A. The day after my return to Australia, I commenced work and was advised by my Director, Mr Reg Worthy that because of Department cuts in staff, there was no further work for me, and that I should find employment in another Government Department. Because of this situation and until I find out exactly what my future plans are, I would like to defer receiving the grant.

Clearly, Worthy valued Alick less, once the work was project-based. Otherwise he would have found ways to keep a man who had been in the public service with the Board, Ministry and now Department and who knew the Aboriginal community intimately.

In his statement to the RCADIC around 1990, Alick also alluded to dissatisfactions stretching back to the Ministry, stating:

> I am a little critical of DAA today. There is very little Aboriginal decision making when submissions are made to the Department by communities. The project officer may recommend an organization's submission but it's whites and their attitudes which decide whether it should be approved. The role of the MAA field officer was to collect submissions from Aboriginal families to be housed. It took a long time. I was concerned that single people and childless couples did not get housing. The Ministry wouldn't take submissions from these two groups. These people lived in humpies. The Ministry hounded them. This attitude flowed onto the DAA.

This devaluing of his skills was most marked during his time at the DAA. Indeed his RCADIC statement in 1990 ended with these three sentences. 'In the past 10 years I only attended a handful of staff meetings. They called the meetings "senior Staff meetings" to exclude me. Younger people were classed as "senior staff"'. Trudi Miteff, a close colleague, referred obliquely to this, commenting, 'towards the end there were some problems work-wise, which he was very unhappy about, but he spent a lot of time just doing his genealogy which was wonderful too, because otherwise it wouldn't have been done anyway'. In Aboriginal organisations the issue of his non-Aboriginality became a problem for Alick by the late 1960s, and within the public service by the late 1970s his lack of education also created difficulties for him. A pale shadow enveloped Alick, whose life was given meaning by helping others. Ever resilient, he forged other ways to feel valued, especially through his passion for travel, Victorian Aboriginal community life, and his interest in Aboriginal photographs and history.

12   Boomerang Diplomacy

Alick, like his Castellorizian forebears, thrived on travel, meeting people and being involved in festivals and public occasions. His time in the boxing tents and his work with the Advancement League and three successive Aboriginal departments kept him on the road. Family holidays were always great treks and as their children grew, Alick and Merle travelled privately, giving Alick greater scope for his gregariousness. His daughter Esmai recently remarked that if Alick entered a room of people he could talk to anyone, and by the time he left he had a friend with whom he corresponded. As often as not on these jaunts, some official and others not related to work, Alick carried a brace of boomerangs to smooth the way.

His first official trip came in late November 1966, when Alick represented the Aboriginal Advancement League on an eighteen-day Maori study tour to New Zealand by 24 people, seven of them Aboriginal. For ten days they heard lectures by Maori leaders on all aspects of Maori history and culture, relations with Pakeha (white settlers and their descendants) and Maori contemporary life and culture. For eight days they visited Maori meeting houses and cultural centres. Alick left no reminiscences about this trip so we cannot know if and how many boomerangs he took. But he did write a two-page official report for the League.

In his report Alick noted the stark differences in the treatment of its indigenous people between New Zealand and Australia: 'the Maori is a national responsibility and New Zealand whose population is smaller than Victoria, spends much more than all Australian states spend on Aborigines'. He noted that they had taken their place in New Zealand's society and economy, but that Maori culture had survived — albeit in changed form — and was a part of New Zealand's culture. 'Maori language is taught at the Universities, old people say that the young must keep language, arts and crafts alive, but to many of the modern Maoris, modern Maori culture is the way modern Maoris live with their football, dancing, singing and integration.' Alick also noted the differing political situation with Maori members of parliament and a lack of discriminatory laws: 'what we are fighting for here in Australia, equal rights, housing, employment, education, and health, the New Zealand Government accepted 30 years ago'. He was impressed too with the Treaty of Waitangi, and he quoted the sections on rights to land. He concluded:

> How many years must Aboriginals wait for the same opportunities?...Australia has 100,000 Aborigines, we have taken so much away from these people, they must be given all the opportunities so that they can take their place in Society and Australia has so much to gain economically and culturally by their advancement.

During his time in the Welfare Board and the Ministry he was kept busy at the grass roots, but once in the federally-based DAA, Alick worked on the funding of community development programs. In the mid-1970s a colleague, Beryl Bergraff, suggested he apply for a Churchill scholarship to study indigenous programs overseas. Alick ordered the form but when it arrived he was overwhelmed by its length and the request for 'about a million references. I said "I can't handle this"', so he filed it away.

A few years later he met Margaret Valadian. She was the first Aboriginal university graduate, and one of Alick's teachers in the Australian National University workshop on Aboriginal culture held in 1971. She urged him to apply for a Churchill scholarship and offered to be a referee. Diane Barwick and Gordon Bryant also lent their support. Alick requested new forms. Mollie Dyer, Margaret Tucker's daughter, who had gained a scholarship to study the removal of children from Indigenous communities in America, offered Alick her contacts. He soon received favourable replies, endured the form-filling, submitted his application, and was successful. Dame Phyllis Frost, who was on the selection panel, commented to Merle at the award ceremony: 'Alick was beyond the eligible age limit. But he left school at 12, spoke three languages, and joined the army, what could I do but appoint him?'

Alick toured from mid-July to mid-September 1977, this time with boomerangs. His itinerary was typically energetic and whirlwind in style. In eight weeks he visited twenty Black and Indian American programs in California, Arizona, New Mexico, Mississippi, Illinois, New York and Washington DC. Five weeks were spent in the cities and three in rural areas. As he stated in his official Churchill report: 'on some occasions, I visited two programs in one day. It is impossible to give an assessment of each program, in reporting each program I have attempted to clarify the aims and objectives of each organization which I visited'.

Alick also visited Hawaii on the way over and Kibbutz Yisreel, near Nazareth, Israel, during his return journey, where he heard 'shells coming over the border [with Lebanon] everyday'. Neither of these two stopovers featured in his official report. In 1998 he stated that the Hawaii stopover was 'a dud', as the programs there were not relevant and most groups were fighting for land. He visited a courtroom with one community, bearing banners, and they were threatened with contempt of court and gaol and ejected. Alick mused at the time, 'I'd better get out of this'. He also found the Israel stopover irrelevant, as most of those on the kibbutz were university graduates, undertaking programs that were 'too advanced for the Aboriginal people I was working with'.

Alick was impressed with the Black American programs he visited in Los Angeles, Mississippi, Washington DC, Chicago and Harlem, Brooklyn, New York. He later recalled they were 'much more powerful than the Indian community, because in all those places they had the numbers, the voting numbers, the power, they had the political power'. In Chicago he visited PUSH (Peoples United to Save Humanity) led by Rev. Jesse Jackson, which advocated educational, health, housing and economic rights to complement the civil rights gains of the 1960s. In New York he observed the Wild Cat Corporation, a non-profit body that provided eighteen months of paid work for those without skills or a work culture. He also visited the urban renewal program run by the Bedford Stuyvesant Restoration Centre. The Program organised low-cost building and renovation, cheap home ownership finance, job training, economic and business development and cultural revival. In 1998, however, Alick recalled that this segment of the trip 'wasn't relevant to Victoria'.

Alick found relevance and inspiration in Arizona and Mississippi among the First Nation peoples, the Apache, Hopi, Navajo and Choctaw. These were the people most like Aboriginal people in their history and current situation. Alick recalled in 1998: 'their land was taken from them, they were put on reservations, a lot of them had alcoholic problems, their kids had been taken away'. In Arizona he was accompanied by Gordon Krutz, an anthropologist, and co-ordinator of Indian programs at the University of Arizona, who gave him background information.

The rural nature of most of his Arizona visit allowed Alick's boomerang diplomacy to shine once again. In 1978 Alick received a letter from E. Harold Keyes, a social worker with the Bureau of Indian Affairs, Choctaw Agency, who had shown him Choctaw programs in Mississippi, and with whom he had stayed. Keyes wrote: 'It was a blessing to have you visit in our home. I only wish it could have been for a longer period of time. The children all enjoyed your visit and especially the demonstration you gave of the proper use of the "boomerang". We shall always appreciate the gift you left with us'.

Choctaw Indian dancers (*Aboriginal and Islander Identity,* July 1978)

In 1984 Gordon Krutz wrote to Alick, recalling their trip to Phoenix, White River and Oraibi Az. Krutz recalled 'you teaching the Apaches how to throw the boomerang, what a sight that was!' In 1985 and again in 1991, Steve and Daisy now living in Vancouver, British Columbia, reminisced in a similar way. In 1991 they wrote that their grandchildren still enjoyed the boomerang, which has been to 'show and tell' so many times. 'I can still see all the children gathered around you Alick, you were the best public relations person any country could have'. Tony and Phyllis Machukay, who exchanged Christmas cards with Alick over the years, did not mention boomerangs, but in 1990 they thanked him for his card 'which brought cherished memories of your visit and the good times we shared'.

In Arizona Alick spent three days in Phoenix amidst 40° C heat, visiting several organisations, one being the Phoenix Indian Center, which aimed to integrate Indian groups to an urban setting. He then travelled to Apache, Hopi and Navajo Reservations where he found 'vast empires' of bureaucrats administering federal funding, although some tribal agencies also administered moneys. The Indian communities wanted to end welfare, and build economic enterprises run by Indians, using the resources on their reserves. 'On the reservations I found direct Indian involvement, Indians doing things for themselves, the way they wanted to do them'. Alick reported in enthusiastic detail the business enterprises, irrigation and development projects, health and employment programs, and cultural activities that were under way. 'Those programs were all positive', he recalled in 1998. He also visited the Choctaw people at the Pearl River Community, ten kilometres outside of Philadelphia in Mississippi. These Choctaws had a proud tradition of resisting removal from their region to Oklahoma in the nineteenth century. Their small reservation did not have any natural resources, so they were developing it into an industrial park, to attract industry.

While visiting the Choctaw community of Mississippi, who numbered fewer than 5000 people, he experienced racism, American-style. Alick recalled in 1998 that he went on a barbeque with two carloads of Choctaw students. They went to a park with a big shed, about twenty tables and barbeques. While their meat was cooking several cars drew up. 'Some whites got out of their cars and stood near them, with their arms across their chests like the "white boss" sign and one of the Indian teachers went over'. He spoke to them for several minutes, then came back and said, '"Look we'd better leave immediately". They told him "they didn't want any Indians here". Yet there was room for everyone. So we packed up and took all the food, half-cooked and everything, took it back to the Pearl River Reservation and finished our barbeque there'.

Alick returned home full of enthusiasm and wrote his 47-page report. It was a detailed factual account of what he had observed, but did not distil any proposals for action back in Victoria. Analysis and policy making were not his forte. He stated in 1998 that 'I made a report and handed it around to various organizations and some of those programs were later implemented'. When pressed by Barry York for an example, Alick could not give one. But he added, 'I know that a lot of projects were copied, programs that DAA eventually was funding for Aboriginal organizations, self-help programs'. The connections he drew between his report and later programs were vague and unconvincing. Merle's memory is that when Alick arrived home, the DAA management did not ask him to present his findings and sat him at a desk for three months with nothing to do. Certainly the month after he arrived home from his Churchill study tour Alick refused an Aboriginal Arts Board grant to write the history of Lake Tyers, because he was told by the Director of the DAA that 'there was no further work for me, and that I should find employment in another Government Department'.

This uncertainty at work was interrupted by a three-month secondment, which involved more travel, but his time within Australia. He was appointed as a project officer to the DAA's Mount Isa office from April 1978. Alick was responsible for an area twice the size of Victoria in far north-west Queensland's Gulf Country, from Boulia and Dajarra south of Mount Isa to Normanton, Burketown and Mornington Island to the north. Aboriginal unemployment stood at over 90 per cent owing to the replacement of Aboriginal drovers by motor bikes and helicopters after the equal wage case in the pastoral industry in 1965. With no work and no rations, people left the stations for towns or reserves. Alick reported that Aboriginal people lived in overcrowded 'humpies' on little money, near stores where prices were marked up 50 per cent on Mount Isa prices, and few were registered for unemployment benefits. Of the 250 Aborigines at Camooweal, '50 to 70 live in some of the most shocking conditions that a human being could be asked to tolerate. Housing provided on the reserve consists of 5 tin huts which lack the bare necessities'. His role was to form housing co-operatives, create works programs and develop economic bases. He no doubt applied some of his Arizona experience here. He assisted the creation of a local store–service station at Dajarra, but his three-month stay was too short to have much impact.

Alick initially stayed with the former Palm Islanders, Iris and Fred Clay. Fred was a DAA field officer whom Alick knew from the boxing tents thirty years previously. Alick then moved into a boarding house where life was less congenial. He experienced the racism directed towards Aboriginal people in far north Queensland and those who associated with them. The time was especially tense, as the Queensland Government was in protracted dispute with the Commonwealth over its management of Aurukun and Mornington Island Aboriginal reserves, which is revealed in the documentary film, *Takeover*. Alick recalled in 1998:

> I stayed in a residential area where we had community use of the kitchen and the dining room. I got a bit of hell there because all the white workers there knew I was working for DAA and they were trying to start a brawl about Aboriginal affairs or about Aurukun or Mornington Island. They'd make some pretty nasty comments but I didn't reply.

Acquainting himself with local Aboriginal people was a pleasure and easy as Fred Clay spread a good word about Alick. He also met another old boxing friend, Tony Sabadine from Thursday Island, who fought as Tony Assan. He was the National Aboriginal Council member for the area and ran a taxi service between the missions in an old 'Combie wagon'. On one occasion, instead of catching the charter flight from Doomadgee Mission near Burketown, Alick was persuaded by Tony to take Assan's taxi the 500 kilometres to Mount Isa with eight or ten other Aboriginal people. Before too long they hit a kangaroo or wallaby.

> They jumped out and grabbed the kangaroo and put it in the combi wagon. We go another fifty miles and "bang", because there are a lot of kangaroos and we had bull bars... Bit further it started to get dark we're still hitting them, 'bang' one of our lights went out...'bang' another light...we got to Mt Isa with no lights and about thirteen kangaroos and there was blood everywhere, but it was good tucker. It was an experience.

Perhaps his most amazing and mind-opening trip occurred a few years earlier. It happened by accident, yet one that Alick made happen by his own gregariousness. He was holidaying with Merle in Europe in 1976, travelling by boat train from London to Dover. He was in the train's corridor and a woman of Malay-Chinese extraction was talking in Malay to a child. Alick joined the conversation in his friendly way, and the woman was so surprised that 'within a short moment she'd left the corridor and called some of the other people from adjoining compartments. It happened to be a group of about twenty people from Brunei who had just visited London and they were going off to Europe on a tour'. Alick spoke to them in Malay which he had picked up in wartime. By coincidence they were heading along the same tourist route and kept seeing each other. Captain Ambran Noor Aston of the Royal Brunei Malay Regiment, his family and in-laws, were among the group. When they parted, Ambran invited Alick and Merle to Brunei, but Alick never for a moment imagined they would catch up again.

When Alick was awarded the Churchill scholarship the following year, however, he decided to visit Brunei on his return journey and notified Captain Ambran Noor Aston of his plans. Alick's arrival at Bandar Seri Begawan in Brunei coincided with Hari Raya Eid Al-Fitr, when the thirty-day fasting of Ramadan ends and a week of festivities begin. Alick's luggage was delayed in transit so the family lent Alick some clothes. As Alick recalled:

> They took me home... and for the next few days we went and visited friends, sometimes we'd visit six, eight, nine, ten families a day, and every family that you went to, they'd put on a feast for you and eventually you had to knock a lot of it back and just have a soft drink.

Alick's Brunei friends Lt-Col Ambran HM Noor Aston and his wife Na'imah Mohiddin with their children (l. to r.) Mariana Ambran Aston, Ridzuan Ambran Aston and Mohammad Ambran Aston (Ambran Noor Aston and family)

Alick was always aware of the importance and power of the gift and handed out some boomerangs in Brunei. Photographs survive of him throwing boomerangs on a Brunei oval.

On the third day of festivities it was open day at the Sultan's Palace and usually about 45 000 people gathered for food and entertainment. Alick dressed in an oversized suit lent to him by Nordin, Ambran's brother. Haji Mohiddin, Ambran's father-in-law, took Alick to join the queue but at the head because of the family's social standing. Alick shook hands with the Sultan, his brothers and other members of the Royal family. Like everyone else, he received a gift of a little plastic box painted with a Brunei royal crest, containing a soft drink and a few cakes or bars of chocolate. To his amazement the event was shown on the television news that night and Alick's handshake with the Sultan was included in the coverage. This trip was the first of more than a dozen trips to Brunei. They represented Alick's quest into a new and fascinating Islamic cultural world beyond the boundaries of his own, in the same manner as he journeyed into the realms

Alick catching a boomerang on a football field in the oil town of Kuala Belait, Brunei, 1977 (Ambran Noor Aston and family)

of Aboriginal Australia from boyhood. Cultural exchanges thrived in these tips. Ambran noted of these later visits:

> he [Alick] always comes with lots of original boomerangs as gifts and I have a collection of his boomerangs and having been instructed by Alick I believe I am the only one qualified in Brunei to throw those boomerangs and to be able to catch them again with my hands when they come back.

Alick undertook several other overseas study tours. In September 1979 he travelled to Davao, on the island of Mindanao in the Philippines, where he inspected development projects among national minorities at Kapalang and Mataneo. Merle accompanied him on this trip. In 1982 it was suggested the DAA investigate indigenous projects in Malaysia. Alick wrote in July to the Director of Development Projects for the Orang Asli, the indigenous people of Malaya, seeking a visit. He was invited to Betan in Pahang State, four hours land journey from Kuala Lumpur. Alick visited in late 1982 or early 1983, recalling in the late 1980s:

> the tribes who are animist, live in the jungle. The only access is by river boat. The Government's program is to bring the Orang Asli out of the jungle into Kampongs (villages) and in a generation or so assimilate [them] into the mainstream of Malay life and Moslem Religion. The only languages spoken were the local dialects and Malay. Without the knowledge of Malay, the study could not have been undertaken.

In 1998 he described the same process of removal and resettlement of the people to allow companies to log their lands, forcing them to live on river banks, where pollution had wiped out fish stocks. 'I stayed there for some ten days with these people, living in a little hut and most of the food that we had there was only vegetables and yams and taro, very little meat and no fish at all'. He thought the trip was 'a little irrelevant to the Aboriginal situation. It's personal knowledge', although he added that Aboriginal people had also been resettled from their land, their religion changed, and assimilation attempted.

Alick relished journeys and new experiences; Merle who did not have the same zest for travel, sometimes accompanied him. They travelled to Castellorizo in 1976 but Alick left no written account of his impressions, except his regret that his parents were too frail to accompany them. Merle recalled that they stayed there for four days and she was entranced by the beauty of the harbour, crowded with whitewashed houses glistening in the sun. No relative remained on the island, but one elderly woman remembered the family. Merle and Alick stayed at a pensione and ate at a restaurant run by Greeks from Australia. They were excited by the place and walked and explored it each day until their ship returned. It was one more trip in an active life. Alick visited the USA and Brunei in 1977, the Philippines in 1979 and Malaya in 1982–83, sending boomerangs skyward each time. He went to China in the late 1970s when it was first opened to tourists, again with a brace of boomerangs. He demonstrated the ancient art at a school. Merle stayed home as it was winter and Alick later admitted the weather in China was bitterly cold.

Alick at a Chinese restaurant dinner hosted by Haji Mohiddin, Ambran Noor Aston's father-in-law, and family, Brunei, September 1977 (Ambran Noor Aston and family)

Boomerang diplomacy always led the way. When travelling in the Middle East in 1985 Alick showed Egyptian children at the foot of the pyramids how to throw a boomerang. Alick and Merle met Mary and Vito Vilate from California while in Tel Aviv. As usual Alick gave them a gift of a boomerang. They wrote in December 1985 that it 'had been a constant source of entertainment for our family and friends'. Alick, always ready to explore new things had read the Book of Mormon on their suggestion. The Vilates wrote to him later:

> [We are] so glad you are taking the opportunity to read the Book of Mormon. We believe that the Aboriginal migrated from S. America some hundreds of years BC and that the Book of Mormon is a history of the ancestors of the Aborigines and other South Sea Island natives and the Indians in the Americas.

They referred to a Mormon program of taking Indian children in for the winter, 'with permission of their parents...We had an Indian girl live with us for 3 winters. It was a most rewarding experience for us'. Alick's view of this account of Aboriginal antiquity, and of extended holidaying by indigenous children in white houses, is unknown, but from his knowledge of the Welfare Board, and his involvement in rescuing children from holiday stays, he probably shuddered.

Alick remained very fit for all this activity. Indeed, while returning from one trip in the 1980s, when aged about sixty, his old skills came in handy. His son Michael recalled the story.

> Some young men were being obnoxious on the plane. When the plane landed Mum and Dad were walking to the baggage area and the young men were still being stupid and they bumped Mum, so Dad said something. One of them had a go at Dad, and Dad threw him over his head. Mum removed her shoe and prepared to thump the young bloke on the ground. The other ran away looking for airport security and to complain that Dad was bashing them up. Dad was quite proud of this.

Another time Alick ran after a robber, who had held up Brashs Music store in Melbourne, and caught and secured him with a head lock. The store rewarded Alick with a pile of classical music LPs. The old wrestling holds, applied thousands of times, were just second nature to Alick and part of the adventure of living. His wrestling days, like boomerangs overseas, paved the way as he moved around Australia.

13 In the Thick of Things

Alick was often in the thick of Aboriginal Affairs, especially in Victoria. He knew all the political leaders and their families in the 1930s, he was a member of the Gore Street church and was Doug Nicholls' offsider; he was also present at the creation of the Victorian Aboriginal Advancement League. His enthusiasm for people and events, a legacy of his sideshow and earlier experiences, led to his involvement in many of the most significant Aboriginal gatherings and celebrations over forty years.

One of the first land hand backs in Australia occurred in Victoria and Alick was in the thick of it at the grass-roots level. The Advancement League and other groups pressured the Bolte Government in April 1970 to hand back 1600 hectares of land at Lake Tyers and 240 hectares at Framlingham under 'perpetual licence' to community trusts. The only previous hand back was the return of Pitjantjatjara lands in South Australia to a trust in December 1966. *The Victorian Aboriginal Lands Act 1970* created two trusts comprised of those registered as being resident there between January 1968 and October 1970. Adults were allotted 1000 shares and children 500. Shares could only be transferred to the trust, another trust member, an immediate family member, or back to the government, at a price fixed by the auditor. The land was held under communal title, which prevented its sale if any one shareholder objected.

The Act proved divisive, however, by creating insiders and outsiders. Those who had left the reserve before January 1968, some being enticed off with housing grants, were not eligible for shares. Alick was involved in compiling these shareholder lists which 'included a lot of guesswork'. Ninety-two people from sixteen extended families — mostly Bulls, Carters, Edwards, Fentons, Harrisons, Marks, and Mobournes — received shares. The rest were excluded, causing

213 people to petition over rights to Lake Tyers they claimed were denied them by the registration period. Many protesters were Gunai (Gippsland people), who were aggrieved that they had no rights as traditional owners or by being born there, whereas others from Ebenezer or New South Wales who were living at Lake Tyers in the registration period, received shares. At Framlingham a similar complex split developed between those with and without rights to the land, and exists to the present day.

Alick was immensely thankful about the hand backs, and proud that he had played a role in the proceedings: 'it was my job to organise catering and lunch for 300 people, marching girls from Echuca, Ralph Nicholls, corroboree dances and hotel accommodation for the marching girls, ministry staff and other visitors'. On Saturday 24 July 1971 the title to Lake Tyers was handed over to Charlie Carter by the Governor, Sir Rohan Delacombe, before seven hundred people. Charlie Carter said to the Governor: 'this is our land and we are proud of it. After all you white fellows weren't the first to discover Australia — we were here first'. Doug Nicholls added: 'we have fought for this with bitter experience but the winds of change are blowing. Now we have the chance to prove ourselves by working for our own destiny'. Alick was there as organiser and no doubt wrote the report of the day printed in the Aboriginal magazine, *Identity*, published by Alick's friend from FCAATSI days, Jack Davis. Dancing, didgeridoos, marching girls, a barbeque and basketball match helped celebrate the occasion.

Alick was also present at the parallel handover at Framlingham, although it was very low key and many people, even Aboriginal people, did not know it occurred. Alick remembered: 'approx. 30-40 people attended, no marching girls, no entertainment, no catering and it was all over in half an hour. That evening a dance was held at the Wangoom Hall to celebrate the event, which was attended by some 60 people'. This lack of publicity was not surprising as Framlingham was never as political as Lake Tyers. The Protection Board had tried to ignore it since its official closure in 1889 and during its partial survival thereafter. The Government was forced to tolerate its continued existence due to white supporters in the region. It was rarely newsworthy, while Lake Tyers had always been so.

In 1968 Alick and Merle attended a conference on Aboriginal issues at Adelaide University and met John Moriarty, a young Aboriginal who was involved in South Australian Aboriginal affairs. Moriarty suggested an Australian Rules football match between South Australian and Victorian indigenous teams. The Advancement League organised a weekend carnival for the following October and Alick was made team manager. Moriarty recalled that he arrived in Melbourne late and with less than a team. Indeed, the ranks were only swelled by a few 'drunken blokes' he picked up at an Aboriginal pub in Angas Street, Adelaide. He commented wryly that he 'was black-birding', referring to the kidnap of Kanakas for the Queensland Sugar industry a hundred years earlier. When those players who were pressed into service awoke bewildered the next morning in Melbourne, Moriarty told them: 'you are on in five minutes'. The Victorian team lent South Australia some players and still defeated them. As the competition grew into a national one the Ministry gave Alick time off to travel to these events as Victorian manager. Matches were played in Adelaide, Perth, Darwin and Alice Springs in successive years for the 'Sir Douglas Nicholls Cup'. Victoria did not win again until 1974 when Mick Dodson was the captain.

Alick's organising skills were called upon when Victoria hosted the carnival in September 1973. A Victorian squad played selection games against teams from Mooroopna, Healesville and Broadmeadows. Mick and Pat Dodson, who walked the national stage in Aboriginal affairs in the 1990s, were among those seeking selection, while standout players included Robert Lowe from Warrnambool and Robert Muir from Ballarat. Alick was in his element. He discussed the football carnival with his Director, Reg Worthy, who 'gave me full time off to organise the carnival', along with Dan Atkinson, an Aboriginal field officer also with the Ministry. Doug Nicholls was patron.

The Carnival, generously funded by the Ministry, ran from Friday to Sunday, 27–29 September, with Saturday for visiting the Royal Show or the races. The Victorian Football Association gave it their support, and the Werribee Football Association lent their ground and their staff on the day, no doubt because of Doug Nicholls' involvement. The Ministry threw a welcome reception, funded several socials, paid for meals and accommodation at Corpus Christi College (now 'Werribee Mansion'), and for buses for several hundred footballers and staff. Alick organised most things as well as marching girls, including an Aboriginal team, for half-time entertainment.

After the 1973 Carnival, a national indigenous team of 21 players and three officials were selected for an immediate six-day tour of Papua New Guinea. Alick was appointed as manager, his wartime friend George Bray from Alice Springs was his assistant, and Bill Roe the coach. Doug Nicholls went as patron. Team members included Robert Muir who was soon to star with St Kilda, Michael Mansell, a future Tasmanian activist, and Gary Murray who trained with North Melbourne. Alick arrived at the airport clutching a brace of boomerangs.

The tour was a great success in the circumstances. Australian team members, who left after playing two games in three days at the recent carnival at Werribee, faced three matches in five days in hot and humid New Guinea conditions. They won one game, defeating Goroka, but lost to Lae by four points and were beaten by the national team. Alick recorded that the Papua New Guinea (PNG) team invited the

Alick heading for Papua New Guinea as manager of the Australian Aboriginal Football team, 1973, with a brace of boomerangs and beside his mentor Doug Nicholls

Australians to afternoon tea, but while the New Guineans had lemon squash, they offered the visitors beer. Alick said 'no', but 'how could I stop 22 players'. The PNG team members were in bed by 9 p.m., but the Victorians were up partying till midnight. They lost to tiredness, the humidity and New Guinea gamesmanship the next day. Before the match Alick recalled, 'I got out on the oval...and started throwing boomerangs. They'd never ever seen a boomerang'. He did the same thing at most other places they visited. Over five hundred people watched one demonstration, 'I was their hero'.

After every game there was native dancing, feasting and tours of the local villages. Alick reported that 'every member brought back to Australia many artifacts which were obtained from the villages which included, bows and arrows, masks, shell work, baskets, carvings, wooden trays, native stone axes and many other items'. Alick's surviving scribbled notes contain the words 'conduct very good, great ambassadors'. The carnival and subsequent tour were also a credit to Alick's organisational skills and his ability to convince Reg Worthy to be generous with funds.

Socialising with Doug Nicholls (front) and others after the Australia v. Papua New Guinea match, 1973 (*Aboriginal and Islander Identity*, June 1974)

By 1973 a National Aboriginal Sports Foundation emerged funded by the Federal Government to oversee these carnivals. Alick organised and managed the Victorian team in a voluntary capacity until 1975 and then he was replaced. Alick commented in 1997: 'there was a little bit of money coming into it [the job] so it was time to move on'. In fact he was replaced by an indigenous person, which was more the issue. This was inevitable and Merle said Alick understood, but it was the way it was done that she said was hurtful. There was no 'thank you', certificate or plaque for eight years of work, simply the words 'we don't need you anymore'. Alick's interest in Aboriginal sport was not dampened by this, and he often visited the annual Yuendumu Sports carnivals. He kept researching the careers of Aboriginal boxers, writing about them with Richard Broome later in his life.

Alick valued history greatly and throughout his life it was his privilege to be at a number of historic occasions. One of the most memorable was the scattering of the cremated remains of Truganini. She was now a famous Aboriginal woman from Bruny Island who accompanied the Tasmanian Conciliator, George Augustus Robinson, as he gathered Aboriginal people to Flinders Island in the early 1830s for their 'protection'. She became an iconic figure in life and then death as allegedly the 'last Tasmanian Aboriginal'. She died in 1876 fearing her body would be kept for scientific study. Her nightmare eventuated and for many years her skeleton sat in a glass case, then in a box at the Tasmanian Museum, until a campaign was mounted to put her to rest. Historical controversy has raged about the meaning of her life, and she has become a symbol of colonial oppression and Aboriginal defiance. Alick saw her ashes scattered from a small launch into D'Entrecasteaux Channel adjoining her Tasmanian homeland of Bruny Island in April 1976. Alick represented the Advancement League and was there with a handful of 'kin'.

The cremation and scattering of the ashes was dogged by myth-making as are all historical commemorations. Alick reported, as did many others at the time, that Truganini was 'the last Tasmanian Aboriginal', although she was not the last, as she was survived by descendants of Tasmanian Aboriginal women who lived with Bass Strait sealers. Mary Clarke and her son Len, both of Warrnambool, were also in the small launch as it cast Truganini's ashes into

D'Entrecasteaux Channel. Mary Clarke, a granddaughter of the redoubtable Louis Briggs, was there as she claimed to be a great-granddaughter of Truganini. This was also inaccurate, confirmed in 1924 by her grandmother Louisa Briggs, and Louisa's blue eyes proved additional proof. Blue eyes by the laws of genetics meant that neither of Louisa's parents could be 'full-blood' Aboriginal people — thus Truganini was not her mother. Rosalind Langford who gave an oration at the cremation, said Truganini will live on 'as one who brought her people together even after death', although the Framlingham community, of which the Clarkes were members, was still bitterly split in 1976 over the reserve's hand back in 1970.

Alick, who was present at the hand backs of Framingham and Lake Tyers in 1970, was appropriately at a 'Back to Lake Tyers' weekend in July 1985, sponsored by the Lake Tyers Aboriginal Trust. The community and 'all past residents' were invited to camp along the Lake's shore. There were speeches, athletics events, softball and football matches for both sexes, a church service, a dance, displays of Aboriginal dancing, art displays and, of course, boomerang throwing. David Kidney, the DAA's Regional Director, handed back some of the late Ronald Bull's landscapes to his brother and Trust Chairman, Murray Bull. A plaque in honour of the Trust's first Chairman, Charles Carter, was also unveiled by the Minister of the Department of Aboriginal Affairs, Clyde Holding. Alick had a hand in these proceedings, as he did when Lake Tyers was handed back. He was photographed on the day with Murray Bull and other members of the community in front of the Carter memorial.

Alick was at other important events as an observer, although little more is known of his involvements. For instance, he is in a photograph taken on 10 April 1976 at the opening of the Aboriginal Embassy at 26 Mugga Way, Red Hill, Canberra, published in the magazine, *Aboriginal and Islander Identity* of July 1976. Alick is sitting clapping his hands at the announcement with his daughter Esmai seated nearby. It was a typical shot, Alick being there after an interstate trip, perhaps at a FCAATSI conference seeing it was Easter, applauding Aboriginal efforts at justice.

The Gippsland Aboriginal community gathered at 'The Knob' reserve at Stratford in November 1987 for a day of understanding with religious and other groups from the region. Alick again was there because of his East Gippsland connections. Photographed by the *Gippsland Times* with a boomerang poised for flight, the caption read: 'Mr Alic Jackomos shows how to throw a boomerang. Mr Jackomos is senior project officer at the Aboriginal Affairs Department, Melbourne, and has been a field officer for 20 years. He has studied the genealogies of every family in Gippsland back to the 1860s'.

Alick was also present when Australia's greatest heritage site and icon, Uluru (Ayers Rock) was returned to the control of the traditional owners in October 1985. The return was controversial as the Rock was a symbol of the land rights fight of the 1980s. Uproar occurred when the Labor Government, without consulting the conservative Northern Territory Government, decided on its return as compensation for the failure of its national land rights push. Conservatives, led by the Territory's Government, opposed the move with the slogan 'Ayers Rock for all Australians', which was trailed behind a plane as the Governor-General, Sir Ninian Stephen announced the handover.

Alick at a Gippsland cultural gathering, Bairnsdale, 1985: in the front row (l. to r.) are Manuel Cooper, Reg Blow, Philip Pepper, Reg Saunders, Alick and Albert Mullet.

Alick travelled to the ceremony with the support of his Department and on his return filed a report in its publication, *Aboriginal Newsletter*. He journeyed in true adventuring style, initially by bus overnight to Adelaide where he met John Moriarty, his old friend and Director of the DAA in South Australia. They travelled by four-wheel drive vehicle for eighteen hours to Uluru. Alick as usual landed on his feet through contacts. He met the Assistant Bishop of North Queensland, Bishop Arthur Malcolm, the Aboriginal who had been the Anglican chaplain at Nowa Nowa and Lake Tyers, when Alick worked there in 1967. Expecting to be in the visitors' camp with 1500 others, Alick was invited to share Bishop Malcolm's unit in the Sheraton Hotel in Yalara, the tourist resort adjoining Uluru. He and the Bishop's photograph appeared on the front cover of the DAA's *Aboriginal Newsletter*, above the caption 'Jackomos at Uluru' — the Bishop was not mentioned. Alick also travelled back to Adelaide with some of the family of Yami Lester, the Master of Ceremonies at the hand back. He simply knew everyone — or soon did! Typically, after eighteen hours drive, he quickly showered at John Moriarty's in Adelaide, and rushed on to an overnight bus to Melbourne, which arrived at 6.30 a.m. He showered again at the terminal and reported for work at 8 a.m. Tuesday — no doubt singing 'Don't Cry for Me Argentina'.

Alick reduced his active involvements in Aboriginal organisations when he joined the public service, due to potential conflicts of interest. Besides, from the 1970s his non-Aboriginal status was an issue for a few Aboriginal people, who were defining their identity in terms of insiders and outsiders. However, Alick maintained a close association with and great love for the Advancement League, as it was the social centre of Melbourne's Aboriginal community and because his family and his mentor Doug Nicholls were so involved with the League. Alick attended Aboriginal functions there on a weekly basis. He often went to the annual general meetings of many Aboriginal bodies, including the Health and Legal services. Merle served on some of these bodies once her family responsibilities diminished with the maturity of her children.

In 1979 Alick served for one year as Chairman of the fledgling Victorian Aboriginal Child Care Agency (VACCA), which caused him some anguish. VACCA was formed in 1976 to insert an Aboriginal voice into child care issues, especially the problems caused by the white fostering of Aboriginal children. Mollie Dyer was the inaugural Director and the group contained Aboriginal and non-Aboriginal members. VACCA aimed to minimise the separation of children from their families, and to ensure that any children removed were placed with Aboriginal families. In 1978 the Victorian Department of Social Welfare accepted VACCA as the official voice of the Aboriginal community on child welfare matters. The organisation also ran a 'link-up' service to reunite fractured Aboriginal families.

By 1980 the organisation had grown to include an Aboriginal social worker, Graham Atkinson, non-professional staff such as Mollie Dyer, and seven Directors, including Alick as chairperson. He had stood as a Director on the insistence of Mollie Dyer. A staff member's car accident precipitated a crisis, the Board deciding to sign a claim form stating that the person had permission to use the car, a decision Dyer opposed. Mollie Dyer resigned, not for the first time, but this time it was accepted by the Board. This led to a split within the Board and the Agency's members, precipitating

At the Aboriginal Child Care Agency Conference, St Kilda, April 1979: (l. to r.) Alick and Merle Jackomos, Colin Bourke, John Moriarty and Elizabeth Hoffmann

three extraordinary meetings and an annual general meeting between June and November 1980. Dyer presented a long letter outlining further issues under dispute within the organisation. Discussion at the meetings focused on tensions between the professional and non-professional staff, and issues of policy direction, financial management and nepotism. Discussion was at times acrimonious and also convoluted because of queries over financial reporting, voting rights, membership and the organisation's constitution. A petition signed by twenty members, including Mollie Dyer, in September, called for the replacement of four of the seven Directors, three from the Atkinson clan who were related to Graham Atkinson, and Alick, whose son Michael was a welfare officer at VACCA.

Mollie Dyer was not critical of Alick personally. Indeed, she had written a long and warm reference for him a little over a year earlier in December 1978. She wrote of Alick and Merle's lifelong work for Aboriginal people and their willingness to take people into their home. She referred to Alick's comprehensive knowledge of the Aboriginal community, and that he 'is constantly being requested for information not only by Government Departments, but by the Aboriginal community itself... his ability to relate and empathize with our families has earned for him the complete acceptance and love from our people. This same acceptance extends beyond the boundaries of Victoria'. More pertinent to the matter at VACCA, Dyer wrote:

> It is significant that whilst the policy throughout the Aboriginal community is that only Aboriginal persons are elected to executive positions on their Management Committees, Mr Jackomos is one of the very few non-Aboriginal persons who is continually sought after and nominated by the Aboriginal to a Committee position. His dedication over the years has earned him Life Membership of our oldest and most important Aboriginal Organisation, the Aborigines Advancement League.

The whole affair at VAACA was typical of splits within community organisations — Aboriginal or not. The charge of nepotism was a product of the smallness of the Aboriginal community and the lack of skilled people available for positions in these newly-emerged community bodies. Motions were put by the petitioners, including one of no-confidence in the four directors and one on nepotism. They failed after twenty people, including Dyer, stormed out of the October meeting.

It was inevitable that such tense discussions raised the issue of Alick's non-Aboriginality. At the Annual General Meeting in November, one of the Directors, Gary Murray, told Alick that 'he should not be in ACCA because he was not an Aboriginal'. Stewart Murray, who had attacked Alick at other meetings over this issue, made a similar comment earlier that night. Several including Colin Bourke vigorously defended Alick, and his defenders included Mollie Dyer herself. The minutes recorded that Dyer stated: 'when ACCA was first established the meetings were attended mostly by white people. She also said that most of the people at the meeting had white relatives, and that it had become a Black and White issue, and that if we could not get on with it in unity that she didn't want anything to do with it'. Alick replied to Gary Murray that

> he could have 'thrown in the towel' and that he was a non-Aboriginal Chairperson because an Aboriginal would not accept the position. He said he did not intend standing for the Board again, and when he was finished he would be out of VACCA. He said that they should make sure that the Chairman they elect next time does not get 'hell'.

At the end of the meeting, a vote of thanks was given to Alick, who simply said 'it had not been an easy job'. Ironically, one of Alick's grandchildren, Yolanda Walker, managed *Link Up* for VACCA in 1997.

These tensions resurfaced when Merle defeated Stewart Murray to become the Melbourne representative on the Ministry's Aboriginal Advisory Council, and increased in September–October 1981, during the elections for the National Aboriginal Conference, an advisory body set up by the Federal Government. In September Stewart Murray complained to Colin Bourke, General Manager of the Aboriginal Development Commission, that Alick who was on secondment there at that time, was supporting his wife's campaign. Bourke replied that officers were forbidden to support candidates in work time, or by using work resources, but otherwise were free to campaign if they so wished. He added, 'it is not clear from your telegram whether Mr Jackomos' participation in his wife's campaign contravenes my instructions'. He asked for any evidence, but none was apparently offered.

Merle Jackomos was elected as the Melbourne Metropolitan representative in October, edging out Stewart Murray, Administrator of the Dandenong District Aboriginal Cooperative. Murray told the *Age* that Mrs Jackomos won because her supporters had the money to spend.

> It was the big power group that stopped us – the bloody socialites of the Advancement League. They treat Aborigines as a hobby. I'm the last person they want to get on the NAC because I'm a socialist. You can't beat them. A fellow like me or poor old Bruce [McGuinness] who come up through the grassroots, has got no hope.

McGuinness, who was also interviewed, accepted the result without complaint. The next day Merle, visibly upset, declared: 'I'm not a socialite. I was born on an Aboriginal reserve, Cummeragunga…I grew up there. That's the only schooling I ever had. I've been involved in Aborigines' rights for 30 years, my husband for 40 years'. She listed some of her community work, including positions on the National Council of Aboriginal and Torres Strait Islander Women, and her Directorship with Aboriginal Hostels Ltd, adding: 'it was only sour grapes. I don't want to get caught up in a mudslinging battle'.

In March 1982 Stewart Murray wrote to Senator Susan Ryan, claiming that 'one family has been favoured with the top salaried positions in two Government Bodies'. He referred to Merle's position on the Board of Aboriginal Hostels Ltd and her sister Elizabeth Hoffman who was on the Board of the Aboriginal Development Commission. He pointed out that Michael and Andrew Jackomos also worked for these organisations. Murray also raised issues about other Aboriginal families who he claimed were favoured. He was misguided, as Alick's family and members of other families were in these organisations because their children were educated and could manage these new positions of responsibility now being placed in Aboriginal hands.

Alick, soft drink in hand, and Merle with Margaret Wirrpunda at an Advancement League function, 1975

This jealous attack by Doug Nicholls' son-in-law must have been hurtful to Alick. Nothing seems to have flowed from these accusations, except that Alick and Stewart Murray exchanged solicitors' letters in early 1982 over alleged abuse and counter-abuse in a public place.

The animosity faded and within a few years Alick and Stewart Murray buried their differences. They had served in the same Army Division at Balikpapan and were united in the greater cause of bringing together Aboriginal servicemen. Murray formed the National Aborigines and Islander Ex-Services Association and wanted Aboriginal and Islander service people to march as one body on Anzac Day, a suggestion the RSL opposed. Alick supported his moves. When Murray died in June 1989 Alick gave a fine eulogy at his funeral. He also gave Murray generous praise in a press interview: he was 'a friend since childhood', whom he met at Sister Ellis' Bethesda Aboriginal Mission in Fitzroy in 1939. Alick was glowing on Murray's achievements. He associated Murray with the reforming of the Australian Aborigines' League, pointed to his membership of the Advancement League and

FCAATSI, his service on various Aboriginal organisations, his work for the Aboriginal Funeral Service, his work as a field officer with the Ministry of Aboriginal Affairs, and his award of the Order of Australia. Alick concluded, 'he has served his country and his people well; his loss is our loss and we shall never forget him'. Stewart Murray's wife Nora wrote to Alick and Merle, thanking them for their support in her bereavement.

One of Alick's great strengths was relating to people and educating them in a non-judgemental way about Aboriginal people. His efforts were often accompanied by boomerang diplomacy. In the mid-1970s he teamed up with Trudi Miteff, the Information Officer at the DAA, to educate the public, especially children, about Aboriginal issues and culture. The Department created a large information caravan which toured the state. Alick and Trudi accompanied it to metropolitan centres and Alick went with Patrick Tuck to the country. Trudi recalled,

Alick flanked by boxers Graeme Brooks (left) and Tony Mundine (right)

he was of course the delight of all school children because he was a very skilled boomerang-thrower. It was always fitted into the program. [The Department received] many, many letters written by people who had asked for help for somebody to come, and how they enjoyed his presence there and what he did.

Alick also gave talks on Aboriginal culture at Camp Jungai near the Rubicon, which was taken over by Aboriginal people who ran adventure camps with DAA funding. Boomerangs of course flew at Jungai. Trudi Miteff and Eleanor Bourke (née Anderson), with whom Alick also worked in the DAA, became particularly involved with Camp Jungai. Eleanor met Colin Bourke there, a Koori teacher whom she later married.

Alick gave educational talks in schools right up to his retirement. Indeed he continued speaking at schools for years after. Miteff remembered that Alick told her when he lunched with her in his retirement, that 'he had more support now than he had before. I think particularly the Education Department was extremely kind to him, they really saw that he was useful and that is what Alick wanted, he just wanted to bring across what he knew, in a most charismatic and charming way'. He always attended when invited, especially when his own family's children requested a school visit. Daniela Parisi, daughter of Alick's niece Yvonne, recalls a visit to her school. 'He gave us a talk on Aboriginal history, and then we went down to the oval and we saw his boomerangs. He showed us how they worked...that was pretty good'. Alick's personal papers contain letters concerning school visits. Grades Five and Six at Kew East Primary School wrote in February 1992:

> Dear Mr Jackomos,
>
> In Grades five and six we are studying a topic called the First Australians. We hope you are able to help us by coming and talking about traditional Aboriginal life, and the people in the book you have written. Some time in the morning will be convenient for us, and we will have two groups ready for you.

Alick with his siblings: (l. to r.) Maisie, Michael, Angelo and Stella, with his parents Asimina and Andrew seated, c. 1985

Tertiary students responded the same way but missed out on the boomerang throwing in lecture rooms. These visits made Alick feel wanted, and useful, which is what drove him throughout his life. Despite always being busy, he went, if it was humanly possible.

Recognition at work finally came from the Department in January 1984 when Alick was awarded an Australia Day Achievement Medal, the first time the DAA had participated in the award because of the sensitive nature of Australia Day for many Aboriginal people. The staff memo written by Harvey Jack, the Acting Secretary of the Department, stated: 'Alick was selected on the basis that his tireless and dedicated effort in advancing the Aboriginal cause has been an inspiration to others and that he was representative of those many departmental officers committed to advancing the Aboriginal cause both inside and outside office hours'. This award sat alongside his life membership of the Advancement League as a comfort in any moments of doubt or rebuff.

In June 1988 Alick lost his mentor of almost fifty years when Sir Doug Nicholls died at the age of eighty-one. Nicholls had been a role model and key public figure, being the first Aboriginal person to receive the MBE (1957), Father of the Year (1962), JP (1963), OBE and knighted (1972), King of Moomba (1973), and Governor of South Australia (1976), a position he was forced to relinquish early in 1977 due to ill health. During his early retirement Nicholls worked in the Aboriginal Church at the League in Cunningham Street, Northcote. At his funeral a friend remarked that Nicholls always claimed his success was because, 'I met a man called Jesus'. After his State Funeral, his family, friends and community motored to Cummeragunja where he was laid to rest. Alick was pictured by the *Bendigo Advertiser* walking immediately behind the pallbearers, a position Stewart Murray had asked him to assume.

In the mid-1980s Alick and Merle were distracted somewhat from Aboriginal community work by assisting Alick's parents. His parents by then lived in Kew, near to Violet Grove, where Alick and Merle bought a house they called 'Cummeragunja'. Both Alick's parents

Escorting Doug Nicholls to the graveside at Cummeragunja, 1988

were frail and his father was now blind. During one visit Alick and Merle discovered that the gas had been left on. Merle decided

> we should take them, they shouldn't be allowed to live here by themselves…So we just packed them up without consulting the rest of the family because we knew they would have been against it. So we just got them and brought them home and they lived with us until she [Asimina] went to hospital. His father [Andrew] was blind at the time so then he went into a place in St. Kilda for the blind.

In March 1989 Alick, then sixty-five, retired from the Department after twenty-one years as a public servant, his public being Aboriginal people. He was farewelled by Gordon Bryant and John Moriarty, as well as his immediate supervisors such as David Kidney. This memorable night was greatly dampened by the news that his father Andrew had just died. The Advancement League held its own testimonial for Alick's retirement on 17 March 1989.

Alick did not dread retirement, for it meant more time with family, grandchildren and community, and more space for his passions: the photographs, genealogy and history of the Victorian Aboriginal Community.

14 A Passion for Photographs

Alick's journey at the age of fourteen to Lake Tyers, his under-age enlistment, his wrestling career, his constant travelling to Brunei and his study tours, all revealed his adventurous spirit. He wanted to be there in the action of life, but not for status or even just the experience. These were journeys of the mind, beyond the boundaries others usually erected of what was normal or acceptable, journeys into Aboriginal Australia, into showgrounds culture, and into other religions. This yearning to know also took more academic forms, through collecting and later researching and writing.

People collect for various reasons: for money and status; to possess and control; to touch and to admire greatness; to protect; to know and to commemorate. Alick collected much in his life, but not for money, status or control. He collected some things — sports memorabilia — to admire and touch greatness. But mostly he collected to conserve, to know and to remember. He also collected to give away in the form of copies or information. If an exchange could occur, that was all well and good. Alick would have eventually given the originals of his collecting away, which culminated in a huge collection of photographs, if death had not taken him by surprise.

His collecting began early in his life. In 1998 he told Barry York he collected stamps and coins, which was rather unremarkable, for most children collect such things to glimpse the exotic and know the other — over there — in some small way. But the manner in which Alick collected these things was typical of his adventurous spirit: 'I used to go down to Prince's Wharf and wherever there were overseas ships… I'd talk to someone there and ask them if they had any good coins and they'd take you inside there and give you some foreign coins and stamps which I used to collect'. Such tactics would give heart failure to most parents these days, but Alick was a free spirit. He kept these collections, adding, 'I've still got that hobby now, I've collected a lot of coins, good coins, but I don't know what I'm going to do with them. Maybe the grandchildren 'll inherit them, but no-one seems to show much interest'.

Alick also squirrelled away photographs at a young age as a sideline to his peanut-selling operation at sporting venues. 'By going to the stadiums I started to collect photos of them [the sportsmen], and in those days, all the boxers and wrestlers had postcards of themselves, it was a form of advertising, good quality photographs...I built up a good collection'. When Alick wrestled in tents and stadiums as an adult, he enlarged his collection, which was dated and placed in albums. He asked visiting American boxers and trainers for cards and contacts in America.

> I got a lot of photos sent over to me from Joe Louis, Jerzey Joe Walcott, Gene Tunney...all those world champions. A lot gave me their addresses and I wrote to them personally, and these are all personal photos from some of the greatest boxers that we've ever had.

His collecting was based on admiration and a connection with greatness beyond himself, but often it was through attachment. He treasured postcards from Chief Little Wolf inscribed 'To my Pal Alick, the best to you, Chief Little Wolf' and one from the Black Bomber: 'With best wishes to my friend Alick from Tiger Williams'.

One of Alick's favourite fan photographs from his pal, 'Chief Little Wolf', Tenario, 1950

During the war many soldiers took photographs: of themselves for those back home, battle scenes and battle destruction, and even photographs of the dead. This recording was aided by the 'Box Brownie', a cheap and efficient camera that produced small, square, black-and-white photographs. Alick captured war scenes and collected photographs taken by others, an interest he continued on his return. He photographed his adventures in the boxing tents and many events in his life thereafter. Photographing one's life became standard in this era of more accessible photography.

When Alick teamed with Doug Nicholls in the Advancement League his photographic interest broadened to include Aboriginal people. No one ever asked Alick why he did this, and he never articulated it in any of his interviews or writing. Perhaps he aimed to conserve the Aboriginal past, which he valued, and to ensure that people he admired were enshrined in images.

We certainly know how he accumulated these photographs. In 1998 he explained: 'I'd visit Aboriginal families in their home and ask them if they've got any old photos. I take them to Kodak, make a copy and return the original photo to the family'. Once the Ministry of Aboriginal Affairs was formed, it employed Ted de Meyer to photograph Aboriginal functions for the Ministry's newsletter. Ted would give a copy to Alick and in turn Alick brought old photographs to Ted who made a copy, one each for the family, Alick, and the Ministry's library. Alick remarked that it was just as well that he kept copies, for when the Ministry was transformed into the Department of Aboriginal Affairs some of those photographs disappeared.

Over time, Alick built up a collection of over four thousand photographs of Victorian Aboriginal people. These were housed in large and expensive black albums, 40 x 37 centimetres and each with 36 double-sided pages. Each album held about three hundred photographs, and every page contained a sheet identifying them. An organised mind compiled these albums and kept their contents safe for over forty years. The photographs are fine, warm representations of Aboriginal community and family life, and form a magnificent heritage collection.

Alick's collecting was occasionally controversial. A few Aboriginal people saw it as an appropriation of Aboriginal cultural material. This is an understandable claim from members of a group that has had its land and children taken from them. Some claimed photographs were not returned by Alick, but no hard or specific evidence has been offered beyond accusations, to counter Alick's version that he borrowed the photographs and returned them. Photographic evidence of some images at the Museum of Victoria that show them to be copies rather than originals, demonstrates that Alick's version is probably correct. His tireless work for Aboriginal people over forty years and his massive drop in income in 1965 to continue this work, suggest there is little reason to doubt his version of events. Perhaps a few were not returned, but some community members claim people gave Alick their originals, knowing he would keep them safe and they could always get them back when needed.

Alick saved many old and irreplaceable images of Aboriginal people and families for descendants and posterity. Those who were poor and lived in humpies on river banks, which were prone to flooding, had minimal places to store photographs safely. Others had reasonable storage, but were tenants who moved frequently, further endangering family possessions and photographs. To families who were without photographs, Alick generously gave copies. Aunty Geraldine Briggs wrote to him requesting a photograph of her late daughter, Hyllus Maris. She wanted it to use in the 1989 photographic exhibition at the Museum, 'Daughters of the Dreaming'. Briggs wrote:

> unfortunately the family has few photographs of Hyllus, those that we do have are snapshots and not suitable for use in an exhibition. I understand that you have a photograph that would be suitable. I would be grateful if you would make the photograph available for use in the exhibitions.

Alick gladly acceded to her request.

The photographs he collected have been privately and publicly used hundreds of times by Aboriginal people for family histories; native title claims; and by those who were separated from their families and who are now trying to reassemble their identities. In particular, they have been of immeasurable psychological assistance to those taken and in search of their roots. Alick related how he was once in conversation with Archie Roach, the singer, who was removed from his family when young. Archie remarked that he did not have a photograph of his father. Alick piped up, 'I have one', and promptly sent a copy to him, much to Archie's Roach's delight. Not all those he helped were Aboriginal. Peter and Maria Keegan of Stanmore, New South Wales, wrote in June 1985 to thank Alick for the information he had sent and added: 'Auntie Christina told me of the photo of Granny Kazaglis and great grandfather you sent her. I can't wait to see them'. Another man, Don Perdrisat, a boxing fanatic, was sent photocopies of most of the nineteen images he had requested from Alick's boxing collection. He was in 'absolute joy and overwhelment [sic] to receive your package of my old favourite boxers and wrestlers'. He promptly sent another list of ten images to be photocopied when Alick had the time!

Photographs from Alick's collection appeared in many temporary and permanent exhibitions around the state, including those at the Koorie Heritage Trust, the Melbourne Museum, and regional galleries and cultural centres around Victoria, such as at Brambuck in Halls Gap. They were exhibited at the Stockman's Hall of Fame in Queensland, the New South Wales 'Hall of Champions' and were also displayed for educational purposes. In 1988 Mollie Dyer asked David Kidney, the Regional Director of the DAA, to allow Alick to attend an Aboriginal welfare course at Ballarat and 'bring with him some photographs of the old people and the missions'. Dyer said some of the students had Aboriginal ancestry, and wanted information about their families and traditional life in Victoria, and she and the other tutors were unable to help them very much. She wrote to Alick, sending the names of the students and the families to which they were related, so he could prepare. She closed, 'thanks friend. Cheers for now and God (or whoever) bless, sincerely Mollie'.

Alick's collection of photographs was taken or compiled in a world of less stringent ethical procedures than today, yet it has survived and exists in our own more rigorous ethical world. Alick claimed that he collected the photographs in good faith; that he never took a photograph of someone without permission; and he always copied photographs and returned the originals to the owners. In other words, he had acted in the best ethical standards of his day, before issues of copyright, moral permission, and even reproduction fees, were imagined.

Alick with Richard Broome at Genealogical Expo at Ballarat, 1996

There is only one mildly unfavourable letter in Alick's papers about photographs, amid many favourable letters. It is from a woman who wrote on behalf of her family in January 1992:

> Dear Alex…the picture you have of our mother…they don't want you to publish as the photo belongs to us. My family they were hurt when they saw that photo in your little magazine a while ago. As she always was a Dressie Lady & that photo was out fishing for the day I thought I'd let you know as I [was] asked to write and let you know. Thank you.

The sin was not great, if sin it was, to picture someone in casual clothes out fishing. However, Alick replied in some distress and bewilderment:

> Dear…and Family…I have 1000's of photos that I have taken over the years & I have never taken anybody's photo without their permission. I have always asked before I snapped a photo & always with their consent. In your letter

you said the family was upset when they saw the photo in my little magazine. I am unaware of publishing a magazine with your Mum's photo, if I did I'm sorry. I have spent the last two days going through all my photos but cannot find a photo of Mum, yet I recall that I may have taken a photo in the late 1960s in Healesville of Mum & either 1 or 2 of your sisters but I've looked everywhere but cannot find it. This may be the photo you refer to. I have also gone thru all the articles I have written plus my book "Vic Abn Liv History" but there [is] no photo of Mum in any of the articles. I would appreciate it if [you] could let me know which magazine & date that I published the photo, so that I can connect it and also apologise to your family, Alick...PS Are you referring to NAP (?) newsletter if so I am not connected with that newsletter. You should write to them.

Alick's distress seems to have been genuine, and his effort to track the photograph and willingness to apologise, sincere.

Photographs from Alick's collection have been used in many books, articles, theses and brochures over the last thirty years to the enlightenment of many, because they reveal Aboriginal people in such a positive light. Colin Tatz, who has written books on Aboriginal sportsmen, remarked of Alick: 'he helped inordinately with a book I wrote in 1995...Obstacle Race, many of the pictures in that book were from Alick's collection...he had a wonderful, rare collection of photos'. Many other authors could express such gratitude for his collecting efforts, including the authors of this book. Tatz again: 'Alick never boasted about any of his collected materials. He would show it to you with great pride, privately, but he never boasted, he never paraded, never pranced around and said: "hey, look at me, I'm a collector"'. But for all his efforts some people were jealous of his popularity as a source of an authentic and comprehensive collection. Tatz added, 'a lot of Aboriginal people wished they had been in the field doing these collections – [and they ask] "why is Alick getting the kudos for doing them?"'

In September 1984 Kevin Gilbert, the New South Wales Aboriginal activist, wrote to Alick:

> What are you doing about your collection of old photographs I'm told you have. You realise they should be published and stored for posterity. I'd like your thoughts on this. Maybe we could do something on the true Aboriginal story for the Bicentenary...[or] some street theatre or plays...I'd appreciate copies of some of your old ones [photographs], especially any Wiradjuri ones, and am willing to pay costs.

Alick informed Gilbert that he was not an Aboriginal person, but 'I am now 60 years old, have been involved in the Aboriginal movement since I was 12 in the mid 1930s when I used to attend the street meetings with Doug Nicholls, William Cooper, Marge Tucker and others'. He added, 'In regards to my photos, the Institute, the Melbourne Museum and others have all asked to copy them. I have verbally told them that they can, but I want to use them first in my story. And maybe a book on photos and this is what you have suggested'. Alick continued: 'The photos over the years have cost me 1000's of dollars. I used to borrow the originals and then get copies made, that is why I want to have first use of them. And then the Institute and others can have them for posterity'. He added; 'my photos are on regular display at various programs in Victoria and some have been borrowed for articles etc...Unfortunately I have trouble with some people who borrow my photos but won't return them or lose them'. He might have added that some were not paid for, and others were returned with marks on them. Even when things went smoothly, copying, posting, and returning still had to be done. He added that he had no photographs of Wiradjuri people to send.

The idea of 'first use' proved elusive. His life story was in rough draft in 1984 and, as he told Gilbert, he hoped to finish it in his retirement in 1989. Spurred on by his correspondence with Gilbert, he sought a grant in late 1984 to complete it sooner, but this failed (see Chapter 15) so he appeared to abandon the idea of 'first use'. He wrote to the Australian Institute of Aboriginal and Torres Strait Islander Studies (AIATSIS) in August 1985 offering to allow the Institute to copy his collection — an offer that was accepted with delight. In 1989 Alick also allowed the Museum of Victoria, which had a

Community photographs found in Alick's magnificent albums: Eric Onus, Bruce McGuinness and Mervyn 'Boomealla' Williams (l. to r.) in tuxedos at Aboriginal ball; 'humpy' at the Flat, Mooroopna; and Lionel Rose and friends at Jackson's Track, Drouin; Auntie Margaret Tucker telling of 'them days'

current drive for Victorian Aboriginal photographic material, to copy some prints from his collection. In the agreement it stated that they were to be 'readily available to the Aboriginal community for personal use excepting where special instructions re copying have been noted'. They were also to be available for use in exhibitions with acknowledgement. Copyright remained with Alick, and thus any use needed his permission, and publication fees were payable to him.

In the early 1990s the Aboriginal Advisory Committee of the Museum urged the Museum to copy Alick's whole collection. Alick readily agreed as he wanted the Aboriginal community to have access to the images, and he realised that the AIATSIS being in Canberra were beyond easy reach of most Victorian people. Besides, the continual direct requests for photographs from researchers, family historians, curators and others, had became a burden for him. The Museum gained a grant of $32 000 from Aboriginal Affairs Victoria, to employ a photographer to copy Alick's Aboriginal photographic collection, excluding those of boxers, Aboriginal returned servicemen, sideshows and his family photographs.

Negotiations began over questions of naming, copyright, fees and access. Alick requested that Merle be included and that it be named the 'Alick and Merle Jackomos Collection'. Copyright was to be held by Alick and Merle. It was also proposed that Alick would receive half the reproduction fees. This caused some unhappiness among the Aboriginal Advisory Committee, the very Committee that had requested that the Museum copy Alick's collection. Some members thought that Alick was profiting from the photographs, whereas the collecting, copying, and conserving in albums of 2200 photographs would have cost him many thousands over the years. Merle recalled that she and Alick were grilled by the Committee about how Alick acquired these photographs. Carefully and calmly Alick and Merle answered their probing questions, arguing that he never photographed without permission and returned the originals once copied. Eventually, frustrated by the Committee's attitude, Alick offered that his half of the reproduction fees should go to the Aboriginal Children's Christmas Tree Appeal, run by the League. Alick and Merle retained copyright and their permission would still be needed for use by non-family members. The Museum also determined to seek familial permission of a moral kind for non-family members where possible. The Museum held a reception in 1996 to publicly recognise Alick and Merle's contribution of 2200 new images to its collection, which cheered Alick and Merle immensely.

Few personal photographic collections in the country are so vast, and few concerning Aboriginal people are more important. The photographs Alick collected cover the hundred years before 1980. They illustrate life at reserves, missions and Aboriginal camps, family and community life, political meetings, and Aboriginal people at work, play, and prayer. Alick was a part of the subjects' world, which makes the images not voyeuristic, but warm and valourising. The photographs' value are beyond measure as people and researchers every month — Aboriginal and non-Aboriginal alike — access them and are enriched by them. Aboriginal people have privileged access, not paying for the first three images at the Museum, with cut-price rates on other images for personal use. A photographic database, containing many images from Alick's collection, is being prepared for use by Aboriginal family members. Such family access, in particular, was always Alick's intention in collecting, to conserve knowledge through pictures for access by the community; although he also wanted to teach all Victorians to respect Aboriginal people through these images.

The only regret about the collection is that, while each photograph of Alick and Merle's collection in the Museum has a caption, Alick's premature death prevented a fuller description of each image. He and Museum Collection Manager, Mary Morris, intended to add more information, but Alick's busy life and Mary's commitments foiled the recording of the richer stories about each photograph.

15 Community Historian

Alick's passion for collecting led him into research and naturally from that to the process of writing. He stored his papers in an ordered manner in several dozen labelled filing boxes. The collection included: Aboriginal affairs in general; government reports and acts of parliament concerning Aboriginal people; papers and pamphlets related to Aboriginal missions; specific boxes on the reserves of Cummeragunja and Lake Tyers/Ramahyuck; materials on Aboriginal leaders; boxes on wrestling and boxing tents; photocopies of historical articles; boxes of programs and brochures he had collected at events, many of them signed; and a box of invitations to Aboriginal dinners, balls, meetings, openings and commemorative events. He also kept orders of service from 80 funerals mostly from the mid-1980s, including those of Doug Nicholls, Ralph Nicholls, Hyllus Maris, Lin Onus, David Anderson, Eric McGuinness, Marge Tucker and others. The material he collected was to remember people, places and events, and assist his own research.

His personal knowledge built up over fifty years, together with his accessibility and willingness to help, made Alick an invaluable source on Aboriginal Victoria for many researchers. Those in universities who have written on aspects of Victorian Aboriginal history — Attwood, Broome, Amirah Inglis, Markus, Taffe to name a few — have had discussions with Alick. Freelance researchers such as Hugh Anderson, who was interested in gum leaf bands, contacted Alick, as did film and documentary makers, writers and playwrights. He also gave many interviews to researchers, including one in 1998 to researchers from Aboriginal Affairs Victoria, while driving around Fitzroy. It will remain a classic account of Aboriginal Fitzroy, all told with Alick's precise memory for details of people and place, including names and street numbers.

Alick assisted researchers whenever he was able because of his belief in the importance of knowledge of the past. In January 1990 Colin Tatz invited Alick on to a panel of seven (all Aboriginal except Alick and Tatz) to select an Aboriginal Sporting Hall of Fame. He sent Alick several hundred names to rank in a top 100 and Alick set to work with zest. He applied his own criteria in close decisions: 'where I could not decide between 2 or 3 nominations all being equal in sporting achievements I gave preference to those that also put something back in Aboriginal Affairs'. Colin Tatz remarked recently, 'there is absolutely no way that you would go beyond Alick as your first choice to be on a voting panel to establish the hall of fame. In fact we produced two books, *Black Diamonds* and *Black Gold*. Some of the pictures and the biographies are in part due to Alick'.

Alick also helped amateur researchers, students and schoolchildren. Ros (Olive) Mason, a former Anglo-Australian member of the Advancement League, requested information in August 1991 on the League's 'Tanderra' holiday units at Queenscliff, for a talk to the local historical society. Her file of her involvement thirty years earlier, including a 'bookings' register, was lost in a move. She was promised help by the Advancement League, but four telephone calls and a letter produced nothing from them. A regional and University library, to her amazement, had never heard of *Smoke Signals* (the League's magazine) or 'Tanderra'. Desperate and within three weeks of her talk, she remembered Alick, who supplied her with material — to her great relief. Occasionally high school students heard of Alick and wrote for help on projects, and received it. Sharon Boyd of Macleod High did so in 1984, receiving much information on Aboriginal servicemen.

Mostly he loved this research involvement with others, but occasionally Alick's patience was tried, when demands became too extreme. His assistance to researchers often went beyond the limits of ordinary endurance. One Canberra researcher, who photographed and researched Alick's collection of boomerangs and carved eggs, visited Alick's home, organised several visits by photographers, and wrote him at least eight letters in about ten months from June 1991, some of which asked for considerable information and long explanations. The requests were always polite, but were nonetheless time-consuming. A year later another letter came:

> I hope you don't mind me writing to you. I recall you said that you didn't have time to help me any more because you wanted to get on with your book on Kooris in the army but friends now tell me your book is published so I am hoping you may be able to spare me five minutes.

The new list of questions asked, of course, demanded more time than that.

Many others benefited from Alick's first hand knowledge, especially Aboriginal people. Alick's superiors in the DAA were regularly asked to release him from his usual work to address groups. In 1982 Aboriginal Education Services of the Victorian Department of Education asked if Alick could share his 'valuable information and photographic collection' at the Preston Technical School before a meeting of 'Aboriginal parents and other interested community members'. In 1986 the Aboriginal Liaison Unit of the Health Department of Victoria requested that Alick attend a week-long pioneer camp at Camp Jungai. It argued that

> when Alec Jackomos attended this Camp on Cup Day (Open Day) in 1985, the Elderly Aboriginal Members of the Community stressed that Alec was not present long enough for them to really look at his photograph album collection, and share in his knowledge of Aboriginal family trees. They requested I write to you requesting that Alec be permitted to attend their camp for the entire week this year 1986.

His supervising officer agreed, but there was to be no travel allowance or a holiday in lieu of Cup Day. In August 1988 the Goulburn Valley Aboriginal Education Consultative Group Inc. requested that Alick lecture to them on the history of the Aborigines Advancement League and also compère their NAIDOC fashion parade on the same day. A month later Mollie Dyer requested his attendance to speak at a cross-cultural awareness seminar directed to public servants working with Aboriginal people.

Alick enjoyed all these research and teaching involvements and was proud to be a member of the research body AIATSIS in Canberra. When Alick's five-year membership of the Institute was due for renewal in 1995, he listed his research in Aboriginal studies. These included the co-authoring of two books with a third in process; the collection of photographs and genealogies already lodged with AIATSIS; employment in Aboriginal Affairs for 24 years; guest lecturing on Aboriginal history at universities, TAFE colleges, and schools: and a lifelong involvement in the Aboriginal community. He was made a life member of AIATSIS (Victorian Chapter) in November 1994 'for committee work and for joint activity with the Koori Community'. His central membership was renewed for five years. In 1998, not long before his death, Alick had listed his achievements in his AIATSIS membership file on a piece of paper under the label 'information re 2000 membership renewal'. He was a most organised man!

His most involved, sustained and controversial research effort was the compiling of hundreds of family trees of Victorian Aboriginal families. It began when Alick was an officer with the Welfare Board and the Ministry of Aboriginal Affairs from 1967 to 1974. Welfare officers kept files on clients, which included family details. Alick recalled:

> on the inside of the file you'd make a fact sheet of Mum, Dad, siblings, where they were born and that's all that went on the fact sheet, so that a future officer, well any officer picking up the file knew who they were dealing [with], how many kids, date of birth. But I went further than that. I'd ask them who their Mums and Dads were, their brothers, their sisters, their cousins. I created my own family trees. I created over a thousand family-trees in Victoria.

It is unlikely that Alick initially had the thought of creating family trees. Rather it was a way of knowing the networks of the community to which he had by then devoted his life. Sometime later the creation of an Aboriginal family heritage for posterity occurred to him.

Alick created over a thousand family trees involving enormous research among the community and occasionally in Births, Deaths and Marriages files. He spent countless spare hours in his study at nights and weekends perfecting them. Television watching held little fascination compared to this. His genealogies evolved into impressive works built upon thousands of hours of unpaid work. There are many books in his collection. Each page was hand done — with lines ruled and names printed in black ink — some containing ballpoint additions. Each sheet contained three generations and perhaps seventy names. They must have taken an hour just to copy out neatly, let alone the many hours of research involved in creating each family tree. Merle's own family book — the Atkinson/Cooper line — contained about 200 sheets. Her line descended from 'Kitty' who was born at Moira Lakes in 1834 and had eight children and sixty grandchildren. The compiling of this one great line was a massive and meticulous achievement. Alick had a mind with the natural ability and determination to achieve anything, but the vagaries of Depression, a migrant family life and a consequent lack of education prevented that. Colin Tatz commented of the genealogies that they had 'second, third, fourth, tenth cousins, you name it and Alick had it. And remember this is an untrained guy. This is not a man with a PhD in anthropology who's doing kinship networks in a professional way, but he did it in a thoroughly professional way'.

Inevitably some errors occurred but when discovered they were quickly refined and corrected. Betty Clements gratefully recalled that Alick did her family tree, although when she met him at a community function she said

> 'Alick the family tree you did me, the wording was wrong'. And he said (a bit guiltily): 'What have I done?' 'You put my father second on the Atkinson family tree, rather than the first. My father was the eldest'. 'Oh, Sister, I'm sorry about that', he said: 'I always thought Clarence was second, and Uncle Dan was first'. I said: "No, my father was the eldest… my *uncle* is second-eldest'. 'Oh good', he said: 'Well I'll tell all the others that I done the family tree for, to do that.' That (laugh) was the only differences we had. Yes.

The ethics of Alick's actions in compiling family trees might be questioned today. Current privacy laws make similar research by non-family members difficult, but Alick received strong endorsement for this work from many quarters at the time — Aboriginal families, and community organisations, which saw the work as valuable. Organisations provided grants for important research. Indeed, there has been overwhelming, although not universal, praise and gratitude from the Aboriginal community for what Alick achieved.

For instance, at an Aboriginal Development Commission Conference on land rights in June 1982, discussion turned to Aboriginal case files and genealogies and their importance in land claims. The consensus was that these DAA files should be open to Aboriginal people and copies made available to the South Eastern Land Council for land claim matters. Hyllus Maris declared to the meeting that Alick was an authority on genealogies, and David Anderson also welcomed his input. The conference then resolved unanimously that:

> This conference recommends that the ADC/DAA make the services of Alick Jackomos available to the South Eastern Land Council for the purpose of compiling genealogy data for the South Eastern Aboriginal community. If the ADC/DAA are unable to second Mr Jackomos' services to the South Eastern Land Council, then we recommend that his duties be to compile the aforementioned data while working directly for the ADC/DAA.

It is unclear whether this was formally done, but the DAA thereafter supported Alick's genealogical work indirectly, through unpaid leave when he won research grants, or allowing his duties to include addressing community groups about genealogy.

In 1984 Alick won a grant of $20 000 from the Australian Bicentennial Authority's National Aboriginal and Torres Strait Islander Program in open competition. It was paid through the Advancement League and allowed him to take unpaid leave from the DAA for six months. The project extended his genealogical work into the Murray border region. He compiled 525 family trees in this project entitled *Genealogies of Victorian and Cummeragunja Aboriginal Families*, which were housed at AIATSIS under restricted access. Relevant family members can view and photocopy their family trees, but others could only view them and not make notes or photocopies without Alick's permission. Alick reported that

> the project was well received wherever I went, especially by young people wanting to know their past history. And I've

since had requests from quite a few people to do their own family tree and from many organizations, Aboriginal elders, youth organizations and the like to talk on Aboriginal genealogies.

He received a 'Bicentennial Certificate of Appreciation' once it was completed, the funding Program Coordinator, Philip Morrissey, commenting: 'I have heard nothing but good reports about it from those members of the Aboriginal community I have spoken to'.

On the other hand, a few Aboriginal people from the region were unhappy about the grant and project. Twenty-one people petitioned the Minister-in-charge to object to Alick receiving this grant: 'for the purpose of writing an article relating to the Aboriginal heritage'. Alick was not writing an article, but collecting raw data for families to use in the future. The grant was scrutinised and awarded by a panel of Aboriginal people and was paid through an Aboriginal organisation. Alick gained nothing financially except for his wages and costs while on unpaid leave from the DAA, and in return worked overtime in his study at nights to perfect the family trees. The petition emerged from misinformation and jealousy. The petitioners asked: 'What materials had he been using to base this article on? Did he have permission from the families of the people involved to use this information?' Alick would have been disappointed with this petition, which he gained under Freedom of Information and quietly filed away, given that all the signatories were known to him, some having experienced his hospitality and help.

Alick received other grants, a small one from AIATSIS and one from the Stegley Foundation to further his genealogies. When applying to the latter in February 1992, Alick outlined his previous genealogical work over forty years. He only requested operating costs, not a salary, as he was now retired on a war pension and superannuation. He pointed to the growing interest in his work from Aboriginal people 'including many children now in their thirties & older who were fostered and adopted out under the Government policies of separating children from their families and placing them in institutions'. Alick was granted $5950 to be administered through the Aboriginal Community Elders' Services (ACES). His final report stated that the project unearthed new sources of information for Lake Tyers genealogies, which he presented to the community in book form and in twenty-five laminated family trees. Alick travelled across Victoria and completed 215 more family trees, which were to be lodged with AIATSIS, under the same strict access protocols as before.

Alick's genealogical work became important in Victorian land rights claims as the 1982 Aboriginal Development Commission Conference had foreseen. Alick stated in his final Stegley grant report, with an irony known only to those (who will remain nameless) who had signed the 1988 petition against his Bicentennial grant or who has read it: 'the Yorta Yorta people (Barmah Region) have lodged a land title claim which will be heard in the courts about March 1994. The claimants have asked me to compile genealogies showing that they are descendants of the former residents of the above lands & that they have had permanent association with the above lands'. Those who had attacked him through ignorance now asked for his help, and he gave it. Other claimants later valued his work. Mirimbiak Nations Aboriginal Corporation, an umbrella body acting for land claimants in Victoria in the late 1990s, asked Alick on behalf of Gippsland families for permission to copy his family trees held at AIATSIS. Sandra Mullett wrote to Alick on behalf of Mirimbiak: 'the work that you have done on the genealogies is important and very valuable to the Aboriginal people of Victoria'.

Opposition occasionally emerged when Alick's family trees sometimes laid bare family secrets. His son Andrew remarked: 'some people were unhappy about knowing the truth. Children have been born out of wedlock', although the restrictions Alick placed on access to family trees at AIATSIS protected families to a degree. Genealogists the world over are apt to find the occasional 'skeleton' when they dig.

Andrew added that there were other unforeseen consequences which flowed from the genealogical work. 'People have been moved around. But Dad only wrote what he was told. It caused him much anguish. They were used by the Government against the people in the Yorta Yorta case'. Andrew referred to the Government's strategy in the native title case of arguing the vital matter of 'continuity' with Yorta Yorta lands by revealing from the genealogies that some descendants were not born at Cummeragunja or nearby, but on other reserves around Victoria. Of course the government had often ordered them to move. It was also the case that some were born away from home while their mothers were visiting kin elsewhere. Alick, who was initially so pleased that his genealogies might assist the fight for land for Aboriginal people, especially the Yorta Yorta, also saw them used against the people. They were just facts he had collected, which both sides employed in the case. The genealogies were not the decisive evidence in the loss of the Yorta Yorta case after a decade of Federal and High Court effort, but it was no doubt disheartening for Alick.

Alick also had the pleasure of seeing many others benefit from his family trees. His private papers contain many requests from Aboriginal people seeking family information and permission to copy his genealogies in Canberra, and others who thought they might be Aboriginal wrote seeking information. He helped where he could. From conversations with Alick he probably took a dim view of one person who, hoping for a government benefit, wrote, 'as I have few job prospects I need to prove the fact that I have aboriginal blood in me'.

As with his photographs, the DAA had numerous requests from Aboriginal organisations across the state for Alick to speak to their meetings. Aboriginal educators often asked for him to talk on family trees and history. Requests came from Swan Hill in 1984, Echuca in 1986, Lake Condah in 1987, and the Murray Valley Cooperative, Robinvale, a year later to name just a few. Alick spoke at the annual Aboriginal Elders camp at Camp Jungai a number of times, staying the whole week at their request in 1988. Alick spoke at many other meetings, with the DAA's indulgence, including an elders' meeting at the Dharnya Centre, Barmah, in 1989. Alick reported to his Department, 'I gave a talk on genealogies and assisted some people in doing their own family trees. Also provided displays of photographs and albums'. He added, sadly, that three young men were charged with theft, after money went missing from the rooms of some visitors. 'Some elders said that the camps should be for elders only, but others said that the young people should attend, otherwise how else would they learn'.

Alick's knowledge was encyclopaedic, but the growing size of the Aboriginal community in Victoria, which numbered 16 570 by 1991, made his work more difficult. He could no longer know every Aboriginal person in Victoria. Yet he still made connections, through names and even faces, which he knew from personal encounters over the sixty years since 1938 and years of poring over his photograph albums. Betty Clements recently related one such story.

> The last time I saw him I introduced him to all my children. They were grown up, but I had introduced him to them when they were kids. He looked at all my children and he said: 'You're Artie, you're just like your father, your father 'll never be dead as long as you're alive, when that time comes'. He looked at Warwick, and said: 'Tch, you're a double-image of your father'. He looked at Kay and said: 'Well, you are two faces, you're a part of your mother and a part of your father. Same with Suzie, you're like your two grandfathers, you are a go between your Grandfather Smith and your Grandfather Atkinson, being short like James Smith, but with the features of Clarence Atkinson'. He then looked at Wade and Thorne and said, 'you are both like your grandfathers too'. He added, 'your name should have been James Clarence or Clarence James, or something like that, because you are, dead-spit of them'. So he just looked at all them like that, and as they grew, and grew into men and women, he still remembered 'em.

Collecting and researching are precursors to writing. Alick did little writing in a formal way in his early years, perhaps due to the intense pace of his paid and voluntary working life, combined with wrestling and other commitments. Yet the act of amassing material set ideas going in his head. He began to write in mid-life while he was at the Ministry, and did not stop thereafter. He never considered he wrote well, but with the help of others and collaborations, his output grew.

Alick's first published piece appeared in the magazine *Identity*, edited by Jack Davis, the Western Australian Aboriginal writer and playwright. It was a short piece of about 600 words, entitled 'Gumleaf Bands'. It told the story of the Aboriginal concert groups that operated in the 1930s and 1940s, entertaining themselves and raising money for charity. He gave vivid descriptions of some of the personalities, especially Pastor Atkinson, who carried musical equipment in his 1929 Chevrolet, pulling a trailer with seats under a canopy. His article ended with a political point. Alick stated that with the move to the cities of many Aboriginal people after the Second World War,

> the new generation has never seen a basket made, an emu egg carved, a gum leaf played or a genuine boomerang made from the root or elbow of a tree. The old people are passing on and their culture is dying with them. The language is being forgotten except for a few words.

He argued that Aboriginal culture had an 'important place' in Australia's past and future and the formation of Aboriginality. He concluded with a statement that summed up his years of collecting pictures and researching genealogies: 'It is our responsibility to preserve this culture. Centres should be formed where the young can be taught Aboriginal skills and language by the older generation. Otherwise, in another decade, all will be lost'.

Two longer articles of about 2500 words each were published by *Identity* in late 1971 and July 1972, on the history of Lake Tyers Aboriginal reserve and of Cummeragunja and Maloga missions. These were very good outlines of each mission's history. The article on Lake Tyers ended with the Lake Tyers hand back, at which Alick was present, and the ringing speeches Charlie Carter and Doug Nicholls made at that ceremony. The history of the other two closely-related missions was also comprehensive and told the story of the political activity of the Yorta Yorta from the 1880s, through to the formation of the Australian Aborigines' League by William Cooper in Melbourne, and the Cummeragunja strike of 1939. It ended with the ongoing struggle to develop Cummeragunja and get title to the land. His writing had a definite political edge. These two articles were published under the authorship of 'Merle Jackomos'. *Identity* at that time sought to be a forum for Aboriginal opinion and Merle recalled that Alick believed it would only publish material by Aboriginal people; Alick thus attributed these two articles to Merle. Whether Faith Bandler, the editor, who knew Alick and Merle through FCAATSI realised this, is unknown.

By the late 1970s *Identity*'s Aboriginal-only policy was relaxed, enabling Alick to publish again under his own name. In July 1978 two articles appeared, the 'Aborigines Advancement League' and 'A Tour of Indian Reservations'. In the January 1979 issue three important short biographical pieces appeared: 'Marge Tucker, MBE'; 'Mrs Hannah Lovett, of Greenvale, Victoria'; and 'Thomas Shadrach James — 1856–1945'. In the first two biographies, Alick inserted Aboriginal women into the history of the Aboriginal fight for freedom, pointing to Marge Tucker's political and organisational work, as well as her family origins and welfare work. He added that her daughter Mollie Dyer 'is carrying on the wonderful work of her mother, a dedicated woman fighting for recognition of her people'. Alick wrote that Hannah Lovett (née McDonald) was a great matriarch, who produced a large number of servicemen and sportsmen out of her twelve children with James Lovett, and her fifty grandchildren. He concluded: 'as a tribute to the part Mrs Lovett's five sons played in the First World War, Lord and Lady Stradbroke when passing through Greenvale paid a visit to Mrs. Lovett's roadside cottage. They complimented her on being the mother of five sons who served their country faithfully'.

Alick also greatly admired Thomas James — 'Grandfather James' — a Mauritian of Indian descent who because of illness did not complete his training as a doctor, becoming Cummeragunja's schoolteacher instead. James tutored a generation of important Aboriginal activists, including Doug Nicholls, Bill and Eric Onus, his son Shadrach James, and others, nurturing a pride and confidence in their Aboriginality. James married Ada Cooper (William Cooper's sister), 'and became one of the Aboriginal people'. Alick might have been wistful as he wrote those words as, in another age, he did not always achieve that status.

Alick aimed at a larger-scale work of Aboriginal history. In October 1975 he wrote to Robert Edwards, Director of the Aboriginal Arts Board, raising the possibility of a grant for six months to publish some of his Aboriginal photographs with appropriate text. Edwards responded favourably, as 'there is absolutely no doubt that you have the ability necessary to conduct the research and bring the material together in an interesting way'. Further discussions did not take place;

but eighteen months later Alick explored resources for a book on Lake Tyers. He wrote to Robert Edwards again in May 1977 outlining his non-Aboriginal status, his credentials in Aboriginal affairs, and his request for funding for six months to write a book on Lake Tyers. Edwards replied in July, offering $4277 to be administered by the Arts Council of Australia, which amount included travel, photographic and typing costs, but salary for only three months due to budgetary restraints.

In October 1977 Alick expressed satisfaction with the offer but asked for a deferment. He advised that he had just returned from his Churchill fellowship to find that 'because of Department cuts in staff, there was no further work for me' at DAA. Edwards was horrified: 'your understanding of the problems faced by Aboriginals is unique and should be used to advantage in these difficult times'. Alick renounced the grant in February 1978 as he could not afford to chance three months leave from the DAA. 'The last twelve months have been very difficult for me, not knowing what my future was with the Department. On occasions, I had been advised of being made redundant, and a few days ago, I was advised of my reappointment as community adviser'. He hoped to write the history in his spare time and perhaps apply later for a small grant to cover typing and administrative expenses. Edwards welcomed such an application.

In 1984 Kevin Gilbert wrote to Alick about a joint photographic publication, as we have seen above. Alick responded to his proposal about the photographs. He also told Gilbert he was writing the story of his involvement with Aboriginal people over the last fifty years. 'The story is in draft, needs some research and needs to be typed. My grammar is not a 100% and I need some help to straighten it out. What I have planned is to do the draft and finish it off when I retire in March 1989'. Alick was spurred on by his September–October 1984 correspondence with Gilbert.

In December 1984 he wrote to Gary Foley, the Director of the Aboriginal Arts Boards, attaching a copy of his previous grant approval of 1977 that he had renounced. He asked for assistance to write a 'book on my life with the Aboriginal community which extends over fifty years'. Alick outlined the highlights of his life from war service, through boxing tents, to service in the Advancement

League, FCAATSI, the public service, and his photographic collection and family tree research: 'I understand that the Arts Board policy is that grants are only for Aboriginals. I am a non-Aboriginal but married to an Aboriginal. I am writing to you [to see] if an application would be considered, if not accepted, I would not be offended as I support your policy'. Alick added with honesty and self-knowledge, as he did to Gilbert:

> I have written a few articles which have been published in the *Identity* and other magazines but I do not have the skills to write a book on my own. I understand that if approved an Aboriginal writer could assist me. I have already spoken to Albert Mullett regarding this project and have also forwarded him a copy of this letter.

Alick recalled that he never received a reply to his letter from the Aboriginal Arts Board; there is certainly none in his well-organised private papers. The loss of this opportunity to record Aboriginal history is evident in a long letter Alick wrote to Amirah Inglis the following year (1985). Inglis was researching Australian involvements in the Spanish Civil War, and especially the work of Helen Baillie. In this letter Alick gave a wealth of detail on Aboriginal activists of the 1930s, and also the assistance given to Aboriginal people by Helen Baillie, politically and through welfare, and by Sister Maude Ellis in a spiritual way.

Alick finished his 54-foolscap-paged life story over the next few years (referred to as 'Memoirs'). The story ended with his work for DAA in the 1980s. It was typed, probably by DAA staff, and sent off to a publisher. The verdict came back in May 1988: 'I'm afraid that the manuscript is not really a publishing proposition. It is a valuable record — and the details of your work should be recorded; but at the end of the day, the books we publish have to find a wide enough market to be commercially viable'. So his 'Memoirs' were filed away, never to be brought into book form.

Alick's writing did not stop there. In the late 1980s and into his retirement he wrote a number of short biographical pieces, which remained in typescript form. These included 'The Aboriginal Community of Melbourne' (three pages, 2 July 1992); 'Memories' (eight

Launch of *Forgotten Heroes* at the Advancement League, April 1993

pages, about 1994), 'The Aboriginal Community of Melbourne and Victoria' (four pages, about 1994); 'Sons of the Gournditch-Mara Tribe' (two pages, no date). There were others, without headings or composition dates. Several handwritten ones found in his papers may have been given as lectures, like his 'Speech at Lake Tyers Workshop 28.8. 1991'.

Between 1991 and 1998 Alick also co-produced three significant books: *Living Aboriginal History of Victoria. Stories in the Oral Tradition* (1991); *Forgotten Heroes. Aborigines at War from the Somme to Vietnam* (1993) and *Sideshow Alley* (1998). The first two were co-authored with Derek Fowell, and supervised by the Museum of Victoria's Aboriginal Cultural Heritage Advisory Committee. The third, Sideshow Alley, was produced with Richard Broome. The first two were oral histories containing wonderful stories related by Aboriginal people and graced by many images from Alick's photographic collection. The third had a large oral history component of interviews with Aboriginal boxers, some done jointly with Alick, and other showground people, as well as much archival and press research. Alick probably did little of the writing for the first two and did none of it

Interviewing old friends for the book *Sideshow Alley*: Alick with 'Young Jimmy' Sharman and Clive Coram at Melbourne Showgrounds, 1995 (photograph by Richard Broome)

for the third, for as he told Kevin Gilbert and Gary Foley ten years earlier, 'I do not have the skills to write a book on my own'. However, Alick was absolutely vital to the creation of all three publications, for he knew the community members to interview; where to find them; knew the background of their lives that made for a good interview; and was trusted by these people, which convinced them to become involved. He also had wonderful recall of past events, a vivid oral turn of phrase, and an unsurpassed collection of photographs. All three books deserve to be republished.

Alick enjoyed co-producing these books and was immensely proud of the outcomes. *Living History* caused him some headaches in production, as not all people interviewed could be squeezed into the book. *Forgotten Heroes* fulfilled a deep personal commitment to his Aboriginal Digger mates, and in particular Stewart Murray. He enjoyed immensely the experience of doing *Sideshow Alley*. When asked in 1994–95 whether he would like to co-author a book on the boxing tents, he took a nano-second to say, 'yes'! The five long inter-

Alick speaking at the launch of *Sideshow Alley*, flanked by Jack Allan (left) and Richard Broome (right) at the Aboriginal All Stars Gym, Fitzroy, August 1998 (photograph by Margaret Donnan)

views he gave, beginning with explanations of his many photographs, were done with zest. When he and Richard interviewed old boxers and show people together, he jumped in the car with relish each time. He always wore his peak cap with a metal Koori badge on the side. He knew inner Melbourne like the back of his hand and directed the journey. During the interview he was transported back in time, exclaiming in excitement when a memory was revived. Back in the car he would look across from under his cap, and ask: 'was that a good one?' He knew it was. He checked each draft of *Sideshow Alley* assiduously, placing yellow stickers in pages that needed to be discussed and facts corrected.

Sideshow Alley was launched from the boxing ring at the Fitzroy Stars Aboriginal Community Youth Gymnasium, in Gertrude Street, Fitzroy. This was within metres of the houses where Alick had first met Aboriginal people sixty years before; where he first fought in Harry Johns' training ring; and where he still trained once or twice a week. The launch on 14 August 1998 was performed by Jack Allan, an old 'showie' in his late eighties, whom Alick had known from the 1940s. And performance it was, for Jack Allan dressed in cowboy-style shirt and hat, and looking magnificent, entertained the crowd with showground talk for at least half an hour. Indeed, he was so wound up that he had to be reminded to launch the book. He died a few months later. Alick also spoke with great animation and with great affection for his time on the showgrounds, saying that if the boxing tents were revived, 'he'd be there'. Both authors spoke together on ABC regional radio about the book and the boxing tents eighteen times over the following weeks. Again Alick was exuberant. It was a golden time for him just as the hour-glass was emptying.

16 In Retirement

At a time when retirement age was determined by statute at 65 for men, Alick knew that he would retire in early 1989. He planned to research and write, perhaps resume his life story, continue with his community engagements and make further trips to Brunei. Alick was never short on ideas of how to fill his day. Besides, he would be free of the disappointments of working in an organisation that lately never fully used his skills. He could also spend more time with Merle, his family and grandchildren. As their own family had grown, Alick and Merle grew prouder of their children's achievements within the Aboriginal community and of their children's own families, which grew to sixteen wonderful grandchildren and to date eleven great-grandchildren.

Esmai their eldest, who finished her schooling at Greythorn High, first worked in the typing pool at the Ministry of Aboriginal Affairs, tried nursing, then became a secretary at the Advancement League from 1969 until 1971 during the black power 'troubles'. She returned to the workforce after her four children, Yolanda, Marika, Yasmin and Alex went to school. Currently she is the Manager of the Koori Business Network in the Victorian Department of Innovation, Industry and Regional Development.

Andrew, their second child, was an exchange student from Greythorn High to Mackinley High School in Washington DC. He did media studies in America and social work in Australia. He then took jobs in various areas of Aboriginal affairs. Andrew has held policy and management positions — some interstate — with Aboriginal Hostels Ltd; the Aboriginal Development Commission; the federal departments of Education; and ATSIC. Currently, he is Director of Indigenous and Diversity issues in the Victorian Justice Department. A recent project at Lake Tyers has been made easier because the community remembers Alick's work there in 1967, and Andrew's boyhood visits in 1938. He has four children, Va Hoi, Naida, Asimina and Kalimna.

Michael, their third child, also completed his secondary schooling at Greythorn High and initially did casual work in youth affairs with Ministry of Aboriginal Affairs before trying Law and Economics at the Australian National University. While in Canberra he stayed at the Aboriginal Tent Embassy in Canberra for three months in 1973. He worked as field officer with the Advancement League, as had Alick, and with the Victorian Aboriginal Child Care Agency. He has since held management positions with Aboriginal Hostels Ltd; the Aboriginal Development Commission; and the Department of Employment and Training. He moved to Queensland in 1989 to work in Family Services and now is Regional Manager for Aboriginal Hostels Ltd. Michael has six children living, Ross, Kesheena, Nancy, Myron, Jarara and Nyari. Sadly two other children, Malcolm and Maryanne died.

Alick and children on the eve of Andrew's departure to the US for a student exchange trip in 1971

Alick loved his children intensely and he often showed work colleagues family photographs and spoke proudly of his children's progress, but his family time was always limited by his high level of commitment to Aboriginal organisations and his long hours of paid work in Aboriginal affairs. As Andrew recalled, Alick rarely watched him play sport or took his siblings to the movies, as he was always going to a meeting: 'we would sometimes cry out "not another meeting"'. Michael agreed that if Alick had a fault it was at times putting community before family, but 'I don't recall being unhappy. As a family our lives were always full on and we didn't spend a lot of time at home'. Michael added:

> Dad was a good father, but definitely a better grandfather. If you spoke to my children they would only have fantastic things to say about their 'Pappou'. The only regret I have in moving from Melbourne with my children in 1989 is that they saw their grandfather less. Dad enjoyed a close relationship with all my eight children.

Some of the grandchildren in 1986: back row (l. to r.): Yolanda holding Alick, Marika holding Cindy the dog; (middle row) Vahoi, Malcolm, Kesheana, Ross; (third row: Maryanne, Nancy, Naida; (front row) Yasmin and Myron

Alick's pride in his children flowed through to a great love for all his grandchildren. He was immensely proud, for instance, when Yolanda the eldest was School Captain of St Catherine's in Toorak, and he listened with great pleasure to her lively valedictory speech. Yasmin recalled that he always came to their school concerts, their 'grandparent' and other special days, and gave talks to their classes whenever requested. Always an Australian, Alick still passed some Greek culture on to his grandchildren, teaching Greek words, how to count in Greek, and about Greek festivals. They called him 'Pappou', a Greek term for 'grandfather'. When Marika, a granddaughter married a Greek man and learnt Greek, Alick was pleased to refresh his Greek in conversation with Marika and her daughter Zoe.

Alick and Merle remained busy in his retirement, and were able to enjoy more activities together. They remained active in Aboriginal organisations, especially the Advancement League, for Merle was on the Executive until the mid-1990s. They never missed a NAIDOC ball, which Alick had compèred in earlier years, and attended many other Aboriginal socials, as well as elders' group activities. Occasionally, they might see a film or watch his beloved Collingwood battle against the odds. Merle enjoyed home life at Violet Grove, and Alick was content in his upstairs study, researching and writing. They were as close as ever and rarely disagreed. They saw family constantly although less of Michael and family when he moved interstate for work. Yolanda and Marika came to live with them during their later high school years. Then Esmai and her two other children, Yasmin and Alex, also moved to 34 Violet Grove in Kew.

They occasionally travelled around Australia, especially visiting Michael in Cairns and other friends — usually such trips were orientated around people. They visited Victorian friends and relatives in Victoria, staying with Priscilla McCrae at Shepparton, who made return visits to Violet Grove. There were many trips to Cummeragunja where Merle's sister Elizabeth Hoffmann lived. They holidayed in Bali regularly, as Merle liked its closeness and the ability to just leave home for ten days. Indeed, she often went to Bali with her cousin Walda Blow and other female friends. Merle disliked longer trips, so she left the Brunei adventures to Alick who went there most

Alick's 70th birthday at 34 Violet Grove in 1994 with Merle and children (l. to r.) Michael, Esmai and Andrew

years in retirement. As they told a journalist for the Greek paper *Neos Kosmos*, who was investigating mixed marriages in 1992, 'we had love, we understood each other's needs, and we had a lot of trust. We gave each other freedom to follow our interests'.

Alick's community involvements remained strong. He maintained contacts with the Showground community by visiting his old friends during the Melbourne Show each September. He would stop for a yarn with Bernice McLure, Jack Allan and his daughter Gail Magdziarz, and other 'showies'. He visited the Aboriginal exhibit while at the Melbourne Show, and research for the book *Sideshow Alley* revived more contacts. From 1995 to 1997 Alick and Richard interviewed people, including 'Young' Jimmy Sharman, the children of Harry Johns, Johnny Harris, Jack Allan and others. In 1995 Alick, his old wrestling 'foe' Clive Coram, and boxing tent boss 'Young' Jimmy Sharman, yarned about the old days for two hours while sitting on the cold steel step of a mechanical ride at the Melbourne Showgrounds. In 1997 Alick remarked of the showgrounds life:

> I loved it. I'd do it again now. Better than work in Aboriginal Affairs. There is strong kinship with the show people. Like Aboriginal people, you are very close, you shared. If you get into a brawl they'd stick with you. It was something that I was sorry to give up [in 1948] but you do it because you have got family.

Alick continued to sell boomerangs at the Warrandyte, Dandenong and other shows near Melbourne, as well as at Moomba. He gave a demonstration as well as patter, if space permitted, to increase interest. Once he gave up the boomerang trade he sold Aboriginal badges, flags, posters and the like at these shows. A few Aboriginal people criticised him over this, accusing him of appropriating Aboriginal culture. However, Alick was doing nothing different from shops in Melbourne, that sold such items. Besides, he was doing it from a lifetime of involvement with and affection for Aboriginal people. He loved the work as it involved meeting a great diversity of people and he was able to practise the art of selling. He once recalled how he sold hats made in China, which were in the Aboriginal colours. He ran short and met another seller who told him the 'Two Dollar' Shop had supplies. Alick hot-footed it to the store and bought up all available stock. He then under-sold the other stall holder and disposed of the lot. Alick expressed real regret once those hats became unavailable, as they were 'much sought after'.

He never missed an Anzac Day ceremony or the chance to march with the $2/14^{th}$ Battalion. Often he carried the banner. Merle recalled : 'Anzac Day was the day he looked forward to when he'd go up and see his old mates…he'd always join his mates after for a cup of coffee or tea in the gardens'. She would walk up the footpath beside the marchers and join Alick in the gardens. Alick supported Stewart Murray's efforts in the mid-1980s to form a National Aborigines and Islander Ex-Services Association, but Murray failed to convince the RSL to allow the group to march as a separate body on Anzac Day. Alick's co-authored book, Forgotten Heroes (1993), expressed his admiration for Aboriginal servicemen.

Alick never socialised much at his local Kew RSL club as he did not drink alcohol and was not one to go out to dinner — not when you could eat at home — but he attended the Annual General

Stewart Murray, flanked by Daryl Wallace and Alick on his right and Charles Perkins on his left, asserts (unsuccessfully) the right for Aboriginal returned servicemen to march on Anzac Day as an Aboriginal group, c. 1988.

Meetings and other key meetings. Len (Linton) Cornish recalled that at one meeting Alick ordered a ginger ale, commenting 'it's about the same colour [as beer]'. Alick also worked tirelessly every year for the RSL button and poppy days, which raised money for RSL social services. He believed in helping needy Returned Servicemen and their families, and once again brought his old selling prowess to the fore. Len Cornish, the Kew Branch Appeals Officer, said, 'Alick just loved it'. Alick knew his market well, for 'he'd usually nominate what he wanted in dollar terms as far as fives and twos and ones in these badges or poppies'.

He excelled in the badge-selling department. To prevent fundraising conflict between RSL branches, the custom developed that button-selling activities were to be confined to the branch's local area, but Alick confessed that he ignored this, as he did other nonsensical rules during his days in the Department. Alick was proud that he always topped the fundraising list at the Kew Branch and he did this by choosing prime spots out of the area. Thus he often sold in Melbourne itself and outside Flinders Street Station. Merle remembered his cry: '"Help the old Diggers, buy a poppy and help the old Diggers", and he'd be so loud you could hear his voice before you saw him'. His old boss, David Kidney, recalled 'that it was very, very hard to get past Alick when he was on the corner of Bourke Street and Flinders, with his thing around his neck, selling those badges'. That 'thing' was the tray holding the various denominations of badges and poppies, and Alick also held a tin for the money. They now sit forlornly in a cupboard at Violet Grove.

Alick's Greek consciousness increased in his retirement, although he had subscribed to the 'Castollerizian Newsletter' since its first typed number was issued in 1983. Alick featured in a biographical article in issue no. 2 of the 'Newsletter', which focused on his Greek upbringing and his visit with Merle to Castellorizo in 1976. He was nominated by his sister-in-law Elizabeth Hoffman, Director of the Advancement League for a Hellenic Distinction in 1983. It is not known whether he was successful. Alick gave papers at two Greek–Australian Oral History Symposia at RMIT, in 1992 and 1994, speaking on 'Greeks in the Australian Armed Forces' and 'Wrestling and Greek–Australian Wrestlers in Australia'. He attended the Greek Masonic Lodge monthly and also the Cassie Club in South Melbourne, for a day each month in his retirement. In 1997 Alick admitted that his Greek language skills had 'drifted a little bit now, because I only speak it when I visit elderly Greeks'. He spoke to one brother in Greek because his wife was born there, but with his other siblings, 'we all just talk in English'.

Alick attended the annual general meetings of Aboriginal organisations with Merle, but retained closest links with the Aborigines Advancement League, of which he was a life member. He was a Board member by right of life membership and attended many functions and lunches. He also helped Merle and others co-found the Aboriginal Community Elders Services (ACES) in 1989, which was led by Iris Lovett-Gardiner, Sissie Smith and Edna Brown. Merle became chairperson of ACES for several years and is a committee member to this day. She and Alick attended discussions, bus trips, luncheons, cultural events and other activities, each week at the Northcote premises during his retirement. Alick also attended the weekly swimming

Alick flanked by singers Ruby Hunter and Archie Roach at the Advancement League, early 1990s

sessions sponsored by ACES. He took an interest in the Fitzroy All Stars Gymnasium, where he gave occasional talks on wrestling, and worked out on equipment once a week.

His community knowledge was often in demand. Alick travelled to Florida, USA, in December 1989, to give evidence about the Welfare Board and its assimilation policy in the highly publicised James Savage murder case. Russell Moore (James Savage) was removed from his mother, Beverley Whyman (née Moore), then aged fifteen, just after his birth on 31 January 1963. Beverley Moore and a family member consented to the adoption on 13 February, under pressure from Welfare Board officers. She revoked the consent within the statutory thirty days, although she was told that such revocation would not necessarily lead to the return of her baby, and that police action might follow her return home to Deniliquin, for her under-age sexual relationship with the baby's father. Beverley Moore signed a second consent form under such pressure. Russell Moore was adopted by a white family, the Savages, who moved to the United States in 1969 but returned in 1983, leaving their adopted son Russell in prison there for car theft. Alienated and removed from his roots and his home country in Victoria, Russell Moore knew he was Aboriginal, but this had little meaning for him away from family, community and country. He was a group of one. Moore drifted into drug abuse and crime, eventually raping and murdering a businesswoman, Barbara-Ann Barber, during a drug-induced robbery in 1988. He was sentenced to death in 1988.

In 1989 an appeal campaign emerged in Australia once the connection between Beverley Whyman and James Savage was made. The Victorian Aboriginal Legal Service as the successor authority to the Aboriginal Welfare Board urged the federal government to fund defence witnesses from Australia. This was eventually agreed upon. Alick was not one of those originally nominated by the Legal Service, who included Mollie Dyer, Marjory Thorpe Onus and several psychologists, but he was included in the final group of expert witnesses about the assimilation policy and its impact on families. The jury voted 11 to 1 for life imprisonment but this was subsequently overruled by a Florida judge. After further legal action, his death sentence was commuted in 1992 to life imprisonment. In 1990 Beverley Whyman and James Savage threatened to sue the State Government over the legality of the adoption, alleging coercion, but dropped the case, perhaps advised that duress would be hard to prove.

Alick's deep community knowledge was also utilised in the books co-authored with Derek Fowell discussed earlier, *Living Aboriginal History* (1991) and *Forgotten Heroes* (1993). He looked back on these two, and *Sideshow Alley*, in 1998 and told Barry York: 'I don't have the academic skills, because I left school when I was twelve… but I've got the knowledge in my head, and people like Derek Fowell and Richard Broome, I just tell them the information and give them contacts and together we put these wonderful books together'. Alick assisted many other research projects. As he pointed out to York:

> I have been kept very busy by researchers and people like yourself and the Museum ringing up for information or some young kid saying: 'look, my Mum was taken away but she doesn't know what her name was, and it could have been Smith or Williams from Lake Tyers, can you help us with the family tree?' I enjoy doing that and there are

always university students ringing up and they are doing a thesis, can they come and interview me. Sometimes we have got to knock them back...Sometimes it gets a little bit hectic when you have got three, four, five people in one week want to come home.

Alick was also kept busy attending funerals especially in the 1980s and 1990s, the tunes of the 'Old Rugged Cross' and 'In the Sweet By and By' often resonating in his brain. He once remarked sadly in the mid-1990s that he was the only one left with knowledge about the 1930s for all his peers had died. Many funerals were in Melbourne, but others were in country areas, particularly Cummeragunja — a two-day round trip. He had funeral service programs for eighty people in his private papers, including those for Lin Onus, David Anderson, Eric and John McGuinness, Hyllus Maris and other notable people. Alick personally gave eulogies or obituaries for Lady Gladys Nicholls (1981), Stewart Murray (1989), Robert Lovett (1994), Eleanor Harding (1996), Margaret Tucker (1996), Len Jackson (1997), Tucker's daughter, Mollie Dyer (1998), and others. He travelled to Stradbroke Island in 1993 to represent the Advancement League at the funeral of Oodgeroo Noonuccal (Kath Walker) in 1993. Alick did not speak at Doug Nicholls' State Funeral in Melbourne in June 1988, as Nicholls' son-in-law Stewart Murray did so, but was in the official coffin escort at Cummeragunja. Alick spoke at a service at the Church of Christ Northcote in 1992 to celebrate the sixtieth anniversary of Doug Nicholls' conversion.

All his eulogies were strongly historical, drawing on his deep personal knowledge to place the departed in the context of the Aboriginal community of their youth and also setting out their achievements in precise detail. They were celebratory of a life but also educative of the audience. For instance, when he celebrated the life of Eleanor Harding (1934–1996), a Torres Strait Islander born in Cooktown, he related how she came to Melbourne in the 1950s and joined the Fitzroy Aboriginal community which was 'very small'. She attended the Aboriginal social at the Manchester Unity Hall, and 'she introduced and taught us Island songs and dances in which everyone participated'. Alick described her work in FCAATSI, being careful to add that it was 'a national organisation which played a major role in removing discriminating legislation, gaining voting rights and equal wages for Aborigines and the 1967 Referendum'. He also highlighted her involvement with the Advancement League, and its women's auxiliary, of which Eleanor was a life member and committee member respectively. He listed her youth, hostel, and prison work, and her involvement in NAIDOC and indigenous women's organisations. It was more than a eulogy and almost a brief history lesson.

In May 1996 Alick was invited to the luncheon at Parliament House in Canberra to launch National Reconciliation Week, but a Canberra fog turned Alick's plane back and he missed the lunch, meeting only Gough Whitlam in the Canberra terminal later that day. He was relaxed with paper sellers and ex-prime ministers. Pat Dodson, the Chairperson of the Council for Reconciliation, commiserated by letter, 'although you spent most of your day in the air and airports I thought you would like to know that the day went very well'. He listed those who made it and sent some materials and the menu for Alick to keep. Dodson, who attended school in Melbourne, had been a member of the Victorian football squads which Alick coached and managed in the years around 1970. The following month Dodson again wrote to Alick, thanking him for a photograph of the 'old Victoria team' that Alick had sent. He looked forward to seeing Alick at the Reconciliation Convention in 1997 where he hoped the question of a 'Document' would move forward. Dodson concluded: 'I often think of you and your family. I hope all are well and doing OK in this world that sometimes seems to be spinning upside down. Thank you for all you have done and continue to do in promoting the pride and justice of the people'.

In 1997 Alick and Merle were thrilled to be on the guest of honour list at the conference in Melbourne, to celebrate the thirtieth anniversary of the Referendum and the current Reconciliation movement. They met many old friends from FCAATSI days, Faith Bandler, Stan Davey, Lowitja O'Donoghue and others. At that conference Prime Minister John Howard spoke, and some turned their backs on him. But Merle and Alick did not as he was, as Merle insisted, an invited guest.

Alick and Merle with Merle's sister Elizabeth Hoffmann and Yvonne Cawley (Goolagong) on the right at the Referendum 30th Anniversary Dinner, 1997

Alick derived great pleasure in his retirement from research and sharing this information with others. He dropped in regularly to the DAA (renamed Aboriginal Affairs Victoria) as Terry Garwood, its Director, encouraged Alick's research and gave him free access to the typing pool and the photocopier for his educational talks. Alick's time in the mid-1990s was spent between home, the homes of his children and friends, days at ACES, the Advancement League, the Fitzroy All Stars Gymnasium, the Greek Lodge and Cassie Club, Aboriginal Affairs, the Museum, speaking engagements, occasional festivals selling badges, hats or posters, or making trips with Merle up to 'Cummera' to see family. He travelled around Melbourne by public transport, as cataracts on his eyes were making driving difficult. An operation made little difference. Alick invariably wore a cap with an Aboriginal badge on its crown. He was still a very fit man in his early seventies and, as an old wrestler, proud of his continued strength. In October 1996 Richard and Alick drove to a family history day in Ballarat to run a booth on Aboriginal family history. When they

'Now how the hell does this work?' Alick on a sewing machine at ACES with his trusty cap and badge of a map of Australia with a Koori motif. His jumper sports the Australian flag, photograph taken in the early 1990s.

arrived and a box of books had to be removed from the boot of the car, Alick rushed in and, moving the much younger Richard aside, chirped, 'I'll get it'.

In his last years with the DAA and in his retirement Alick gained the recognition he desired, both from the Aboriginal community and the general public. His yearning was not by way of pride or status, but a recognition that he belonged and was of value — to the Aboriginal community, to Aboriginal Affairs, and to the community of scholars — after the slights he had endured along the way. He received the Australia Day Achievement Medallion in 1983 for services in the DAA, which was presented by the Minister Clyde Holding. He and Merle were also invited to a Canberra reception by the Governor-General, Sir Ninian Stephen, in 1983. Their company was requested several times to receptions given by Victorian Governors and many times to those of Melbourne Lord Mayors in the 1980s. They were guests of Prime Minister Paul Keating and Mrs Keating at the 25th Anniversary of the 1967 Referendum, held in the Great Hall of Parlia-

A good opportunity to pass on a book: Alick with Prime Minister Paul Keating, Canberra, at the 25th Anniversary of the Referendum, 1992

ment House, Canberra, in May 1992. While there Alick, who always knew the importance of a gift, presented Prime Minister Keating with a copy of *Living Aboriginal History*. Alick proudly hung a photograph of that occasion in his hallway, 'true-believer' that he was.

Recognition from the Aboriginal community took pride of place in the hallway. The Fitzroy All Stars Gymnasium recognised Alick for 'the good work over the many years to our Aboriginal communities'. The Aboriginal Legal Service acknowledged 'your invaluable contribution and tireless commitment to the Victorian Aboriginal Legal Service Cooperative Ltd'. And in 1990 the NAIDOC Ball Committee declared its appreciation for his services in running twenty-one annual balls. Aboriginal Affairs Victoria named its library the 'Alick Jackomos Library' and AIATSIS in Canberra named one of its research rooms after Alick, in acknowledgement of the gift of his photographic and genealogical collection.

Alick received the Medal of the Order of Australia (OAM) in June 1993, for 'service to the Aboriginal Advancement League and for

Alick shows his Australia Day medal to daughter Esmai and granddaughter Marika, 1984.

researching and recording Aboriginal family genealogies'. It matched the one received by Merle in 1987 for services to the Aboriginal community and committees, including FCAATSI, National Council of Aboriginal and Torres Strait Islander Women, the League, Aboriginal Hostels Ltd., National Aboriginal Conference, and many others. They were a much honoured family.

Alick's OAM was nominated by ACES and it was seconded by the Echuca Aboriginal Cooperative. The latter referred to Alick's fundraising and welfare work with Doug Nicholls, his work for the Advancement League, his continuing work for the community while working in Aboriginal Affairs by running dances, balls, football carnivals, and button day appeals for the League. It also stated that he was one of only five life members of the Advancement League. The reference did not mention Alick's ethnicity, whether he was Aboriginal or non-Aboriginal. That would have pleased Alick the most, for he always wanted to be treated as a person offering assistance, wanting to belong. He welcomed the emphasis on his work with Doug Nicholls and the Advancement League, for in 1998 he commented of his life membership of the League: 'That to me is just as good an honour as the OAM and all these other honours, because that was my life, the Aborigines' Advancement League, not only the Advancement League, [and] the Australian [Aborigines] League, but it was the association with Doug Nicholls'.

Alick continued to travel in his retirement, sometimes with Merle although her asthma and less adventurous spirit kept her more at home. They visited Michael and his family regularly in Cairns. Michael recalled that 'whenever he visited us in Queensland he would always have someone to visit and would talk to us about how he met this one or knew that one'. When in Cairns Alick would often day trip to Tinaroo Dam where he trained with the $2/14^{th}$ Battalion during the war. There is a memorial there and Alick paused to remember fallen comrades. Michael recalled of these visits to Cairns: 'I got on very well with Dad. Interestingly, I think my relationship with my father became a lot closer after I moved to Queensland. I am not sure why, but possibly because I did not see Mum or Dad as often and therefore we valued our time together or our phone discussions more'. Alick visited many old friends in Queensland, including Becky Thomson (Newfong) in Brisbane. Becky recalled:

> after my parents moved to the 'Home' Alick would come and stay with me and my children, Rebecca, Ben and Bernadette and the talking and reminiscing continued. My kids would be intrigued by Alick to hear of his travels, now going outside of Australia and the mementos that he bought…The years passed and Alick mainly came by himself due to Merle's ill health and his routine never changed, visiting friends, never accepting a lift, always on foot or public transport. Even in his last twelve months he came to see me at Amity Point, Stradbroke Island, which I still treasure to this day.

Brunei proved to be a world of Alick's passionate experience that was locked away from daily inspection even by Alick's family and friends. Alick's Brunei friends included in particular Lt Colonel Ambran H. M. Noor Aston, his wife Naaimah and three children Mariana, Ridzuan and Mohammed, Ambran's parents-in-law, Haji Mohiddin his wife Hajah Norhani and their circle of friends.

The chance meeting with Ambran, the Mohiddins and their extended family on a train in Europe in 1976 led to a friendship over the next twenty years. Alick became almost one of Ambran's extended family, and was called 'Uncle Alick', the same name he carried within the Koori community. There was nothing secret about these trips, but they represented something inside Alick that was deeply personal to him. He visited many times, every two years at first, then yearly in the 1990s. Esmai reflected in 2004:

> going back to Brunei and Asia, I think he was searching for something, for answers in his own life, there were many parts that he couldn't discuss with us…he found peace when he was there…as if that's where he belonged…if there is an afterlife, that's where he is.

Alick's few reminiscences about Brunei centred on his first presentation to the royal family, along with 45 000 others, and the miraculous coverage on television of his personal handshake with the Sultan. More miraculous was that in the summer of 1978–79, Alick again shook hands with the Sultan and again his handshake was aired on Brunei television. The coincidence tickled his sense of humour. During that second palace visit Alick and Haji Mohiddin Abdul Kadir's family were also presented to the Sultan's daughter in her own chambers. More gift-giving followed, Alick emerging with an envelope with a $100 note inside. The Haji Mohiddin's family received far more, often receiving jewellery and once a gift from the Sultan's daughter of $60 000 towards furniture for their new home. These were fabulously memorable events to Alick. The Sultan's palace with its thousands of rooms and golden minarets was breathtaking. Alick recalled of these visits to Brunei families, 'I met so many Bruneians, visited friends and ate so much food, that when I return to Australia I have to go on a diet!' He once confided that the visiting was almost overwhelming, for new meetings brought forth more invitations to stay. Yet he loved it.

Alick visited Brunei fourteen times and Ambran and Naaimah Noor in turn visited Australia twice in the 1980s. Alick took Merle to Brunei in 1982. She went only once as, unlike Alick, she did not speak the language, and was never someone who relished overseas travel.

Eleanor and Colin Bourke went with Alick during the Merdeka (Independence) celebrations in 1984. Alick paved the way for their sightseeing, and Eleanor recalled that 'all the way along we were meeting people'. She was amazed at the laxity of the security arrangements, as President Marcos of the Philippines and Prince Charles were just an arm's length away. Eleanor Bourke was again moved to compare Alick to a 'human version of the World Wide Web…he just couldn't stop making connections, he was always interested in people and places'.

Alick spoke little of the cultural aspects of his visits, but clearly they were a key element. His great friend Ambran Noor remembered that Alick had mastered Malay during the war, and 'he was keen to meet people of all walks of life and to study our Malay culture and history'. Ambran added:

> he loved to meet people and he loved to taste all types of our food. He loved to try all kind of Malay, Chinese and Indian foods and never complained of any of them. He even liked Durian fruit, remarking 'it smells like hell but tastes like heaven'. He loved to attend all of our family functions such as weddings and other cultural or social gatherings. At home he loved to wear the sarong and to live just like one of us. He would enjoy our dinner or lunch with us and then liked to sit having tea or coffee and to join in our family discussions.

There are many photographs of Alick just relaxing in bare feet with Bruneian friends in their living rooms.

Once his stay with Haji Mohiddin and Ambran in Bandar Seri Begawan ended, Alick would visit other families. He usually journeyed by ferry for six hours, then by local bus, to visit a Kadazan friend who worked in the Sabah Railway Company and lived in Kota Kinabalu in neighbouring Sabah. It is most likely that Alick met him while travelling. He also visited an Indian family whom he met in Sabah, and who lived in Kuala Lumpur. Alick also stayed in Palembang in Sumatra with a friend of Ambran, Kiai Dr Yusuf Abdul Aziz, an Islamic religious scholar who ran a school for young children. This stay entailed a two-day ferry and bus journey from Jakarta in Java.

Alick travelling with some companions on a train from Kota Kinabalu, Sabah

Thus the Brunei trip was in fact part of a regular south-east Asian adventure, that saw Alick packed with locals on ferry or on buses on jolting roads, sharing their bunches of bananas and ramutans and talking endlessly. As his daughter Esmai remarked: 'He had no fear of meeting anyone. Introduce him to a room full of people and he would mix in. Within a short time he would find a friend, and then he would write to them'.

There was also a spiritual dimension to Alick's journeys. He was as tolerant of religious difference as he was of cultural difference. He would attend any church with anyone and frequently did so — Greek Orthodox, Church of Christ, Anglican and Catholic — he was totally ecumenical. Ambran Noor recalled: 'He was particularly interested to study about Islam and I gave him a copy of the English translations of the holy Koran and he read them regularly. He also read the life story of our Prophet Mohammed and the history of the Islamic religion'. Alick attended mosques in Brunei and visited the religious scholar Kiai Dr Yusuf Abdul Aziz in Sumatra. Islam, like Aboriginal culture, was a new intellectual and spiritual adventure for Alick, not by way of a conversion, but to be explored and incorporated into Alick's becoming 'a man of all tribes'.

This spiritual quest was in essence Alick's passion to know diverse people, to reach out and touch others. His years in the army were explorations of digger mateship; his times on the showgrounds impressed upon him the warmth and camaraderie of the 'showies'; his ventures into Aboriginal Fitzroy revealed to him the warmth of Aboriginal kinship. Brunei was a similar experience. Alick remarked in 1996: 'Since my first visit, I have come to understand and appreciate the Islamic Religion, the five pillars of Islam and most importantly, the love and brotherhood of Brunei people'. Life for Alick was a journey to oneness — unity with a soul mate like Merle, and with his fellow humans.

17   Watching the Hour-Glass

At some stage in 1998 Alick began to feel unwell. For such a vigorous and active man, who had been strong and fit all his life, he would have been at first incredulous. Then denial seems to have set in about the tightness he was feeling in his stomach; after all, he had never been ill in his life or taken a day of sick-pay, and he was only in his seventy-fifth year. But he might have noticed a changed drawn look in the mirror or even consulted a doctor. If he did, he remained silent about it. Was he scared and willing the problem, if problem there was, to go away? Or was his 'martyr complex', a trait Esmai thought he inherited from his mother Asimina, coming to the fore? Esmai also wondered whether he was angry at some stage: Alick had never smoked or drunk alcohol and always kept himself fit. There was still so much to do and his fitness promised more than seventy-four years. If there was anger, no one detected any.

In retrospect, some signs were evident, but they were dismissed by all, not the least by Alick. Merle recalled that sometimes in that year he uncharacteristically lay on the bed. When she asked if he was sick, he would leap to his feet and cry 'No Mum!' — as he affectionately called Merle. Esmai, who was living with Alick and Merle at the time, recalled that he was unusually active, 'like he had unfinished business…and was going to every single event that was on…but he was bushed'. Michael remembered that when Alick came for his regular visit in mid-1998, 'we knew then that Dad was not well. For the first time, when he came to our house, he just sat around most of the time'. Len Cornish, a member of Alick's Kew Branch of the RSL, said that Alick came to see him late in 1998, to inquire on behalf of an unnamed serviceman friend who was very ill, about the care of his wife. Len assured him that Legacy always looked after the widows of veterans in need.

His personal papers reveal that he was extremely busy in the second half of 1998 as if he was racing against the hour-glass. In late June he attended a two-day meeting in Darwin as the Victorian representative of an Aboriginal and Torres Strait Islander War Veterans taskforce, created by the Commonwealth Department of Veterans Affairs. His status as a non-Aboriginal person seems not to have been an issue. (The group met again in Brisbane in late November for a further two days.) At the end of July he travelled all day by car around Fitzroy, Carlton and Northcote, being interviewed about Aboriginal Fitzroy of the 1940s and 1950s. His recall and memory for rich detail was as acute as ever. Two weeks later, after several preparatory meetings, Alick and Richard appeared at the launch of *Sideshow Alley*. They met at the ABC studios in Southbank on many occasions for radio interviews over the next two weeks. Alick arrived by tram each time, was full of sparkle for each interview, and did not always let Richard drive him home to Kew, insisting on taking the tram. At the end of August he journeyed to New Guinea for an army reunion.

The pace did not slacken in early September. Barry York of the Australian National Library fortuitously interviewed Alick over two days about his life — making six 90-minute tapes — an enormous mental and physical task. Again his clear recall was there and also a sense of urgency. When York at one stage wondered whether they both should rest, Alick was keen to press on and 'do another tape'. He later said that the process exhausted him — as three tapes a day for two days would surely do — but he wanted to get it down. In October 1998 Alick and Merle were featured by the Immigration Museum in Melbourne. They were honoured in a panel, which is still exhibited today. It related the story of their marriage, their contributions to society recognised by each gaining an OAM, and discussed their mixed marriage. Alick must have been pleased with such resolutions to his life. Esmai recalled that in 1998 Alick would often say, 'come here, there is something I want to show you', as if he wanted to pass knowledge on. Her daughter Yasmin experienced the same thing and Merle recalled that he was often busy annotating family photographs.

Loose ends were tied up in 1998. Aboriginal Fitzroy was described as never before; *Sideshow Alley*, which described the boxing tents,

Photograph of Alick and Merle taken beside their beloved house name — 'Cummeragunja' — for the Immigration Museum exhibition, October 1998

had been published; details of his life story not recorded in his own 'Memoirs' and other writings were on tape with Barry York. He had been to Cairns to see Michael, Sue and family, and also Becky Thomson and others in Brisbane. The New Guinea trip 23–28 August 1998 was a further bonus.

The trip was arranged by the 2/14th Battalion Association, of which Alick was a member, and called 'The Last Parade'. Forty-six veterans of the Battalion were flown by the RAAF to New Guinea and by Caribou to Isurava on the Kokoda Trail, to commemorate the 56th anniversary of the four-day battle in late 1942 at Isurava when the 2/14th, along with other battalions, turned back the Japanese advance on Port Moresby, despite being out-numbered six to one. It was the turning point of the Kokoda campaign. The 2/14th lost more men than any other unit in the Papua New Guinea campaign. Alick was spared these traumas as he was not posted to New Guinea until late 1943 and, just after he transferred into the 2/14th in the hope of seeing action, the unit was sent home to Australia for recuperation

Alick on the 'Last Parade' at Isurava, Kokoda Trail, New Guinea, with some unidentified locals

and training. But Isurava would have been embedded in his memories from the talk around the battalion ever since. Lt-Colonel Phil Roden, who became the 2/14th commanding officer at the age of 27, described this 'Last Parade' as a journey to a 'sacred place'.

Hundreds of New Guinea villagers also came to honour the men who saved their district. At Isurava Alick played a gum leaf solo for a crowd of villagers and their children, who looked on in delight. Alick was presented with a string bag as a gift by an Isurava villager. It contained this note, printed in a clear hand:

> Dear Sir,
> I appreciate for the freedom of this country which you have spend 4 days battle in this place Isurava and continues through the Kokoda Trail till you won the victory at Idribaiva near Soberi. I will remember this day as your last respect to those who give their lives at Isurava. May your journey safely bring back home under our good Lord's care. This string bag may remind you of this time we spend there at Isurava. May you write back on the above address when get back home.
> Zedee I. Kiloki

It is not known whether Alick wrote, but a betting man would think it a sure thing. Certainly, he wrote to his assigned New Guinean carer at Isurava, Gerod Lovi, and sent him photographs. Lovi thanked Alick in response, said he was so happy to have 'a friend with white man', and asked for 500 kina to start a business. Alick's reaction is unknown.

Not feeling very well, at least as Esmai recalled, Alick was determined to make his usual visit to Brunei, which he did in February 1999. Ambran Noor recalled that Alick complained of a swelling in his stomach, but added that there was no pain. While there he talked much of his family and his grandchildren.

> On the last visit he tended to travel around Brunei alone. He would go by bus to the other end of the state, the oil town of Seria, and also by boat to the interior district of Temburong right into the Borneo jungle. I remember he came home soaking wet that evening after the jungle trip as there was a heavy tropical rain downpour and he had to walk about half a km for the bus stop to our house.

The lone journeys into the forest brought Alick face to face with his mortality and calmed him for the final adventure. Alick decided to see his Kadazan friend on the way home. Ambran, his wife Naaimah and their daughter Mariana drove Alick to the ferry terminal. Filled with emotion, Alick insisted they did not come into the terminal. 'We all gave him a hug as it is in our Islamic culture to give a hug to a departing family or friend on a journey...We could see the tears in his eyes and likewise we cannot also stop our tears as he is more than a friend to us'. Their last image was Alick in tropical hat, suitcase in one hand, waving back with the other, but not looking back. 'We could feel that this is the way he wished his departure to be' — walking to his greatest adventure.

Alick returned home via Kuala Lumpur where he became ill. He was given antibiotics, and more when he arrived home. Richard saw him a day or two after his arrival home. They looked forward to working together on Alick's planned life story. Richard remarked that he looked unwell, but Alick shrugged it off as a chest problem that antibiotics would fix. He was cheery as usual. Little did we then know that the book would be completed without Alick's personal involvement. Within a week he was admitted to St Vincent's Private Hospital.

The family has mixed feelings about the amazing scenes that followed. Once the news of his serious illness spread, Alick's hospital room was filled each day with a procession of people conveying their last farewells. Flowers and greetings from across Australia festooned the room. Alick wanted all this and he even welcomed a visit from an estranged close relative, for he wanted to resolve grudges. Those who came spoke their parting words before a crowded bedside. Alick remained strong through these days and joked to the end. He pondered the hospital menu one day, and asked Andrew with a twinkle in his eye whether he should have a wine and break his lifelong pledge not to drink alcohol. He decided to hold the line. Despite Alick's great love for people, and his desire to see so many at the end, he was exhausted by the visitors as his final days neared. Only at the end, when the crowds thinned or were excluded, was there more time for the family. Sadly Yolanda, his eldest grandchild, was unable to arrive from America in time, which distressed Alick: he called for her near the end. Less than two weeks after he was admitted to hospital with cancer, Alick slipped into a coma and was at rest on 4 March 1999, just twenty days short of his seventy-fifth birthday.

He accepted Greek Orthodox rites in hospital, but wished to be buried from the Advancement League but, as it was being rebuilt, his funeral was held at the Northcote Town Hall on 12 March, the scene of many Aboriginal Balls that Alick had organised. Andrew planned the service 'as a parting gift to my father to send him off in style, with candles and flags on the wall, the Greek flag, the Koori flag and the Australian flag'. The Northcote Town Hall is immense, and yet it was filled with seated guests, others banked three deep around the walls, and more choking the foyer and steps. About a thousand people crammed inside, and many hundreds more milled about outside, unable to squeeze in. As a tribute to Alick, the Museum of Victoria went to enormous trouble to display the precious and recently acquired Harry Johns boxing-troupe truck nearby in a vacant allotment. The old cry of 'who'll take a glove' was on the wind.

A traffic jam developed near the Town Hall. Andrew later commented that 'there had never been a bigger funeral in the Koori community in Victoria'. The crowd was swelled by people from many communities to honour 'a man of all tribes', as Arnold Zable named him in his large obituary of Alick in the *Age*. Alick had been a loved part of all these tribes: his Greek and Aboriginal family; his many, many friends, including people from interstate; representatives and members of Aboriginal communities and organisations; Aboriginal Affairs colleagues; Museum staff and academics; representatives from the Greek Lodge and the RSL; friends from the 'showie' community and former wrestlers. Some of his Greek relatives were over-awed, others struck dumb. His niece Yvonne Parisi remarked, 'maybe we didn't know Uncle Alick as well as we should have. Once he passed away we realised what he had achieved in his life'. Theo Conos, his cousin, simply said: 'that big funeral stunned me'.

Alick lay in state for viewing and touching by streams of people; he appeared smaller and thinner than in life, but at rest. David Kidney, his old boss, read a piece which included the words 'to know your past is to admire the man'. Eulogies were given by Andrew for Merle and the children — he termed Alick 'my hero' — by Yolanda for the grandchildren, by Terry Garwood for the Aboriginal community, Alf Bamblett for the League, by Richard Broome on Alick's research contribution, and by others. Bruce McGuinness spoke in a hard-hitting manner from his wheelchair. He said that while Aboriginal people were born into their community without a choice, and that some over the years had been diffident about identifying with the community, Alick had by choice always wanted to belong. He was in McGuinness' estimation: an 'honorary Koori'. The 'Old Rugged Cross' was sung, the Cummeragunja choir sang: 'Shall We Gather at the River', and the 'The Last Post' passed shivers of emotion through the congregation.

Community singing spontaneously burst forth at the afternoon tea wake that followed, led by Lowitja O'Donoghue, Alick's old friend from FCAATSI and the Referendum days, and the Cummeragunja women. The Order of Service for the day contained two images of Alick, one in the uniform of the AIF and the other of Alick stripped bare in wrestling pose. The family had looked desperately around the family home for his slouch hat to place on the coffin, but it eluded them on the day. Alick would have been pleased about the service, as he liked a good celebration, but he would have been most proud to hear the affection in the eulogies, and McGuinness' conferred title of 'honorary Koori'. He would have been pleased at the 'slap up' afternoon tea that was served and would have been disappointed if no one had collected the 'left-overs' in a bag, as was his way. Some days later Alick was laid to rest in a quiet ceremony at the Melbourne General Cemetery, beside his parents. The service was conducted by the Aboriginal Evangelical pastor, Neville Lilley.

Merle had lost her soul mate of forty-eight years. She suffered an irrevocable blow with Alick's passing, but has battled on as Alick would want her to do. She continues in 2005 as matriarch of her growing family and has taken a keen interest in the writing of his life history. How then do we finally measure Alick's life? Surely we can do so only by understanding his past in all its richness as David Kidney suggested in his eulogy. Through the writing of his life story, a journey of speaking, listening, reading and writing, we have come to know his past.

Many people we have spoken to or communicated with around the state and beyond — family, friends, colleagues and community

Alick in the 2nd AIF in 1944, a man of all tribes, but above all an Australian: the photograph chosen by the family for the cover of the Order of Service at Alick's funeral

members — reach for superlatives when describing Alick. Several wept as they talked to us. George Tongerie from Oodnadatta's Antikirinya people, a fellow serviceman and mate from FCAATSI days, wrote: he was 'sincere, dedicated, honest, highly respected and accepted as a brother by everyone'. Walda Blow, Merle's cousin, commented that Alick was a 'beautiful and generous person'. Becky Thomson, his Brisbane friend, remarked that 'people were enriched by knowing Alick. His zest for life was contagious'. To many others in the Aboriginal community he was simply 'Uncle Alick', a sign of quiet respect. Colin Tatz, a research collaborator, who also knew him in the Welfare Board days, observed: 'He was a humanitarian spirit. He was a moral man…whenever I was in Alick's presence I always came away feeling cleansed. I'd been in the presence of somebody who was a moral being'. Trudi Miteff, a workmate in the DAA, commented: 'he was charismatic, he was understanding, he would have bent backwards for you'. Ambran Noor in Brunei believed he was 'a wonderful man, like a true example of a Muslim'. Myra Grinter, whom Alick and Merle chaperoned when in the Girls' Hostel, remarked, 'you didn't even think of him as Greek; as far as I was concerned he was Aboriginal, he'd lived it'.

Alick lived a life of adventure, exploring beyond cultural boundaries, excited by difference as Zable eulogised: he was 'a man of all tribes'. His journeys to Lake Tyers when fourteen, and his voyaging to Brunei sixty years later, symbolised this spirit. He was devoted to and loved his children Esmai, Andrew and Michael, and their offspring. He absolutely adored Merle to the end, as she did him. But his commitment to community, and in particular the needs of Aboriginal people, took him away from family for a great part of his adult life. His tireless collecting and research was to preserve cultural knowledge for the community he so admired. He rarely did things for himself, as he was always working; but his wrestling, his history work and his Brunei journeys were his great personal delight. Alick was always warm and genial, which his signature greeting — 'G'day Brother' — affirmed. Asked how he saw himself six months before his death, he replied that he was proud of his Greek heritage, and that while he had most contact with the Aboriginal community, 'I am Australian, that's where it starts and that's where it ends'.

Notes

1 Growing up Greek

Castellorizo: Alick Jackomos, 'Memoirs', pp. 1–6; York–Jackomos interview, Tape One, 9 September 1998, transcriptions from NLA tapes in possession of the authors; Alick and Merle Jackomos interview with unidentified granddaughter of Nellie Stewart of Swan Hill, no date but internal evidence suggests late 1997–early 1998; Profile of Andrew Jackomos, Castellorizian Newsletter, March/April 1983; Profile of Athanasios Auguste, unpublished materials, n.d; Nicholas G. Pappas, *Castellorizo: an illustrated history of the island and its conquerors*, Rushcutters Bay, N.S.W, Halstead Press, 1994, pp. 12–128.

Migration: York–Jackomos interview, Tapes One and Two, 9 September 1998; Alick Jackomos, 'Memoirs', p. 6; Alick and Merle interview with unidentified granddaughter of Nellie Stewart, c. 1997; Profile of Andrew Jackomos, Castellorizian Newsletter, March/April 1983; Richard Broome, *Arriving*, Sydney, Fairfax, Syme and Weldon, 1984, pp. 128–30, 150–7.

Greek community in Australia: Dominique François De Stoop, *The Greeks of Melbourne*, Melbourne, Transnational Publishing Company Pty. Ltd, 1996, pp. 19–35, 49–67; James Jupp, *Arrivals and Departures*, Melbourne, Lansdowne Press, 1966, pp. 176–7; Charles Price (ed.), *Greeks in Australia*, Canberra, Australian National University Press, 1975, pp. 4–5, 69–70, 122–6; Anastasios M. Tamis, *An Illustrated History of the Greeks in Australia*, Melbourne, Dardalis Archives of the Greek Community, La Trobe University, 1997, pp. 3–13, 29–61; Eleanor Bourke interview, 29 July 2003; Alick and Merle interview with unidentified granddaughter of Nellie Stewart c. 1997; Profile of Andrew Jackomos, Castellorizian Newsletter, March/April 1983.

Fish and chip shops: Jackomos, 'Memoirs', pp. 6–7; York–Jackomos interview, Tapes One and Two, 9 September 1998; Yvonne and Daniela Parisi interview, 17 July 2003; Alick and Merle interview with unidentified granddaughter of Nellie Stewart, c. 1997.

Schooling: Alick Jackomos, 'Memoirs', p. 6; York–Jackomos interview, Tape One, 9 September 1998; Eleanor Bourke interview, 29 July 2003; Alick and Merle interview with unidentified granddaughter of Nellie Stewart, c. 1997.

Religion: York–Jackomos interview, Tape One, 9 September 1998; Alick and Merle interview with unidentified granddaughter of Nellie Stewart, c. 1997.

Football: Jackomos, 'Memoirs', pp. 6–7; Yvonne Parisi interview, 17 July 2003.

Difficult living conditions and social intolerance: York–Jackomos interview, Tape One, 9 September 1998; York–Jackomos interview, Tape Two, 9 September 1998.

Racism and meeting Aboriginal people: York-Jackomos Interview, Tape One, 9 September 1998; York-Jackomos Interview, Tape Two, 9 September 1998; Alick and Merle Interview with unidentified granddaughter of Nellie Stewart, c. 1997; Alick Jackomos, 'The Aboriginal Community of Melbourne and Victoria', n.d.

2   Youth and the Great Depression

The Great Depression: Jenny Lee, 'Depressions', in Graeme Davison, John Hirst and Stuart Macintyre (eds), *The Oxford Companion to Australian History* pp. 183–5; Jackomos, 'Memoirs', pp. 8–9; Jackomos, 'Memories'; York–Jackomos interview, Tapes One and Two, 9 September 1998; Yvonne and Daniela Parisi interview, 17 July 2003; Theodore Conos interview, 31 July 2003; Alick and Merle interview with unidentified granddaughter of Nellie Stewart, c. 1997.

Fish and chip chops: Jackomos, 'Memoirs', pp. 6–7; York–Jackomos interview, Tapes One and Two, 9 September 1998.

Money management: Jackomos, 'Memoirs', pp. 7–8; Jackomos, 'Memories'; York–Jackomos interview, Tape One, 9 September 1998.

Alick's early employment: Jackomos, 'Memoirs', pp. 7–8; York–Jackomos interview, Tapes One and Two, 9 September 1998; Alick and Merle interview with unidentified granddaughter of Nellie Stewart of Swan Hill, c. 1997; Broome–Jackomos interview, 25 May 1995.

Meeting Aboriginal people in Melbourne and activism: Alick Jackomos, 'The Aboriginal Community of Melbourne and Victoria', n.d.; Jackomos, 'Memoirs', pp. 9–18; Mavis Thorpe Clark, *Pastor Doug: The Story of an Aboriginal Leader*, Adelaide, Rigby, 1965; York–Jackomos interview, Tapes One and Two, 9 September 1998; Alick and Merle interview with unidentified granddaughter of Nellie Stewart, c. 1997.

Boxing: Jackomos, 'Memoirs', p. 9; Theo Conos interview, 31 July 2003; York–Jackomos interview, Tapes One and Two, 9 September 1998; Alick and Merle interview with unidentified granddaughter of Nellie Stewart, c. 1997; Broome–Jackomos interview, 25 May 1995; Richard Broome and Alick Jackomos, *Sideshow Alley*, Sydney, Allen and Unwin, 1998.

Lake Tyers: Jackomos, 'Memoirs', pp. 13–18, Alick Jackomos, 'Memories; Alick and Merle interview with unidentified granddaughter of Nellie Stewart, c. 1997.

3   Off to War

Australia and Britain at war, Japanese threat: Peter Cochrane, Australians at War, Sydney, ABC Books, 2001, pp. 92–3, 96, 129; Menzies Virtual Museum, http://www.menziesvirtualmuseum.org.au/1930s/1939.html#MenziesEvents; York–Jackomos interview, Tape Two, 9 September 1998; Alick Jackomos, unpublished writing, 19/2/1996.

Alick's enlistment: York–Jackomos interview, Tape One, 9 September 1998; Theodore Conos interview, 31 July 2003; Alick Jackomos, unpublished writing, 19/2/1996; Jackomos, 'Memoirs', p. 19; Attestation Form in his military service record NAA, Series B883, Item VX71917.

Military service in Australia: NAA — military service record, Series B883, Item VX71917; York–Jackomos interview, Tape Two, 9 September 1998;

Linton Cornish interview, 11 July 2003; Jackomos, 'Memories'; Jackomos, unpublished writing, 19/2/1996; Jackomos, 'Memoirs', pp. 19–22.

Aboriginal workers for the Army in the Northern Territory: see R. M. and C. H. Berndt, *End of an Era. Aboriginal Labour in the Northern Territory*, Australian Institute of Aboriginal Studies, Canberra, 1987, p. 164.

Meeting Indigenous Australians: Jackomos, 'Memories'; York–Jackomos interview, Tapes Two and Three, 9 September 1998; Jackomos, unpublished writing, 19/2/1996; Jackomos, 'Memoirs', pp. 19–22.

Military service overseas: York–Jackomos interview, Tape Three, 9 September 1998; NAA — Military service record, Series B883, Item VX71917; Theo Conos interview, 31 July 2003; Jackomos, unpublished writing, 19/2/1996; Jackomos, 'Memoirs', p. 22.

Learning new languages: York–Jackomos interview, Tape Three, 9 September 1998; Jackomos, unpublished writing, 19/2/1996; Jackomos, 'Memoirs', p. 21.

Boxing for the Army: York–Jackomos interview, Tape Three, 9 September 1998; Broome–Jackomos interview, 1 June 1995.

Money management: York–Jackomos interview, Tape Three, 9 September 1998; Broome–Jackomos interview, 1 June 1995.

Hiroshima and Nagasaki: Cochrane, *Australians at War*, p. 177.

Alick's demobilisation and return home: Discharge Papers, Defence Records, NAA, series B883, item VX71917; York-Jackomos interview, Tape Three, 9 September 1998.

4 Tent Wrestler

The decision to go tent boxing: Jackomos, 'Memoirs', p. 34; and Broome–Jackomos interview, 1 June 1995.

The showgrounds: For more on sideshows see Richard Broome with Alick Jackomos, *Sideshow Alley*.

Aboriginal boxers: Richard Broome, 'Professional Aboriginal Boxers in Eastern Australia 1930–1979', *Aboriginal History*, vol. 4, part 1, pp. 49–71; Richard Broome, 'David Sands', in *Australian Dictionary of Biography*, vol. 16, pp. 174–5.

Alick and the Sands: Jackomos, 'Memoirs', pp. 34–5.

Alick's time with Harry Johns: Broome with Jackomos, *Sideshow Alley*, chap. 4; Broome–Jackomos interview, 1 June 1995; Affidavit in the matter of Shane Kenneth Atkinson by Alick Jackomos taken by Kate Auty, undated, but taken during Alick's retirement and while he was living at 22 Lemon Drive, North Balwyn, making it about 1990, Jackomos Papers.

Alick as wrestler: Jackomos, 'Memoirs', p. 35; Broome–Jackomos interview, 25 May 1995; Bernice McLure interview, 4 August 2003.

'Showie' values: Broome–Jackomos interviews, 25 May, 6 June 1995; see also Broome with Jackomos, *Sideshow Alley*, pp. 27–45.

Alick as a wrestler with John Sampson and Clive Coram:: Broome–Jackomos interview, 25 May 1995; Jackomos, 'Memoirs', p. 36; York–Jackomos interview, 9 September 1998; Gail Magdziarz interview, 23 August 2003; Clive Coram interviews, 25 September 1995, 28 July 2003, 19 March 2004; 'Young Jimmy' Sharman interview, 11 March 2004.

Alick as 'gee': *Shepparton News*, undated, in Alick Jackomos scrapbook; Broome–Jackomos interview, 25 May 1995; Bernice McLure interview, 4 August 2003; Magdziarz interview, 23 August 2003.

Alick in Tasmania: Broome–Jackomos interview, 25 May 1995.

'Takes': Broome–Jackomos interview, 25 May 1995.

Alick and 'Kiss the Girl' and as Betty Clements' protector: Broome–Jackomos interviews, 1 and 6 June 1995; Jackomos, 'Memoirs', p. 39; Betty Clements interview, 4 February 2004.

The Sharmans: See Broome with Jackomos, *Sideshow Alley*, pp. 101–40; Broome–Jackomos interviews, 25 May, 1 June 1995; Broome–Jackomos–Iris Lovett Gardiner interview, 11 August 1995; Broome–Jackomos–Sharman–Coram group interview, 14 November 1995; York–Jackomos interview, 9 September 1998.

Rud Kee: *Daily Telegraph*, 3 April 1976; Broome–Jackomos interview, 25 May 1995; Broome with Jackomos, *Sideshow Alley*, pp. 107–9.

The 'Black Bomber': Broome–Jackomos interview, 1 June 1995; Broome–Jackomos–Lovett Gardiner interview, 18 August 1995; Broome with Jackomos, *Sideshow Alley*, pp. 177–8; Broome–Jackomos–Sharman–Coram group interview, 14 November 1995.

'Chief Little Wolf': Broome–Jackomos interviews, 25 May, 1 June 1995, Jack Allan interview, 8 May 1997; Gail Magdziarz interviews, 8 May 1997, 23 August 2003; York–Jackomos interview, 9 September 1998.

'Joe Blow'/Mick Allen: Broome–Jackomos interview, 25 May 1995; Johnny Harris interview, 12 August 1996.

Rush Milling's words: Fan photo, Alick Jackomos' photographic collection.

Clarence Reeves/'Alabama Kid': *News* (Adelaide), 6 December 1947; *Sun*, 6 February 1950; see Clarence Olin Reeves file, Australian Archives (Melbourne), Series Mp484/1, item 53/34/34444 Reeves 1953.

5 Just Like Hollywood

Alick's determination to marry a Koori girl: Betty Clements interview, 4 February 2004; Roma Connors interview, Shepparton, 17 September 2003.

Alick and Merle's first meeting: Merle Jackomos interviews, 21 May, 11 June 2003.

Courtship and the family's concerns: Merle Jackomos interview, 21 May 2003; Yvonne Parisi interview, 17 July 2003; Theo Conos interview, 31 July 2003; York–Jackomos interview, 10 September 1998; Merle and Alick Jackomos interview with unidentified granddaughter of Nellie Stewart of Swan Hill, *c.* 1997, Jackomos Papers.

In-marriage rates: Broome, *Arriving*, p. 219; Diane Barwick, A Little More Than Kin, PhD thesis, Australian National University, 1961, pp. 54–8, 267–72.

Wedding and honeymoon: Merle Jackomos interview, 28 May 2003; Merle and Alick Jackomos interview with unidentified granddaughter of Nellie Stewart of Swan Hill, *c.* 1997, Jackomos Papers; York–Jackomos interview, 9 September 1998.

NOTES (PAGES 75 TO 97)   267

6 Entrepreneur and Family Man

Alick's hamburger joint: Broome–Jackomos interview, 1 June 1995; York–Jackomos interview, 10 September 1998; Jackomos, 'Memoirs', p. 39; 'Alick Jackomos, Dynamic Greek Grappler', *Australian Ring*, September–October 1958, pp. 40–1.
Seller of fruit and vegetables: Jackomos, 'Memoirs', p. 26; Yvonne Parisi interview, 17 July 2003; York–Jackomos interview, 10 September 1998; Roma Connors interview, 17 September 2003; Andrew Jackomos interview, 28 March 2004; Michael Jackomos written communication, March 2004; *Coburg Courier*, 5 September 1961; Richard Barwick, Canberra, written communication, 8 December 2003.
Dyer reference: Mollie G. Dyer, Program Director Victorian Aboriginal Child Care Agency, 'To Whom It May Concern', 5 December 1978, in Jackomos Papers.
Basic wage in 1953: *The Australian Encyclopedia*, The Grolier Society of Australia, Sydney, 1963, vol. 1, p. 446.
The St Phillip's Street house: York–Jackomos interview, 9 September 1998.
Asimina's new name: Merle Jackomos interview, 28 May 2003.
Property matters: York–Jackomos interview, 10 September 1998.
Domestic life: Merle Jackomos interview, 28 May 2003, Yvonne Parisi interview, 17 July 2003; Walda and Reg Blow interview, 22 July 2003; Roma Connors interview, 17 September 2003.
Alick and food: Roma Connors interview, 17 September 2003; Yvonne Parisi interview, 17 July 2003, quoting Esmai Manahan (née Jackomos).
Greek family gatherings: Esmai Manahan interview, 27 March 2004; Andrew Jackomos interview, 27 March 2004; Michael Jackomos, written communication, March 2004; Yvonne Parisi interview, 17 July 2003.
Introducing Merle to Fitzroy: York–Jackomos interview, 10 September 1998.
Football, humility and dinner: Andrew Jackomos interview, 27 March 2004; John Moriarty interview, 18 March 2004; Merle Jackomos conversation, 31 March 2004.
Becky Thomson (Newfong's) memories: letter to the authors, 17 December 2003.
Holidays and Alick's fathering: Esmai Manahan interview, 27 March 2004; Andrew Jackomos interview, 27 March 2004; Michael Jackomos, written communication, March 2004.

7 The 'Greek Grappler'

Tent wrestling: Broome–Jackomos interviews, 1, 6 June 1995.
Tent boxing and family life: 'Young Jimmy' Sharman to Clive Coram, 15 March 1959, in Clive Coram's scrapbook; Broome–Jackomos interviews, 1 and 2 June 1995.
Stadium wrestling: Broome–Jackomos interviews, 25 May, 1 and 6 June 1995; York–Jackomos interview, 9 September 1998; Manning–Coram interview, 28 July 2003; Broome–Coram interview, 19 March 2004; 'Alick Jackomos,

Dynamic Greek Grappler', *Australian Ring,* September–October 1958, pp. 40-1; Clive Coram personal papers and newspaper cuttings; Jackomos Papers; Andrew Jackomos interview, 28 March 2004; Michael Jackomos written communication, March 2004.

Greek wrestling boom: *Castellorizian Newsletter*, no. 22, September 1984, p. 7.

End of wrestling and last wrestle: Broome–Jackomos interview, 25 May 1995; York–Jackomos interview, 9 September 1998; Jock Austin to Alick Jackomos, 6 June 1983, Jackomos Papers.

Working the showgrounds: Broome–Jackomos interview, 1 June 1995; Bernice McLure interview, 4 August 2003; Gail Magdziarz interview, 23 August 2003.

8 Teaming with Doug Nicholls

Doug Nicholls and Alick's apprenticeship: Mavis Thorpe Clark, *Pastor Doug: The Story of an Aboriginal Leader*, Adelaide, Rigby, 1965; and in Jackomos Papers the following: Program, 'Celebrating the 60th Anniversary of the Conversion of the Late Sir Douglas Nicholls at Northcote Church of Christ…5th July 1992'; Alick Jackomos, 'Lady Gladys Nicholls 1908–1981.

Life Member of the Aborigines' Advancement League; Jackomos, 'Memoirs', p. 26; Alick Jackomos statement taken by Kate Auty in the matter of Shane Kenneth Atkinson, no date, about 1990; Merle and Alick Jackomos interview with unidentified granddaughter of Nellie Stewart of Swan Hill, *c.* 1997, in Jackomos Papers.

Aboriginal community of Fitzroy and also Barwick's research: See Richard Broome, *Aboriginal Victorians. A History Since 1800*, Allen and Unwin, Sydney, 2005, pp. 287–99.

Manchester Unity Dances: Esmai Manahan interview, 27 March 2004; Jackomos, 'Memoirs', p. 40; Andrew Jackomos, 27 March 2004; Michael Jackomos, written communication, March 2004.

Coburg Courier **profile:** *Coburg Courier*, 5 September 1961.

Aboriginal hostels: Myra Grinter interviews, 14 October 2002, 4 February 2004.

Australian Aborigines' League Ball 1962: Minutes of Ball Sub-committee 10, 31 July, 7 August, and Ball report, 2 October 1962, Jackomos Papers; *Aboriginal News*, no. 1, August 1963.

9 Political Activism

Australian Aborigines' League: For the League in the 1930s see Bain Attwood, *Rights for Aborigines*, Allen and Unwin, Sydney , 2003; Australian Aborigines' League, 'Victorian State Program for Aborigines and Aborigines Castes. Campaign — Objectives and Demands', no date, Jackomos Papers.

Bill Onus and corroborees: Program of 'Corroboree Season 1949' in the author's possession; Jackomos, 'Memoirs', pp. 25–7; York–Jackomos interview, 10 September 1998.

The League's creation: Alick Jackomos, 'The Aborigines Advancement League', *Identity*, July 1978, pp. 4–5; Miller–Jackomos interview, 12 December 1996;

Alick Jackomos, 'Lady Gladys Nicholls 1908–1981. Life Member of the Aborigines Advancement League (Vic)' in Alick Jackomos Papers.

League's policy and activities: For its integration policy, see *Smoke Signals*, October 1959. See also its brief history, Anon., *Victims or Victors? The Story of the Victorian Aborigines Advancement League*, Hyland House, Melbourne, 1985, chap. 4; Alick Jackomos, *Curriculum Vitae*, 1993, Jackomos Papers. See also the League's magazine, *Smoke Signals*, 1957–1970s.

Membership survey: *Smoke Signals*, December 1965.

Bill Onus' plaque: *Smoke Signals*, February–March 1967.

Alick and politics: York–Jackomos interview, 9 September 1998; Broome–Jackomos interview, 25 May 1995.

Alick on Aboriginal–Police relations: 'Statement in the Matter of Shane Kenneth Atkinson by Alick Jackomos taken by Kate Auty', no date, in Jackomos Papers.

Australian Aborigines' League activities: Minutes of an interview between AAL Executive and Ray Meagher, 15 August 1962. Minutes of the Annual Meeting, May 1963, Jackomos Papers.

Alick as mediator: Colin Tatz interview, 14 August 2003.

'Aboriginal News': Issues 1–14 in Jackomos Papers.

First Aboriginal Congress: Program of First Congress, 13–14 June 1964; Report on First Aboriginal Congress by Chairman Alick Jackomos, in Jackomos Papers.

Second Aboriginal Congress: Invitation to Second Aboriginal Congress from Alick Jackomos, 21 June 1965; 'Resolutions Passed at Second Aboriginal Congress', Minutes of Second Victorian Aboriginal Congress, in Jackomos Papers; reports also in *Truth*, 20 June 1964; *Smoke Signals*, August–September 1965.

Aboriginal interest and unity: Alick Jackomos to Pauline Pickford, 14 December 1965, CAR Papers, SLV PA 222, item 3646; Fran Russell to Pauline Pickford, 19 July 1964, CAR Papers, SLV PA 222, item 3306.

Involvement with FCAATSI: Jackomos, 'Memoirs', p. 27; Merle Jackomos interview, 11 June 2003; Jack Horner to Alick and Merle Jackomos, 14 December 1989, in Jackomos Papers; Esmai Manahan interview, 27 March 2004; John Moriarty interview, 18 March 2004. For FCAATSI see Jack Horner, *Seeking Racial Justice. An Insider's Memoir of the Movement for Aboriginal Advancement, 1938–1978*, Aboriginal Studies Press, Canberra, 2004, and Sue Taffe, *Black and White Together. FCAATSI: The Federal Council for the Advancement of Aboriginal and Torres Strait Islanders 1958–1973*, University of Queensland Press, Brisbane, 2005. See also *Identity*, vol. 2, no. 9, July 1976, p. 10, which pictures Alick at the annual conference April 1976 and lists him as newly appointed State Convenor.

FCAATSI socials: Miller–Jackomos interview, 12 December 1996; Broome–Jackomos interview, 6 June 1995.

FCAATSI policies and the Referendum: Joe McGinness (President of FCAATSI) 'Birth of the Federal Council for the Advancement of Aborigines and Torres Strait Islanders', FCAATSI Minutes and Proceedings of the Twentieth Annual Conference 9th and 10th April 1977, Canberra, pp. 21–3; Faith Bandler, *Turning the Tide. A Personal History of the Federal Council of Aboriginal* *and Torres Strait Islanders Affairs*, Canberra, Aboriginal Studies Press, 1989; York–Jackomos interview, 10 September 1998.

Decision to join the League: Jackomos, 'Memoirs', pp. 28–9; Merle and Alick Jackomos interview with unidentified granddaughter of Nellie Stewart of Swan Hill, c. 1997, in Jackomos Papers.

Rumbalara: For the opening of both settlements see *Age*, 12 April 1958, 12 March 1960. See also Corinne Manning, 'Humpies' to Houses: Victoria's Transitional Aboriginal Housing Policy 1957–1969, PhD thesis (revised), La Trobe University, 2001, chaps 4–5; Alick Jackomos, letter to the editor, *Age*, 3 February 1967; 'Statement in the Matter of Shane Kenneth Atkinson by Alick Jackomos taken by Kate Auty', no date, in Jackomos Papers.

Morwell transit village: 'Resolutions Passed at Second Aboriginal Congress', Minutes of Second Victorian Aboriginal Congress, in Jackomos Papers; 'Morwell Village. TV Programme — 'Watch This Space', transcript in NAA, series B357, item 77, Districts: Gippsland, 1963–1965, 17 September 1965.

Lake Tyers Inquiry: 'Report of the Lake Tyers Planning and Action Committee on Rehabilitation and Training for Aborigines at Lake Tyers Reserve' in Jackomos Papers; Colin Tatz interview, 14 August 2003.

Alick's Aboriginal idiom: Colin Tatz interview, 14 August 2003; Myra Grinter interview, 14 October 2003.

Murray rejects Alick: Colin Tatz interview, 14 August 2003; Miller–Jackomos interview, 12 December 1996.

Attempts to oust him from FCAATSI: Moriarty interview, 18 March 2004; Andrew Jackomos interview, 28 March 2004; Merle Jackomos discussion, 31 March 2004; Alick and Merle Jackomos interview with unidentified granddaughter of Nellie Stewart of Swan Hill, c. 1997, Jackomos Papers.

Alick's views on expulsion of non-Aboriginals: Alick and Merle Jackomos interview with unidentified granddaughter of Nellie Stewart of Swan Hill, c. 1997, Jackomos Papers; Yvonne White–Jackomos interview, December 1981, Jackomos Papers.

The League's split: For Roosevelt Brown's visit and reactions to it, see *Herald*, 28, 29 August 1969, *Age*, 30 August 1969; the League's definition of black power in *Herald*, 3 October 1969; Myra Grinter interview, 14 October 2002; Miller–Jackomos interview, 12 December 1996.

10   Welfare Board Officer

Application to the Welfare Board: Jackomos, 'Memories', p. 3.

The Welfare Board: Mark Harris, A 'New Deal' for Victorian Aborigines 1957–68, MA thesis, Monash University, 1988, chaps 5–7: 'Aboriginal Policies of the Aborigines Welfare Board', in *Report of the Aborigines Welfare Board*, 1967, Appendix 1. For the controversy over the Board see *Herald*, 4, 6, 8, 17, 23 March 1967. For Tatz see *Herald*, 11, 15 April 1967.

Alick's secondment: Aborigines Welfare Board Minutes, 10 March 1967, NAA B314/5, box 2, item 11.

Alick at Swan Hill: Jackomos, 'Memoirs', pp. 41–5; York–Jackomos interviews 9–10 September 1998; 'Statement in the Matter of Shane Kenneth Atkinson by Alick Jackomos taken by Kate Auty', no date, in Jackomos Papers; Alick and

Merle Jackomos interview with unidentified granddaughter of Nellie Stewart of Swan Hill, *c.* 1997, Jackomos Papers.

Conditions of the people: Jackomos, 'Memoirs', p. 43.

Work at Swan Hill: Alick and Merle Jackomos interview with unidentified granddaughter of Nellie Stewart of Swan Hill, *c.* 1997, Jackomos Papers; RCADIC statement, Jackomos Papers; Alick Jackomos weekly reports from Swan Hill, NAA, B2009, staff reports, 1967–68.

Specific work practices: Close analysis of weeks beginning 3 April and 23 and 30 July 1967 and analysis of all Mondays and Fridays between 23 April and 4 August, NAA B2009, staff reports 1967–68.

Alick's appointment to Welfare Board: AWB Minutes, 21 April 1967, NAA B314/5, box 2, item 11.

The decision to send Alick to Lake Tyers: Jackomos, 'Memoirs', p. 45, and York–Jackomos interview, 10 September 1998.

The state of Lake Tyers: 'Report of the Lake Tyers Planning and Action Committee on Rehabilitation and Training for Aborigines at Lake Tyers Reserve' in Jackomos Papers; Jackomos, 'Memoirs', pp. 46–9.

The Harrisons: *Herald*, 27 May 1961; see also *Sun*, 26 October 1959; Jackomos, 'Memoirs', p. 50.

Dances and fighting: Jackomos, 'Memoirs', p. 49; RCADIC statement, Jackomos Papers; AWB Minutes, 27 October 1967, NAA B314/5, box 2, item 11.

Alick's report on Lake Tyers: 'Lake Tyers Report – 14.12.67' to the Aborigines Welfare Board, Jackomos Papers.

End of his Lake Tyers role: AWB Minutes, 10 November 1967, NAA B314/5, box 2, item 11.

11 Public Servant

Ministry's new broom: Ministry of Aboriginal Affairs, *Annual Report* to June 1968, p. 9; see also the Ministry's annual reports, especially to June 1973.

Ministry and end to the removal of children: *Age*, 10 June 1968. See three reports of Worthy's speech in *Age*, *Sun* and *Herald* for 25 June 1968; *Herald*, 25 June 1968; *Sun*, 26 June 1968.

Alick 's work among fostered children: Jackomos, 'Memoirs', pp. 53–4.

East Gippsland Field Officer: Alick Jackomos, weekly reports as a field officer in the Ministry of Aboriginal Affairs, 1 January–21 June 1968, National Archives of Australia, B2009, staff reports, 1967–1968; Sandra Neilson interview, 12 August 2002, and conversation February 2004.

Lake Tyers adventure camp: Report of Adventure Camp, Lake Tyers 1969, January, in Jackomos Papers.

Alick and consultations: York–Jackomos interview, 10 September 1998; Peter Renkin interview, 23 July 2003; John Moriarty interview, 18 March 2004.

Worthy's view of Aboriginal responsibility and Maza and Anderson's criticisms: *Age*, 27–28 January 1969; *Age*, 29 March 1972 respectively.

Alick's contribution to the Ministry: Peter Renkin interview, 23 July 2003; Philip Felton interview, 18 August 2003; York–Jackomos interview, 10 September 1998.

Ministry's end: See the *Aboriginal Affairs (Transfer of Functions) Act* 1974, no. 8606.

Department's role: Jackomos, 'Memoirs', p. 54; Renkin interview, 23 July 2003.
Alick's help to staff: Eleanor Bourke interview, 29 July 2003; John Moriarty interview, 18 March 2004; Peter Renkin interview, 23 July 2003; David Kidney interview, 9 July 2003.
Lake Tyers visit: Eleanor Bourke interview, 29 July 2003.
Alick's place in the Department: Jackomos, 'Memoirs', p. 52; Andrew Jackomos interview, 28 March 2004.
Alick's work in the Department: Trudi Miteff interview, 18 July 2003; Peter Renkin interview, 23 July 2003; David Kidney interview, 9 July 2003.
Threatening officer: Andrew Jackomos interview, 28 March 2004.
Problems with the 1981 Census: *Age*, 3 September, 18 December 1982, 22 March 1983; Australian Bureau of Statistics, Information Paper, n. 2164.0 and 2153.0, 17 August 1982; Clyde Holding, *Commonwealth Parliamentary Debates*, 1 December 1983, p. 3234.
ABS position: *Commonwealth of Australia Gazette*, no. PS 44, 14 November 1985.
Work with the ABS 1986 and 1991: Alick Jackomos, 'Report by Census Field Officer, Melbourne', 3 July 1986, and 'Report by Alick Jackomos Census Field Officer', 9 August 1991, in Jackomos Papers.
Letter to the Aboriginal Arts Board: Alick Jackomos to Bob Edwards, Director, Aboriginal Arts Board, 10 October 1977, in Jackomos Papers.
Work troubles: Trudi Miteff interview, 18 July 2003; Peter Renkin interview, 23 July 2003; David Kidney interview, 9 July 2003; 'Statement of Alick Jackomos in the Matter of Shane Kenneth Atkinson', in Jackomos Papers.

12 Boomerang Diplomacy

Maori study tour: Alick Jackomos, 'Maori Study Tour November–December 1966', typescript in Jackomos Papers.
Churchill scholarship: York–Jackomos interview, 10 September 1998; Merle Jackomos conversation, 31 March 2004; Alick Jackomos, 'Study Tour of Indian and Black Communities in the U.S.A. July–September 1977'.
Boomerang diplomacy: E. Harold Keyes to Alick Jackomos, 23 October 1978; Gordon Krutz to Alick Jackomos, 18 December 1984; Steve and Daisy ? [surname unknown] to Alick Jackomos, 9 September 1985, 22 October 1991; Tony and Phyllis Machukay to Alick Jackomos, 24 December 1985, 18 December 1987, 11 December 1990, all in Jackomos Papers.
Reception of Alick and his report after Churchill tour: York–Jackomos interview, 10 September 1998; Merle Jackomos conversation, 31 March 2004; Alick Jackomos to Bob Edwards, Director, Aboriginal Arts Board, 10 October 1977, in Jackomos Papers.
Mount Isa secondment: Alick Jackomos, 'Secondment to Area Office Mt. Isa, Queensland', 22 September 1978.
Mount Isa experiences: York–Jackomos interview, 10 September 1998; Broome–Jackomos interview, 1 and 6 June 1995.
Brunei connection begins: Jackomos, 'Memoirs', pp. 22–3; Alick Jackomos, untitled 4-page typescript of Balikpapan and Brunei, 19 February 1996, in Jackomos Papers; York–Jackomos interview, 10 September 1998; email to

Corinne Manning, March 2004, from Ambran Noor, in possession of the authors.

Philippines and Orang Asli trips: Itinerary of Philippines trip, September 1979; letters re Orang Asli trip, Jimin Bin Idris to Alick Jackomos, 25 October 1982, and Zoll Helpi Bin Ismail to Alick Jackomos, 2 February 1983, in Jackomos Papers; foolscap biographical notes, no date (about 1988), p. 4; York–Jackomos interview, 10 September 1998.

China trip: David Kidney interview, 9 July 2003.

The Vilates: Mary and Vito Vilate to Alick and Merle Jackomos, 14 December 1985, in Jackomos Papers.

Airport wrestling and robber catching: Michael Jackomos, written communication, February 2003; Andrew Jackomos interview, 28 March 2004.

13 In the Thick of Things

Lake Tyers and Framlingham hand back: *Age,* 1 April 1970, *Sun,* 20 July 1971; *Aboriginal Lands Act 1970,* no. 8044; *Victoria Government Gazette,* no. 56, 9 June 1971; Jackomos, 'Memoirs', pp. 51–2; Ministry of Aboriginal Affairs, 'Lake Tyers Land Title', Melbourne, 1971; 'Lake Tyers Celebrates', in *Identity,* October 1971, pp. 4–5.

Carter's and Nicholls' speeches: Quoted in Alick Jackomos, 'The History of Lake Tyers', *Identity,* October 1971, p. 6.

Football carnivals, Victorian selection and Papua New Guinea trip: Jackomos, 'Memoirs', pp. 32–3; Merle and Alick Jackomos interview with unidentified granddaughter of Nellie Stewart of Swan Hill, *c.* 1997; York–Jackomos interview, 10 September 1998; John Moriarty interview, 18 March 2004; and in Jackomos Papers see 'Durrung Aboriginal Newsletter Aborigines Advancement League', no. 8, August–September 1973, Alick Jackomos, 'Report of the Victorian Aboriginal Football Carnival and Papua New Guinea Tour', PNG v Australia Souvenir Programme, and scribbled notes re tour, see also *Papua New Guinea Post Courier,* 3 and 4 October 1973; Merle Jackomos interview, 28 May 2003.

Truganini's history: L. Ryan, *The Aboriginal Tasmanians,* Sydney, Allen & Unwin, 1996; Lyndall Ryan and Neil Smith, 'Trugernanner', in *Australian Dictionary of Biography,* Melbourne University Press, 1976, vol. 6, p. 305.

Truganini's cremation: Alick Jackomos, 'Truganini to be Disturbed No More', in Jackomos Papers.

Mary Clarke's claim: Mary Clarke's claim is found in Mary Clarke, 'An Open Letter to Those Who Are Interested in Aborigines and their Descendants', Queen Victoria Hospital, 2 December 1951, in VAG papers, SLV ms 9212. It was also made to Richard Broome on 16 August 1978 during an interview with Mary and Ray Clarke at Framlingham. It was indirectly analysed by Diane Barwick in her exhaustively researched article on Louisa Briggs, 'This Most Resolute Lady: A Biographical Puzzle', in D. E. Barwick, J. Beckett and M. Reay (eds), *Metaphors of Interpretation. Essays in Honour of W. E. H. Stanner,* Australian National University Press, Canberra, 1985, pp. 185–239. A salient fact here, besides Louisa's own claim in 1924 that she was not Truganini's descendant, was that she was observed to have light blue eyes, a recessive gene, which depends on a genetic inheritance from both parents, meaning Louisa could not have been the daughter of a 'full blood' Tasmanian, Truganini or any one else, as blue eyes are not part of their genetic make-up. She was still an Aboriginal Tasmanian, but descended from people of mixed descent, from unions between Aboriginal women and European sealers.

Back to Lake Tyers: 'Lake Tyers Aboriginal Trust Celebrations, Program, July 1985', in Jackomos Papers; '"Back to Lake Tyers" — Emotional Scenes', *Aboriginal Newsletter*, October 1985, p. 3.

Gathering at 'The Knob', Stratford: *Gippsland Times*, 3 November 1987.

Uluru hand back: 'the hand-over of Uluru at Alice Springs was a Significant Step in the Struggle for Aboriginal Land Rights. DAA Project Officer Alick Jackomos Was There and Filed This Report', *Aboriginal Newsletter*, February 1986, pp. 6–7.

Mollie Dyer's reference: Mollie G. Dyer, Program Director Victorian Aboriginal Child Care Agency, 'To Whom It May Concern', 5 December 1978, in Jackomos Papers.

VAACA Chairperson: 'Introduction to VACCA' and 'Aboriginal Child Placement Principle', typescript VAACA, in possession of Richard Broome. Minutes of VAACA meetings, 10 June, 8 September, 15 October, 14 November 1980; petition of twenty members; Mollie Dyer, 'Reasons for the Resignation of Program Director of Aboriginal Child Care Agency', in Jackomos Papers.

Merle's NAC election: *Age*, 21, 22 October 1981.

Stewart Murray's accusations: Colin J. Bourke to Mr Murray, 16 August 1981, cc to Alick Jackomos; Stewart Murray, Administrative Officer Dandenong and District Aborigines Co-operative Society Ltd to Senator S. Ryan, 10 March 1982; solicitors' letters in Jackomos Papers.

Stewart Murray's eulogy and obituary: Order of Service, 6 June 1989, and obituary in *Sun Herald*, cutting undated, in Jackomos Papers.

Educational work: Trudi Miteff interview, 18 July 2003; Eleanor Bourke interview, 29 July 2003; Yvonne and Daniela Parisi interview, 17 July 2003; Grades Five and Six, Kew East Primary, to Alick Jackomos, 14 February 1992, in Jackomos Papers.

Australia Day Award: 'Australia Day Medal Awarded to DAA Officer', *Aboriginal Newsletter*, no. 133, February/March 1984; Staff Memo from Harvey Jacka and Invitation to testimonial, in Jackomos Papers.

Sir Douglas Nicholls' funeral: *Age*, 11 June 1988; *Bendigo Advertiser*, 11 June 1988.

14 A Passion for Photographs

Coin, stamps and card collecting: York–Jackomos interview, 9 September 1998.

Methods of collecting Aboriginal photographs: York–Jackomos interview, 9 September 1998.

Geraldine Briggs Request: Geraldine Briggs to Aleck [sic] Jackomos, no date, in Jackomos Papers. The Exhibition was held in 1989.

Private users: Peter and Maria Keegan to Alick Jackomos, 25 June 1984; Don Perdrisat to Alick Jackomos, two letters, no date, in Jackomos Papers.

Dyer's request: Copy of Mollie Dyer to David Kidney, 7 September 1988, with attachment to Alick, in Jackomos Papers.

Fishing photograph: R. W. to Alick Jackomos, 15 January 1992, and Alick to R. W. and family, 20 February 1992, Jackomos Papers.
Tatz's view: Colin Tatz interview, 14 August 2003.
Gilbert correspondence: Kevin Gilbert to Alick Jackomos, 28 September 1984; Alick Jackomos to Kevin Gilbert, 11 October 1984, in Jackomos Papers.
Donation of collection: Alick Jackomos to AIATSIS, 14 August 1985, and in reply Carol Cooper to Alick Jackomos, 27 August 1985; Agreement between Alick Jackomos and Museum of Victoria, 6 December 1989; Andrea Appleby, 'Museum Copies Jackomos Photo Collection', in unidentified magazine cutting, in Jackomos Papers; Mary Morris interview, 19 May 2004.
Aboriginal Advisory Committee: Merle Jackomos, personal communication, 31 March 2004.
Importance of the collection: Mary Morris interview, 19 May 2004.

15 Community Historian

Fitzroy driving interview: Steve Brown and Steven Avery, 'Remembering Aboriginal Fitzroy', Historical Places Section, Heritage Service Branch, Aboriginal Affairs Victoria, typescript, 1998. The interview took place on 31 July 1998.
Aboriginal Sporting Hall of Fame: Colin Tatz to Alick Jackomos, 8 January 1990, and Alick Jackomos to Colin Tatz, 8 February 1990, with attached listing, in Jackomos Papers; Colin Tatz interview, 14 August 2003.
'Tanderra' information: Ros (Olive) Mason to Alick Jackomos, 21 August 1991, and her letter of thanks, 4 September 1991, Jackomos Papers.
Research help: Series of eight letters from Sylvia Kleinert to Alick Jackomos, 20 June 1991–5 May 1992, 25 March 1993, Jackomos Papers.
Requests for information or to talk: Sharon Boyd to Alick Jackomos, 30 July 1984; Edna Graham, Aboriginal Teacher Aide, Preston Technical School to Director, DAA, 14 October 1982; Joan Vickery, Aboriginal Liaison Unit, Health Department, Victoria, to David Kidney, Director, DAA, 9 September 1986; M. J. Atkinson, Chairperson GVAECG, to David Kidney, Head DAA, 9 August 1988; Mollie J. Dyer to DAA, 23 October 1988, in Jackomos Papers.
AIATSIS membership: J. A. Lambert to Alick Jackomos, 16 December 1994, 1 May 1995; copy of Alick's 1995 renewal application; Victorian Chapter of AIATSIS to Alick Jackomos, 29 November 1994, conferring life membership, in Jackomos Papers.
Alick on making family trees: York–Jackomos interview, 19 September 1998.
Accuracy of: Betty Clements interview, 4 February 2004: Colin Tatz interview, 14 August 2003.
Secondment motion: 'Proceedings of the Aboriginal Development Commission Conference on Victorian Land Needs', Aborigines Advancement League, 17–18 June 1982, pp. 26–8.
Bicentennial Authority grant: 'Family Trees Flourish', *Newsletter of the Bicentennial National Aboriginal and Torres Strait Islander Program*, no date, received by Alick, 2 February 1988; Philip Morrissey to Alick Jackomos, 8 December 1987, with certificate attached, in Jackomos Papers. The petition, undated, is also found in the Jackomos Papers, stamped 'Released under the Freedom of Information Act'.

Stegley Foundation Grant: Alick's application, 27 February 1992; progress report, 13 October 1992, final report, 21 December 1993, grant notification, Fiona Moore to Fay Carter, Manager ACES, 13 July 1992, Jackomos Papers. See c. 1987 petition listed immediately above.

Miriambiak nations request: Sandra Mullett to Alick Jackomos, undated; Ian Keen to Alick Jackomos, 4 June 1997, Jackomos Papers.

Family skeletons and Yorta Yorta case: Andrew Jackomos interview, 28 March 2004.

Genealogical help: Jill Pattenden, resource teacher, Swan Hill, to Alick, 10 August 1984; Mavis Egan, Echuca Aboriginal Education Committee, to Alec [sic] Jackomos, 18 November 1986; Sandra Bell, Cultural Liaison Officer, Lake Condah Aboriginal Cooperative, to David Kidney, 5 November 1987; Joan Vickery, Melbourne Coordinator Aboriginal Elders Camp, Health Department, Victoria, to David Kidney, June 1988; Darcy Pettit, Murray Valley Aboriginal Cooperative Ltd to Alex [sic] Jackomos, 7 October 1988; Alick Jackomos, 'Report on Elders Cultural Camp Dharnya Centre Barmah', 3 November 1988.

Reading faces: Betty Clements interview, 4 February 2004.

Articles in *Identity*: See Select Bibliography.

Lake Tyers history grant correspondence between Robert Edwards and Alick Jackomos: RE to AJ, 11 November 1975; AJ to RE, 20 May 1977; RE to AJ, 11 July 1977; AJ to RE, 10 October 1977; RE to AJ, 25 October 1977; AJ to RE, 6 February 1978; RE to AJ, 9 February 1978, in the Jackomos Papers.

Gilbert correspondence: Kevin Gilbert to Alick Jackomos, 28 September 1984, Jackomos Papers.

Aboriginal Arts Board request, 1984: Alick Jackomos to Gary Foley, Director, AAB, 13 December 1984, Jackomos Papers.

Letter to Inglis: Alick Jackomos to Amirah Inglis, 26 August 1985, Jackomos Papers.

Publisher's opinion: Matthew Kelly to Alick Jackomos, 26 May 1988, Jackomos Papers.

Three co-authored books: See full details in the Select Bibliography.

16 In Retirement

Children's careers and relations with grandchildren: Esmai Manahan interview, 27 March 2004; Andrew Jackomos interview, 27 March 2004; Michael Jackomos, written communication, March 2004; Yasmin Jackomos interview, 27 March 2004.

A relationship of trust: Kindly translated by Dimi Delimitrou, Vivian Morris, 'Mixed Marriages, part 6. I Chose a Dark Woman But Didn't See the Colour', *Neos Kosmos*, 27 February 1992.

Showgrounds community: Alick and Merle Jackomos interviewed by unidentified granddaughter of Nellie Stewart of Swan Hill, c. 1997, Jackomos Papers.

RSL activities: Len Cornish interview, 11 July 2003; Merle Jackomos interview, 28 May 2003; David Kidney interview, 9 July 2003.

Greek-speaking decline: Alick and Merle Jackomos interviewed by unidentified granddaughter of Nellie Stewart of Swan Hill, c. 1997, Jackomos Papers.

Russell Moore case: *Age*, 21 September 1989; and the video 'Savage Indictment', which follows the court case and appeal. Alick is visible in the courtroom. Copies of consent form, 13 February 1963, social worker's report, 22 February 1963, and adoption form, 4 March 1963, signed by the Savages; Phillip Cooper Aboriginal Legal Service to Senator Michael Tate, no date; and other legal briefs and opinions related to the case in Jackomos Papers; *Age*, 19 May 1991.
Alick's research efforts: York–Jackomos interview, 10 September 1998.
Eulogies: See the many funeral programs and eulogies in Jackomos Papers.
Reconciliation celebrations: Patrick Dodson to Alec [*sic*] Jackomos, 28 May 1996; Patrick Dodson to Alick Jackomos, 24 June 1996, Jackomos Papers.
Awards: See citations and plaques in Jackomos Papers, including Directors of Echuca Aboriginal Cooperative to Ruth Weaver, Honours Secretariat, April 1990.
Interstate visits: Michael Jackomos, written communication, March 2004; Becky Thomson (née Newfong), written communication, 17 December 2003.
Brunei trips: York–Jackomos interview, 10 September 1998; Eleanor Bourke interview, 29 July 2003; Alick Jackomos, untitled notes on Balikpapan and Brunei, 19 February 1996, in Jackomos Papers; notes in an email by Ambran Noor to Corinne Manning, March 2004, in possession of the authors; Esmai Manahan interview, 28 March 2004.

17 Watching the Hour-Glass

1998: Michael Jackomos, written communication, March 2004; Len Cornish interview, 21 July 2003; Esmai and Yasmin Manahan interview, 27 March 2004; Barry Telford, Veterans Affairs to Alick Jackomos, 29 October 1998, Jackomos Papers.
PNG 'Last Parade': see *Post Courier*, 28 August 1998; *Geelong Advertiser*, 26 September 1998.
Last Brunei trip: Notes in an email by Ambran Noor to Corinne Manning, March 2004, in possession of the authors.
Last days: Esmai and Yasmin Manahan interview, 27 March 2004; Andrew Jackomos interview, 27 March 2004; Michael Jackomos, written communication, March 2004; Eleanor Bourke interview, 29 July 2003.
Funeral: Yvonne Parisi interview, 17 July 2003; Theo Conos interview, 31 July 2003.
Obituary: Arnold Zable, 'Alick Jackomos, A Man of all Tribes', *Age*, 18 March 1999.
Final assessments: George Tongerie to Corinne Manning, 28 December 2003; Walda and Reg Blow interview, 22 July 2003; Becky Thomson (née Newfong), written communication, 17 December 2003; Colin Tatz interview, 14 August 2003; Trudie Miteff interview, 18 July 2003; Ambran Noor to Richard Broome and Corinne Manning, 22 July 2003; Myra Grinter interview, 4 February 2004.

Select Bibliography

Alick Jackomos private collection

Jackomos, Alick, Private Papers. These contain 25 boxes in the following categories: official reports/acts of parliament; Cummeragunja and personalities; Missions/languages; Aboriginal leaders; Lake Tyers/Ramahyuck/Gippsland; FCAATSI; Football carnivals; Wrestling; Sideshow Alley; Castellorizo; Brochures; Invitations; Referendum/Census/NAC/.

Jackomos, Alick and Merle, Photographic Collection. This comprises eight large black photographic albums with over 4000 photographs depicting Aboriginal people of Victoria from the 1860s to the 1970s. It was compiled by Alick Jackomos for over thirty years. It has been copied by both AIATSIS Library in Canberra and Museum Victoria.

Jackomos, Alick and Merle, family photograph albums

Jackomos, Alick, Genealogical Collection. This consists of over 600 family trees of Victorian and southern New South Wales Aboriginal families. It was compiled over twenty years from the late 1960s, and has been copied by AIATSIS Library for restricted access. It had not been accessed by these authors, except for a brief inspection of the Atkinson–Cooper family line from which Merle Jackomos (née Morgan) is descended.

Alick Jackomos unpublished writing

'Study Tour of Indian & Black Communities in the U.S.A., July–September 1977', 47pp, typescript, 1977.
'Memoirs', 54pp, foolscap typescript, c. 1989.
'Speech at Lake Tyers Workshop', 9pp handwritten, 28 August 1991.
'The Aboriginal Community of Melbourne', 3pp typescript, 2 July 1992.
'Memories', 8pp typescript, c. 1994.
'The Aboriginal Community of Melbourne and Victoria', 4pp typescript, c. 1994.
'Sons of the Gournditch-Mara Tribe', 3pp typescript, no date.

Alick Jackomos published articles

'Gumleaf Bands', *Identity*, July 1971, pp. 33–4.
'Merle' (Alick), 'The History of Lake Tyers', *Identity*, October 1971, pp. 5–8.

'Merle' (Alick), 'The History of Cummeragunga and Maloga', *Identity*, July 1972, pp. 29–32.
'Aborigines Advancement League', *Identity*, July 1978, pp. 4–5.
'A Tour of Indian Reservations', *Identity*, July 1978, pp. 23–5.
'Marge Tucker, MBE', *Identity*, January 1979, pp. 14–15.
'Mrs Hannah Lovett, of Greenvale, Victoria', *Identity*, January 1979, p. 12.
'Thomas Shadrach James — 1856–1945', *Identity*, January 1979, pp. 10–11.

Alick Jackomos co-authored books

Jackomos, Alick, and Fowell, Derek. *Living Aboriginal History of Victoria. Stories in the Oral Tradition.* Museum of Victoria, Aboriginal Cultural Heritage Advisory Committee, Cambridge University Press, Melbourne, 1991.
Jackomos, Alick, and Fowell, Derek. *Forgotten Heroes. Aborigines at War from the Somme to Vietnam.* Victoria Press, Melbourne, 1993.
Broome, Richard, with Jackomos, Alick. *Sideshow Alley.* Allen & Unwin, Sydney, 1998.

Manuscripts and archives

National Australian Archives Series B2009, Staff Reports, Aborigines Welfare Board Weekly Work Record Sheet, 3 April–4 July 1967.
National Australian Archives Series B2009, Staff Reports, Ministry for Aboriginal Affairs Weekly Work Record Sheet, 1 January–21 June 1968.
National Australian Archives, Series B314/5 box 2, item 1, Aborigines Welfare Board Minutes, 1967.
National Australian Archives, Series B355/0, item 1, Correspondence Aborigines Welfare Board.
National Australian Archives, Series B357, item 77, Districts–Gippsland 1963–1965, 'Morwell Village, TV Programme — 'Watch This Space'.
Council of Aboriginal Rights Papers, State Library of Victoria, manuscripts, LV PA 222.
Clive Coram press cuttings and memorabilia.
Alick Jackomos military service record, NAA, Series B883, item VX71917.

Interviews by Richard Broome

Clements, Betty, Mildura, 4 February 2004
Coram, Clive, Ashwood, 19 March 2004
Grinter, Myra, 4 February 2004
Jackomos, Alick (5 tapes), Kew, 25 May, 1 and 6 June 1995
Jackomos, Andrew, East Malvern, 28 March 2004
McClure, Bernice, Murrumbeena, 4 August 2003
Magdziarz, Gail, Bulla, 23 August 2003
Manahan, Esmai, East Malvern, 28 March 2004
Moriarty, John, Melbourne, 18 March 2004
Sharman, Jimmy, Randwick, 11 March 2004

Interviews by Corinne Manning

Blow, Reg and Walda, Melbourne, 22 July 2003
Bourke, Eleanor, Melbourne, 29 July 2003
Connors, Roma, Mooroopna, 17 September 2003
Conos, Theo, Melbourne, 31 July 2003
Coram, Clive, Ashwood, 28 July 2003
Cornish, Len (Linton), Melbourne, 11 July 2003
Felton, Philip, Melbourne, 18 August 2003
Jackomos, Merle (3 tapes), Kew, 21, 28 May, 11 June 2003
Kidney, David, Melbourne, 9 July 2003
Miteff, Trudi, Melbourne, 18 July 2003
Parisi, Yvonne and Daniela, Melbourne, 17 July 2003
Renkin, Peter, Melbourne, 23 July 2003
Tatz, Colin, Carlton, 14 August 2003

Other Interviews

Jackomos, Alick, with Yvonne White, North Balwyn, December 1981, in Alick Jackomos Private Papers.
Jackomos, Alick, with Leanne Miller, 12 December 1996 for FCAATSI Oral History Project, copy supplied to the authors by Dr Sue Taffe.
Jackomos, Alick and Merle, with unidentified granddaughter of Nellie Stewart of Swan Hill, no date, but internal evidence suggests late 1997–early 1998, Alick Jackomos Private Papers.
Jackomos, Alick, with Steve Brown and Steven Avery of Aboriginal Affairs Victoria, 31 July 1998, 'Remembering Aboriginal Fitzroy', typescript in Alick Jackomos Private Papers.
Jackomos, Alick (6 tapes), with Barry York of the National Library of Australia, 9 and 10 September 1998, transcriptions made from NLA tapes, in possession of the authors.

Written communications

Barwick, Richard, letter, 8 December 2003
Bisset, Stan, letter, 8 October 2003
Jackomos, Michael, statement, Cairns, February 2004
Noor Aston, Ambran H. M., Lt-Col, letter, 22 July 2003, 26 July 2004, emails, 29 January, 25 May 2004
Stirling, John, letter, 19 December 2001
Tongerie, George, Enfield, South Australia, letter, 28 December 2003
Thomson, Becky (née Newfong), letter, 17 December 2003

Index

Page references printed in italics refer to illustrations and captions which are not discussed elsewhere on the page or surrounding span of pages.

Abbotsford, 75, 84–5
Aboriginal activism, *see* political activists
Aboriginal Affairs Act (1967)(Vic.), 153
Aboriginal Affairs Advisory Council, 155, 160, 196
Aboriginal Affairs Department, *see* Department of Aboriginal Affairs
Aboriginal Affairs Ministry, *see* Victorian Ministry of Aboriginal Affairs
Aboriginal Affairs Victoria, *see* Department of Aboriginal Affairs
Aboriginal and Islander Identity, 186, 191, 224–6
Aboriginal and Torres Strait Islander Commission (ATSIC), 170, 233
Aboriginal and Torres Strait Islander Water Veterans taskforce, 255
Aboriginal Arts Board, 170, 226–8
Aboriginal Balls, 113–15, 116, 119, 212
Aboriginal Child Care Agency, 193–6
Aboriginal Children's Christmas Tree Appeal, 111, 122, 152, 213
Aboriginal Community Elders Services (ACES), 221, 240–1, 246, 248
Aboriginal Congresses, 124, 125–8, 134
Aboriginal Cultural Heritage Advisory Committee, Museum of Victoria, 213–14, 229
Aboriginal culture, talks about, *see* educational talks
Aboriginal Deaths in Custody Royal Commission (RCADIC), 124, 152, 171
'Aboriginal Destruction Board,' 117
Aboriginal Development Commission, 165, 167, 196–7, 220, 234
Aboriginal Embassy, 234
 Red Hill, 191

Aboriginal friends, 65–6, 67, 90, 259–62
 from childhood, 21–6, 28, 33, 41, 90, 198
 fruit and vegetable delivery customers, 81
 funerals, 243
 met through FCAATSI, 94, 244, 262
 met when in army, 33–4, 73, 78, 91–3
 met while boxing/wrestling, 43–6, 58–9, 61–2, 70, 178–9; Carter, Charlie, 152
 at Pascoe Vale South, 87–8, 90
 see also Moriarty, John; Nicholls, Sir Doug
Aboriginal Funeral Service, 199
Aboriginal hostels, 94, 111–12, 122, 123, 216
Aboriginal Hostels Ltd, 122, 123, 197
'Aboriginal News,' 115–16
Aboriginal newsletter, 193
Aboriginal/non-Aboriginal divide, 135–40, 155, 159, 190, 196
Aboriginal people, 31–4, 45, 106–16
 Alick's photographs of, 206–14
 Alick's writings about, 224–30
 boxers, 42, 43–5, 102–3, 178–9, 229–30; Williams, Irwin ('Black Bomber'), 58–9
 Broadmeadows, 80
 communities visited on Jackomos family holidays, 93
 counting in Census, 168–70
 footballers, 187–90
 fruit and vegetable delivery customers, 81, 83
 hitchhikers, 150–1, 166
 police and, 124
 public servant working for, 143–86, 196–7, 203, 217, 218

281

see also child removal; football and Doug Nicholls; genealogical knowledge; political activists; Torres Strait Islands and Islanders
Aboriginal policy, 130–2, 154, 162
  New South Wales, 106
  Queensland, 178
  Western Australia, 121
  see also land rights; Victorian Aboriginal policy
Aboriginal Protection Board, 117, 118, 121, 149, 186
  New South Wales, 106
  see also Victorian Aborigines Welfare Board
Aboriginal rights, 130–2, 142
Aboriginal self-determination, 155, 160–1
Aboriginal servicemen, 33, 216, 262
  Atkinson, Otway ('Otty'), 28
  First World War, 226
  Forgotten Heroes, 229, 230
  Murray, Stewart, 198
  Nicholls, Doug, 107
Aboriginal Sporting Hall of Fame, 216
Aboriginal Tent Embassy, 234
Aborigines' Advancement League, *see* Victorian Aboriginal Advancement League
Aborigines Welfare Board, *see* Victorian Aborigines Welfare Board
ACES, 221, 240–1, 246, 248
Adams, Ray, 126
Adelaide, 21, 129, 187, 193
Adelaide Show, 47, 103
Adelaide University, 187
African-Americans, *see* Black Americans
Age obituary, 260
AIATSIS, *see* Australian Institute of Aboriginal and Torres Strait Islander Studies
AIF, *see* army service
'Alabama Kid' (Clarence Reeves), 41–2, 48, 62
Alice Springs, 33, 187
'Alick and Merle Jackomos Collection,' 213–14
All Stars Gymnasium, 102–3, 231, 241, 247
Allan (Magdziarz), Gail, 49, 105, 237
Allan, Jack, 60, 105, 231–2, 237
Allen, Mick, 60–1
Anderson, Alan, 147
Anderson, David, 160–1, 220, 243

Anderson (Bourke), Eleanor, 164–5, 200, 251
Anderson, Hugh, 215
Anderson's hosiery mills, 65, 69
Andrews, Shirley, 126
Annual Aboriginal Balls, 113–15, 116, 212
Anzac Day, 38, 79, 198, 238
Apache Indians, 175, 176
APM mills, Fairfield, 80, 84
apprentice, 21, 22, 39
Aristokelous, George, 72
Aristokelous (Jackomos), Maisie, 5, 11, 30, 89, 201
  at Alick's wedding, 71, 72
  wedding, 73–4
  see also Parisi, Yvonne
Arizona, 175, 176
army service, 27–39, 79, 249, 261
  Jackomos, Angelo, 38, 76
  see also Aboriginal servicemen; 2/14th Battalion
Arthur, Bruce, 101
articles in magazines, 115–16, 224–6
Arts Council of Australia, 227
ASIO, 120
Assan, Tony, 178–9
assimilation policy, 121, 134, 142, 146, 241–2
Atherton Tablelands, 34
Atkinson, Pastor, 225
Atkinson (Clements), Betty, 55–6, 64, 219, 224
Atkinson, Clive, 88
Atkinson, Dan, 187
Atkinson, Elizabeth, 64
Atkinson, Graham, 194, 195
Atkinson, Joyce, 142
Atkinson, Lucy, 56
Atkinson (Grinter), Myra, 111–12, 114–15, 136–7, 139, 262
Atkinson, Otway ('Otty'), 28, 33–4
Atkinson, Rosalin, 128
atomic bombs, 37–8
atomic testing, 121
ATSIC, 170, 233
Augustes, Asimina, *see* Jackomos, Asimina
Augustes, John, 19
Augustes, Manuel, 3
Augustes, Peter, 3
Augustes, Theo, 35, 37
Austin, Jock, 102
Australia Day Achievement Medal, 201, 246

Australian Aborigines' League (Aboriginal Branch), 23, 107, 113–21, 124–8, 141–2, 198
  Aboriginal Congresses, 124, 125–8, 134
  'Aboriginal News,' 115–16
  Alick's article on, 225
  'Objectives and Demands,' 118
  Social Sub-committee, 113–15
  Worthy's 1968 address to, 155
  see also Victorian Aboriginal Advancement League
Australian Bicentennial Authority, 220–1
Australian Bureau of Statistics, 167–70
Australian Constitution referendum, *see* referendum
Australian Department of Aboriginal Affairs, *see* Department of Aboriginal Affairs
Australian Imperial Force, *see* army service
Australian Institute of Aboriginal and Torres Strait Islander Studies (AIATSIS), 217–18, 221, 247
  Alick's genealogical works housed at, 220, 222
  copy of Alick's photographic collection, 211
Australian National Library, 255
Australian National University, 161, 162, 173, 234
Australian Ring, 76, 98, 99–100
Australian Rules football, *see* football
Australian Security Intelligence Organisation (ASIO), 120
author, *see* writings and publications
awards, 201, 246–9
  Murray, Stewart, 199
  Nicholls, Sir Doug, 202
  nomination, 240
Ayers Rock, return to traditional owners, 192–3
Aziz, Kiai Dr Yusuf Abdul, 251

'Back to Lake Tyers' weekend, 191
badge seller, 38, 239–40
Bailey, 'Headlock,' 46–7
Baillie, Helen, 228
Bairnsdale, 152, 158, 192
Balaclava, 5
Bali, 236
Balikpapan, 35–8, 198
Ballarat, 187, 208
  Genealogical Convention, 209, 245–6

Ballarat Orphanage, 118
Balranald, 145
Balwyn, 94
Bamblett, Alf, 260
Bandar Seri Begawan, 179–80, 249–51
Bandiana, 38
Bandler, Faith, 129, 225, 244
Banka Banka, 31–2
baptisms, 9, 89, 107
Barber, Bernice, 64
Barber, Elizabeth, 64
Bargo, Billy, 119
Barmah Lakes, 90, 112, 222–3
Barwick, Diane, 108, 161, 173
Barwick, Richard, 82
Batman Re-enactment Committee, 124–5
Bedford Stuyvesant Restoration Centre, 174
Belf, Harold, 98
Belgrave, 119–21
Bell, Roy, 49
Bendigo Show, 56
benevolent ideals, 17–18
Bergraff, Beryl, 173
Betan, 181–2
Bethesda Aboriginal Mission, 116, 198
Bigelow, Doug, 102
Bill T. Onus (Boys) Hostel, 111, 122
birth, 4, 8
Black Americans, 34, 62, 174
  Reeves, Clarence ('Alabama Kid'), 41–2, 48, 62
'Black Bomber', 58–9, 205
Black Diamonds, 216
Black Gold, 216
Black Power, 139
Blackburn, Doris, 121
Blind Society, 21
Blow, John Joe Aloysius, 60–1
Blow, Reg, 86, 192
Blow, Walda, 86–7, 88, 236, 262
body slams, 100, 101
Bolte Government, 154, 185
Bombala Show, 42
Bonang, 133, 158
Bonner, Senator Neville, 167
books, *see* writings and publications
boomerang throwing, 119–20, 191, 192, 200
  contests, 120, 125
  Onus' boomerangs, 104
  overseas, 175–6, 181, 182–3, 189
boomerang trade, 104–5, 167, 238

boomerangs, 125, 172, 180, 181, 188, 216
  on Alick's wrestling gown, 49
Borneo, 35–8, 198
Brunei, 179–81, *183*, 236–7, 249–53, 258
Bourke, Colin, *194*, 196–7, 200, 251
Bourke, Eleanor, 164–5, 200, 251
Bouverie Mob, 24
boxing and wrestling, 41–63, 65, 75, *87*, 92, 178–9, *199*
  Alick's history papers on, 240
  Alick's photograph collection, 11–12, 62, 205, 208
  in army, 35
  as a boy, 20, 21, 24
  to catch a thief, 184
  'Jaw Jarring Jackomos,' 158–9
  after marriage, 77, 93, 95–103; on honeymoon, 73
  Museum of Victoria tribute to Alick, 259
  peanut selling at local matches, 18–20, 59
  Sideshow Alley, 73, 229–32, 242–3, 255
  see also Johns' boxing tent; Sharman troupe
Boyd, Sharon, 216
Boys Hostel, 111, 122
Bracken, George, *87*
Bracken sisters, 128
Bradley, Archie, *59*
Bransen, Wynnie, 129
Brashs Music store, Melbourne, 184
Bray, George, 188
Bray, Harry, 32, 33
Briggs, Geraldine, 70, *123*, 139, 207
Briggs, Kenny, 70, 71, 72
Briggs, Louis, 191
Briggs, Louisa, 191
Briggs, May, 67
Briggs, Selwyn, 70
Briggs sisters, 128
Brisbane, 34, 61–2, 73, 255
Brisbane Show, 59, 61, 93, 95
Britain, 179
  atomic testing, Maralinga, 121
  Occupation Force in Japan, 38, 76
Broadmeadows, 80–1, 83, 108, 187
Brooks, Graeme, *199*
Broome, Richard, 258, 260
  Genealogical Convention, 209, 245–6
  Sideshow Alley, 229, 231, 232, 242, 255
Brown, Edna, 240
Brown, Roosevelt, 139
Brunei, 179–81, *183*, 236–7, 249–53, 258

Bruny Island, 190
Bruthen, 158
Bryant, Gladys, 110
Bryant, Gordon, 121, 123, 125–6, 173, 203
Builders' Arms Hotel, Fitzroy, 124
Bull, Murray, 191
Bull, Ronald, 191
Bungalow, 34
Burdeau, Arthur, 125
Bureau of Statistics, 167–70
Burns, Margaret, 113
Burnt Bridge Aboriginal Reserve, 44
Burnum, Burnum, 139
Bux, Edgar, 119
Bux (Nicholls), Gladys, 107, 108, 111–12, 122–3, *123*, 243

Cabbage Tree, 133
Cairns, 34, 92, 249
Cairns Show, 48
California, 174
Camberwell, 16
Camooweal, 178
Camp Jungai, 200, 217, 223
Canberra, 234, 244, 246–7
  Aboriginal Embassy, Red Hill, 191
  Aboriginal Tent Embassy, 234
  Australian National University, 161, *162*, 173, 234
  Federal Council for Aboriginal and Torres Strait Islanders (FCAATSI) conferences, 129, 130
caps and hats, 238, 245, 246
Carlton, 4, 6, 12, 22, 84
  153 Elgin Street, 12–13, 39, 89
Carnera, Primo, 97, 98
Carroll, Flo, 57
cars, *see* motor vehicles
Carter, Charlie, 124, 149, 152, 186, 191
Carter, Phyllis, 149, 152
Carter, Thelma, 152
Carver Club, 34
Cassidy, Stan, 22
Cassie Club, 10, 240
Castellorizian Newsletter, 98, 240
Castellorizo and Castellorizians, 1–3, 10, 89, 182, 240
  marriage, 68
Castle, Tommy and Shirley, 55
Cawley, Yvonne, 245
Cedar, Pancho and Kappa, 34
Census, 167–70
Channel 7, 101

charitable ideals, 17–18
Charles, Bernice, 64
Chester, Jack, 156
Chicago, 174
'Chief Little Wolf,' 59–60, 205
child removal, 117, 155–6, 194, 207–8, 221
  Ballarat Orphanage, 118
  James Savage (Russell Moore) murder case, 241–2
child welfare, 155–7, 183–4, 193–6
childhood and youth, 4–26, 204
  see also family life
children, see Jackomos, Andrew Morgan; Jackomos, Esmai; Jackomos, Michael Stafford
Children's Christmas Tree Appeal, 111, 122, 152, 213
China, 182
Choctaw Indians, 175, 176–7
Christie, Chris, 72, 80
Christie, Margarita, 72
Christie (Jackomos), Mary, 5, 30, 73, 84
  at Alick's wedding, 71, 72
  childhood, 6, 11
Christmas Tree Appeal, 111, 122, 152, 213
Christophers, Barry, 126
Churchill Fellowship, 173–7, 179
Cinesound newsreels, 101
Citizen Military Forces, 38, 79
citizenship rights, Aboriginal, 131–2
Civil Construction Corps, 31
Clark, Geoff, 169, 170
Clark, George, 22
Clarke, Albert ('Bert'), 20, 24
Clarke, Frank, 24
Clarke, Henry (Banjo), 24
Clarke, Jack, 22
Clarke, Len, 190
Clarke, Mary (Warrnambool), 190–1
Clarke, Norm and Mary (Fitzroy), 24, 41
Clarke, Norman (son), 24
Clay, Fred, 178
Clay, Iris, 178
Clements, Betty, 55–6, 64, 219, 224
Club Terrace, 133, 157
Coburg, 65, 81, 83, 89
Coburg Courier, 81, 82, 110–11
Cockerill, Bob and Nora, 152
Cocky Roberts Island, 25
coin collection, 204–5
Cole, 'Killer,' 54
collector, see genealogical knowledge; photograph collection

Collingwood, 6–7, 9, 10–11, 15, 21
  Manchester Unity Hall, 108–10, 243
  newspaper boy, 18
Collingwood Football Ground, 12, 19, 131–2
Collingwood Football Team ('Magpies'), 12, 91, 165
Collingwood Technical School, 8
Collingwood Town Hall, 98
Commonwealth Department of Aboriginal Affairs, see Department of Aboriginal Affairs
Commonwealth Industrial Gases, 40
community dances, 108–10, 243
community historian, 215–32
  see also genealogical knowledge
Connors, Clare, 88
Connors, Roma, 70, 83, 87, 88
Conos, Theo, 8, 20, 24, 96, 260
  Alick's family's request 'to talk him out of' wedding, 69–70
Constitution referendum, see referendum
Cook, Bob, 32
cooking, 87
Cooper, Ada, 226
Cooper, Lynch, 126, 128, 129
Cooper, Manuel, 192
Cooper, William, 107, 116, 117
Coram, Clive, 49–50, 95–102, 230, 237
Cornish, Len (Linton), 239, 254
Corpus Christi College, 187–8
'Corroboree Season 1949,' 119
Costello, Colley and Joan, 73
Council for Aboriginal Rights, 126, 127
courtship, 65–70
criminals, 78, 184
Cummeragunja, 91, 106, 127, 236, 260
  Alick's articles on, 225, 226
  Atkinson, Otway ('Otty'), 28, 33–4
  concert party tour members, 128
  farm project, 126
  genealogies, 220–1, 223
  Merle's childhood and youth, 64, 65
  Nicholl's burial, 202
  walk-off, 23, 65
'Cummeragunja' (34 Violet Grove), 202–3, 236, 237, 256

Dajarra, 178
dances, 108–10, 126, 186, 243
  Aboriginal Balls, 113–15, 116, 119, 212
  Lake Tyers, 152
Dandenong Show, 104

Darwin, 187, 255
Davao, 181
Davey, J. H., 142
Davey, Stan, 121, 122, 128, 139, 244
Davis, Jack, 94, 224
Davis, Johnny, 102
Day, Melva, 66, 67, 71, 72
de Meyer, Ted, 206
death, 259–61
  funerals attended and eulogies given, 34, 198–9, 202, 243–4
  Jackomos, Andrew, 203
debutante balls, 113–15, 116, 119, 212
Delacombe, Sir Rohan, 186
delivery business, 80–3, 95, 108, 132
D'Entrecasteaux Channel, scattering of Truginini's ashes in, 190–1
Department of Aboriginal Affairs (DAA/ Aboriginal Affairs Victoria), 162–7, 173–82, 193, 208, 217, 245
  Alick Jackomos Library, 247
  Australia Day Achievement Medal award, 201, 246
  handback of Ronald Bull's landscapes, 191
  information caravan, 199–200
  Mount Isa Office, 177–9
  redundancy, 170–1, 227
  retirement from, 203
  support for Alick's genealogical work, 220, 223
Department of Education, 233
  Victorian Department of Education (Vic.), 200, 217
Department of Employment and Training, 234
Department of Health (Vic.), 217
Department of Innovation, Industry and Regional Development (Vic.), 233
Department of Justice (Vic.), 233–4
Department of Social Welfare (Vic.), 194
Department of Veterans' Affairs, 255
Depression, 12–26, 83
Dimboola, 43
discrimination, 23, 31–3, 34, 45, 130–2
Dixon, Brian, 164–5
Doctor Washington Carver Club, 34
Dodson, Mick, 187
Dodson, Pat, 187, 244
domestic life, *see* family life
Don Football Club, 12
"Don't Cry For Me Argentina," 166
'Doug Nicholls Centre,' 123, 128

dragging ('gees'), 50–5, 60–1
Drouin, Jackson's Track, 90, 91, *113*, 212
Dunnolley, Tom and Rose, 90, *112*
Dunwich, 33–4, 92, *131*
Dyer, Jack, 20
Dyer, Mollie, 173, 242, 243
  Alick's writings about, 226
  courses run by, 208, 217
  reference written for Alick, 81
  Victorian Aboriginal Child Care Agency (VACCA) member, 194–6

earnings, 21, 85
  Aboriginal, 32–3, 126, 155
  with Aborigines' Advancement League, 132
  boomerang sales, 104–5
  fruit and vegetable deliveries, 83
  from hamburger shop, 78–9
  research grants, 170, 220–2, 226–8
  washing shirts, 55
  from wrestling, 95, 102; in army, 35
East Gippsland, *see* Gippsland
East Gippsland Cooperative, 169
East Kew, 89
East Melbourne, 122
  Greek Orthodox Church, 3, 9
Echuca, 65, 223
Echuca Aboriginal Cooperative, 248
economic development, 176, 178
Edmonds, Frank, 127
education, 6–8, 141, 154
  Alick's children and grandchildren, 233, 234, 236
  apprentice, 21, 22, 39
  Australian National University workshop on Aboriginal culture, 161, *162*, 173
  Cummeragunja boys, 226
  Jackomos (Morgan), Merle, 64
  language learning, 6, 8, 35, 182
  overseas study tours, 172–7, 179–82
educational talks, 199–201, 217, 245
  Nicholls, Doug, 118, 121–2
Edwards, Con, 142, 143
Edwards, Robert, 226–7
Egypt, 183
Elgin Street, 12–13, 89
Ellis, Sister Maud, 28, 116, 228
  Bethesda Aboriginal Mission, 116, 198
employment, 39–40, 75–83
  Aboriginal people at Mataranka Army Camp, 32–3

with Advancement League, 132–4, 140, 141, 146
Alick's children, 140, 195, 197, 233–4
army service, 27–39, 79, 249, 261
boomerang seller, 104–5
childhood and youth, 18–21
Jackomos (Morgan), Merle, 64, 65
public servant, 143–82, 196–7, 203, 217, 218
rural dwellers, 144, 149–50, 177–8
with Welfare Board, 141, 143–53
see also boxing and wrestling; earnings; fish and chips; public servant
entrepreneur, see salesman
Essendon 'Bombers,' 91
European holidays, 179, 182
Exhibition Building, 98
Exhibition Youth Club, 20, 21, 24

Fairfield, 60, 80, 84
family life, 84–97
during childhood, 5–18
in retirement, 235–7
when working, 145–6, 151, 235
family trees, see genealogical knowledge
Farnham, Bob and Cora, 158
Farnham, Sandra, 158
Faye, Monty, 42
Federal Council for Aboriginal and Torres Strait Islanders (FCAATSI), 94, 128–32, 243–4, 262
exclusion of non-Aboriginal people from meetings, 137–8, 139
Federal Council for the Advancement of Aborigines (FCAA), 128–9
Federal Department of Aboriginal Affairs, see Department of Aboriginal Affairs
Felton, Philip, 142, 145, 148, 151, 161
speaker at Aboriginal Congresses, 126, 127
Festival Hall, 97, 101, 103
First Nation peoples, US, 175–7, 183–4, 226
Tenario, 'Chief Little Wolf,' 59–60, 205
First World War, 226
fish and chips, 2, 4–5, 12–13, 39
'Magpie Fish,' 15–18, 21
Fisher, Cyril, 128
Fitzroy, 21, 41, 70, 80, 243, 255
Bethesda Aboriginal Mission, 116, 198
Builders' Arms Hotel, 124
McKinnon's transport to East Gippsland, 24–5
see also Gore Street Church of Christ
Fitzroy AFL team, 106
Fitzroy All Stars Gymnasium, 102–3, 231, 241, 247
Fitzroy High School, 125
Flannery, Frankie, 53
the 'Flat,' Mooroopna, 64–5, 90, 212
Flinders Street Station, 140
Florida, 241–2
'flying scissor' hold, 100
Foley, Gary, 227–8, 230
food appreciation, 87
food sector, 75–81
peanut selling, 18–20, 59
see also fish and chips
football, 12, 13, 15, 91, 165
Dyer, Jack, 20
indigenous teams, 187–90, 244
peanut selling at, 18–19
wrestling matches for, 98, 102
football and Doug Nicholls, 106, 107, 187, 188, 189
Constitution referendum campaign, 131–2
Northcote Football Ground, 108, 121
Forbes, 57
Forgotten Heroes, 229, 230
Foster, Tom and Ada, 25
foster homes, Aboriginal children in, 155–7, 194
Fowell, Derek, 242
Framlingham, 142, 169, 185–6, 191
Fraser, Pat, 148
Frater, 'Nugget,' 58
'fringe camps,' 64–5, 90, 144, 171, 177–8, 212
Frost, Dame Phyllis, 173
fruit and vegetable delivery business, 80–3, 95, 108, 132
fundraising, 94, 123
Aboriginal Balls, 114, 115
Christmas Tree Appeal, 111, 122, 152, 213
Nicholls, Gladys, 108, 111, 122–3
for RSL, 38, 239–40
wrestling matches, 98, 102
Yarra Bank, 23
funerals, see death

Galbraith, Fred, 22
Garwood, Terry, 245, 260
'gees,' 50–5, 60–1

genealogical knowledge, 164–5, 207–8, 217, 218–24, 242–3
  'Aboriginal News,' 116
  award for, 248
  Ballarat Genealogical Convention, 209, 245–6
  Genealogies of Victorian and Cummeragunja Aboriginal Families, 220–1
'Gentleman Gunboat Jack,' 62
Gilbert, Kevin, 210–11, 227, 230
Gippsland, 133, 134, 156, 157–9, 169
  cultural gathering at 'The Knob,' 191–2
  land claims, 222–3
  see also Lake Tyers
Gippsland Times, 192
'girlie shows,' 55–6
Girls Hostel, 94, 111, 122
Glenroy, 81
Golden Fleece Hotel, Melbourne, 57
Goolagong, Yvonne, 245
Gore Street Church of Christ, 107–8, 117, 243
  Aboriginal Youth Club, 110
Goroka, 188
Goulburn Valley, 127
Goulburn Valley Aboriginal Education Consultative Group Inc., 217
Grafton Show, 46–7, 73
Grayden, Senator Bill, 121
Great Depression, 12–26, 83
Greek–Australian Oral History Symposia, 240
Greek culture, 5–6, 8–10, 47, 89, 236, 240
  see also Castellorizo and Castellorizians
Greek school, 8
Greek wrestlers, 47, 98–100, 240
  'Greek cook' routine, 51–2
gregariousness, 86–8, 252
Grinter, Myra, 111–12, 114–15, 136–7, 139, 262
Gully, Walter, 84
gum leaf playing, 128, 130, 152, 215
  Alick, 121, 257
  Alick's article about, 224–5
  Ted ('Chook') Mullet and band, 26, 119
Gympie Show, 48
'Gympie Tiger,' 59

hamburger shop, Russell Street, 75–9, 119
'Happy Hammond' show, 101
Harcourt, Rex, 124
Harding, Eleanor, 130, 243–4
Harmes, Rita, 71, 72
Harris, Johnny, 45, 47, 50–1, 60, 237
Harrison, Dick, 151, 152
Harrison, Mary, 151–2
Hassen, Jack, 44
hats and caps, 238, 245, 246
Hauser, Joan, 92
Hawaii, 174
Hawkins, Lyn, 163
Hayes, Ken, 25
Healesville, 187
health, 13, 21, 245–6, 254, 258–9
  Banka Banka hospital, 31–2
  boxing/wrestling injuries, 54–5, 63, 100–1
  Merle's asthma, 86, 94, 97, 249
  near miss at Balikpapan, 36–7
  tropical infection, 38, 100
Heidelberg, 81
height, 46, 99–100
Henger, Ralph, 160
Hicks, Ray, 145, 147
Higgins, Clarrie, 71, 72
Hildebrand, Sister, 151, 152
historian, 215–32
  see also genealogical knowledge
hitchhikers, 24–5, 150–1, 166
Hoffman (Morgan), Elizabeth, 65, 66–7, 129, 194, 236, 245
  membership of organisations, 197, 240
  Merle's bridesmaid, 71, 72
  nomination of Alick for Hellenic Distinction, 240
Holden, Arthur, 142
Holding, Clyde, 191, 246
homes, 81, 83–8, 94
  childhood, 5, 6, 8–9, 12–13, 15
  'Cummeragunja' (34 Violet Grove), 202–3, 236, 237, 256
  Harrison, Mary and Dick, 151–2
  see also family life
homes, Andrew and Asimina Jackomos, 5, 6, 8–9, 15, 89, 202–3
  Elgin Street, 12–13, 39, 89
  Station Street, 16, 83
honeymoon, 73
honours, *see* awards
Hopi Indians, 175, 176
Horner, Jack, 129
hostels for young people, 94, 111–12, 122, 123, 216
housing, 127, 133–4, 142, 144, 146

Lake Tyers, 149
Manatunga, 144, 145, 146, 147
Ministry of Aboriginal Affairs policy, 155, 171
Queensland Gulf Country, 177–8
United States Black American programs, 174
see also homes
Howard, John, 244
Howe, Don, 134, 142
Huggard, Charlie, 124, 142
Hullick, Jim, 148
'humpies,' 64–5, 90, 144, 171, 177–8, 212
Hunter, Ruby, 241

Identity, 186, 191, 224–6
Illinois, 174
Immigration Museum, Melbourne, 255, 256
immigration to Australia, 1–5
income, *see* earnings
indigenous communities, overseas, 172–3, 175–7, 181–2, 183–4, 226
indigenous rights, 130–2
Maori, 173
Indonesia, 35, 38, 40–1
Indonesian language, 35
Inglis, Amirah, 228
Ipswich, 92
Ipswich Show, 52
Islam, 252–3
Islam, Margaret and Pat, 92
Israel, 174, 183
Isurava, 256–8

Jack, Bindi, 110
Jack, Harvey, 201
Jackomos, Alexios (Alexi), 1, 2, 3, 4, 47
Jackomos, Andrew (Andreas), 1–5, 6, 13, 26, 201, 202–3
Alick's enlistment, 29
Alick's marriage, 68, 74
at Rickett's Point, 89
social life, 9–10, 15, 17
sport, 12, 24
work, 2, 4–5, 17, 21
Jackomos, Andrew Morgan, 115, 233–4, 237, 259
birth, 84–5
childhood, 81, 82, 88, 89–94, 101, 112, 235; Manchester Unity Hall dances, 109–10
employment, 197, 233–4

eulogy given by, 260
Lake Tyers adventure camp, 158
Jackomos, Andrew Morgan, recollections of Alick, 93–4, 235
boomerang trade, 167
fruit and vegetable seller, 81, 83
genealogical work, 222–3
public servant, 165
when asked to leave FCAATSI meetings, 138
wrestling, 101
Jackomos, Angelo (brother), 5, 30, 38, 71, 73, 201
childhood, 6, 11, 18–19
hamburger shop, Russell Street, 76–7, 79
Jackomos, Angelo (uncle), 1
Jackomos, Areti, 1
Jackomos, Asimina, 3–6, 13, 21, 26, 201, 202–3
Alick's enlistment, 28–9
Alick's marriage, 68–70, 73–4
family gatherings at Christmas and Easter, 89
'martyr' complex, 254
money management, 15–16, 35
religion, 8–9, 17–18, 69
Jackomos, Asimina (great-grandchild), 234
Jackomos, Basil, 1
Jackomos, Esmai (Asimina Elizabeth), 233, 234, 237, 248
Aboriginal Ball, 114, 115
birth and childhood, 84, 85, 88, 89–96, 104; Manchester Unity Hall dances, 109, 110
employment, 114, 140, 233
at Federal Council for Aboriginal and Torres Strait Islanders (FCAATSI) meetings, 129
at opening of Aboriginal Embassy, Red Hill, 191
Jackomos, Esmai (Asimina Elizabeth), recollections of Alick, 254, 255
at Federal Council for Aboriginal and Torres Strait Islanders (FCAATSI) meetings, 129
food appreciation, 87
gregariousness, 252
on holidays, 93
showman, 96
travel to Brunei and Asia, 250
Jackomos, Jack (Yakomi), 1, 47
Jackomos, Jarara, 234
Jackomos, John, 1

Jackomos, Kalimna, 234
Jackomos, Kesheena, 234, 235
Jackomos, Maisie, *see* Aristokelous, Maisie
Jackomos, Malcolm, 234, 235
Jackomos, Mary, *see* Christie, Mary
Jackomos, Maryanne, 234, 235
Jackomos, Megthalia, 1
Jackomos, Merle, 64–74, 83–92, 110, 115, 194, 261
  'Alick and Merle Jackomos Collection,' 213–14
  Alick's wrestling, 73, 95, 96–7, 101
  Alick's family and, 68–74, 202–3
  Alick's retirement, 236–7, 240
  asthma, 86, 94, 97, 249
  'author' of *Identity* articles, 225
  awards and recognition, 246–7, 248; referendum 30th anniversary conference, 244, 245
  Bali trips, 236
  family book compiled by Alick, 219
  Immigration Museum panel featuring Alick and, 255, 256
Jackomos, Merle, membership of organisations, 122–3, 193, 196–7
  Aboriginal Community Elders Services (ACES), 240
  Aboriginal Hostels Ltd, 111–12, 197
  Aborigines Advancement League, 121, 126, 140, 198, 236
Jackomos, Merle, recollections of Alick, 84
  Anzac Day, 238
  cancer, onset of, 254, 255
  Churchill scholarship, 173
  at Department of Aboriginal Affairs (DAA), 177
  on Federal Council for Aboriginal and Torres Strait Islanders (FCAATSI), 129, 138
  first meetings, 65, 66–7
  food appreciation, 87
  helping Aboriginal families move to Broadmeadows, 80
  replacement as Victorian football team manager, 190
  RSL badge and poppy seller, 240
Jackomos, Merle, travels with Alick
  Aboriginal issues conference, Adelaide University, 187
  Federal Council for Aboriginal and Torres Strait Islanders (FCAATSI) conferences, 129
  Mooroopna, 124

  overseas, 179, 181–4, 236, 250
  in retirement, 236
Jackomos, Michael, 5, 73, 201
  childhood, 30, 46, 69
Jackomos, Michael Stafford, 115, 237
  birth and childhood, 85, 88, 89–94, 101, 112, 235
  employment, 140, 195, 197, 234
  recollections of Alick, 94, 235, 249, 254; wrestling, 101, 184
Jackomos, Mick, 1
Jackomos, Myron, 234, 235
Jackomos, Naida, 234, 235
Jackomos, Nancy, 234, 235
Jackomos, Nyari, 234
Jackomos, Panayota, 1, 3
Jackomos, Ross, 234, 235
Jackomos, Stella (Christella), 5, 11, 30, 71, 73, 201
Jackomos, Va Hoi, 234, 235
Jackson, Daryl, 90
Jackson, Eddie, 91
Jackson, Rev. Jesse, 174
Jackson, Len, 243
Jackson's Track, 90, 91, 113, 212
James, Thomas Shadrach, 226
Jansen, Captain, 55
Japan, British Occupation Force in, 38, 76
'Joe Blow,' 60–1
Johns, Harry, 41, 45–7, 48, 237
Johns, Stella, 45
Johns' boxing tent, 41–8, 49, 61, 95, 152
  Merle's introduction to, 73
  Museum of Victoria display in tribute to Alick, 259
Johnson (Day), Melva, 66, 67, 71, 72
Johnson, Ronny, 83
Johnsons, 40

Kadazan, 251, 258
Kapalang, 181
Keating, Paul, 246–7
Kee, Rud, 57–8
Keegan, Peter and Maria, 208
Kempsey Show, 41–2, 44, 45, 73
Kew, 89
  34 Violet Grove, 202–3, 236, 237, 256
Kew East Primary School, 200
Kew RSL, 238–40
Keyes, E. Harold, 175
Kibbutz Yisreel, 174
Kidney, David, 164, 166, 191, 208, 240, 260
Kiloki, Zedee I., 257–8

'Kiss the Girl,' 55–6
'The Knob,' 191–2
Knox, Sir George and Lady, 119
Kokoda Trail, 256–8
Koori Business Network, 233
'Koori(e)', 135
Kruger, Alec, 32, 33
Krutz, Gordon, 175, 176
Kuala Belait, *181*
Kyneton, 97

Lae, 188
Lake Condah, 59, 223
Lake Tyers, 109, 124, 127, 128, 166–7, 233–4
  Alick's first visit, 24–6
  Alick's writings on, 170, 225, 227
  Australian Aborigines League 'Objectives and Demands,' 118
  'Back to Lake Tyers' weekend, 191
  boys adventure camp, 158–9
  Dixon's visit to, 164–5
  fight to prevent closure, 116, 124, 127, 134–5, 142, 149
  genealogies, 222
  land hand back, 185–6
  Ministry of Aboriginal Affairs policy, 155
  music tradition, 119, 152
  welfare officers at, 143, 148–53, 159
Lake Tyers Aboriginal Trust, 191
Lake Wallaga Mission, 152
Lakes Entrance, 102, 149, 150–1, 153, 158
land rights, 220, 222–3
  hand backs, 185–6; Uluru, 192–3
  Maori, 173
Langford, Rosalind, 191
languages, 6, 8, 35, 179, 182
'The Last Parade,' 256–8
Laughton, Mick, 32, 33
Leach, Bill, 61
Lemon Road, 94
Lester, Yami, 193
Lilley, Neville, 261
Lilydale Show, 104
Lindenow, 133
Link Up, 196
Little, Jack, 101–2
Livery, Mary, 72
Livery, Pino, 72
Living Aboriginal History of Victoria, 229, 230, 242–3, 247
Londos, Jim, 98
Lonos, Tony, 49

Los Angeles, 174
Lovell, Keith, 159
Lovett, Ebenezer, 22, 23
Lovett, Hannah, 226
Lovett, Iris, 59
Lovett, May, 119
Lovett, Robert, 243
Lovett-Gardiner, Iris, 240
Lovi, Gerod, 258
Lowe, Robert, 187
Luna Park, *30*

McCrae, Sister Priscilla, *160*, 236
McDonald, Alec, 32, 33
McDonald, Hannah, 226
McGuinness, Amy, 130
McGuinness, Bruce, 120, 197, 212
  Alick's eulogy given by, 260
  Australian Aborigines' League/Aborigines' Advancement League, 113, 125, 139, 140
  Esmai Jackomos' recollections of, 109
McGuinness, Eric, 243
McGuinness, Joe, 120, 129, 130
McGuinness, John, 120, 243
Machukay, Tony and Phyllis, 176
Mackay Show, 51
McKinnon, Jim, 24
McKinnon, Joyce, 119
McLure, Bernice, 47–8, 52–3, 103, 104, 105, 237
McLure, Kitch, 103
magazine articles, 115–16, 224–6
Magdziarz, Gail, 49, 105, 237
'Magpie Fish,' 15–18, 21
Malay language, 35, 179, 182
Malaysia, 181–2, 251, 258
Malcolm, Bishop/Captain Arthur, 150, 193
Maloga Mission, 225
Manatunga, 144, 145, *146*, 147
Manchester Unity Hall, Collingwood, 108–10, 243
Mansell, Michael, 188
Maori, 43, 172–3
Maori-kiki, Albert, 114
Maralinga, 121
Maris, Hyllus, 123, 207, 220, 243
Marks, Danny, 42, 43
Marks, Ivy, 152
marriage, 64, 67–74
  Jackomos, Andrew and Asimina, 3
  Nicholls, Doug and Gladys, 107
Marshall, Harry, 22
'martyr' complex, 254

Mason, Ros (Olive), 216
Mataneo, 181
Mataranka Army Camp, 32–3
Maza, Bob, 139, 160
Meagher, Ray, 124
mechanic, 21, 22, 31
Medal of Order of Australia, 247–9
Melbourne, 1, 3, 80
  Aboriginal Advancement League offices, 122
  badge and poppy selling outside Flinders St Station, 140
  Brashs Music store, 184
  Golden Fleece Hotel, 57
  Greek school, 8
  hamburger shop, Russell Street, 75–9, 119
  Immigration Museum panel, 255, 256
  poliomyelitis epidemic, 21
  Royal Children's Hospital, 60, 158
  Shields Motor Company, 21, 22
  'Spring House,' 65
  Stadiums Ltd office, 98
  Yarra Bank, 23
Melbourne 'Demons,' 91
Melbourne General Cemetery, 261
Melbourne Olympic Swimming Pool, 99
Melbourne Show, 95–6, 103, 237
Melbourne Stadium, 19–20, 59, 97–8
Melbourne Town Hall, 28, 98
Melton, 82–3
'Memoirs,' 228
memory and recall, 7
  see also genealogical knowledge
Menzies, Robert, 27
Middle East, 174, 183
migration to Australia, 1–5
military service, see army service
Miller, Mickey, 75–6
Milling, Rush, 62
Milne, Bruce, 102
Mindanao, 181
Ministry of Aboriginal Affairs, see Victorian Ministry of Aboriginal Affairs
Mirimbiak Nations Aboriginal Corporation, 222
Mississippi, 174, 175, 176–7
Miteff, Trudi, 161, 165–6, 167, 170, 199–200, 262
Mitty, Fred, 18
'mixed descent,' 117, 118, 149
Moffatt, Gena, 25

Moffatt, Laurie, 24, 25, 130
Mohiddin, Haji, 180, 183, 249
Moira Lakes, 219
Moore, Russell, 241–2
Moore, Sandy, 52, 73
Moore, Selby, 73
Mooroopna, 90, 187, 212
  Alick and Merle's wedding reception, 72, 73
  Rumbalara settlement, 124, 133–4, 142
  'Flat,' 64–5, 90, 212
Moran, Al, 75
Morgan, Des, 71, 72
Morgan, Elizabeth, see Hoffman, Elizabeth
Morgan, Kaleb, 23
Morgan, Maude, 64
Morgan, Merle, see Jackomos, Merle
Morgan, Mick, 64, 71, 72, 85
Moriarty, John, 91, 159, 187, 193, 194, 203
  recollections of Alick, 129–30, 164;
  exclusion from FCAATSI meetings, 137, 138
Mormons, 183–4
Morotai, 35, 38
Morphett Creek, 31–3
Morris, Mary, 214
Morrisey, Philip, 221
Morwell, 134
Moss Vale Show, 62
motor vehicles, 91, 92, 109
  Assan's taxi service, 178–9
  Atkinson, Pastor, 225
  delivery business, 80–1
  Johns, Harry, 45–6
  McKinnon, Jim, 24–5
  mechanic, 21, 22, 31
  Nicholls, Doug, 118
  Sharman, 'Old Jimmy,' 57
Mount Isa, 177–9
Moyle, Aunty Maud, 80
mudwrestling, 102
Muir, Robert, 187, 188
Mullett, Albert, 192
Mullett, Euphemia, 90
Mullett, Nora, 25
Mullett, Sandra, 222
Mullett, Ted ('Chuck'), 25, 26, 119
Mullins, Agnes, 33
Mullins, Archie, 33
Mundine, Tony, 199
Murray, Gary, 188, 196
Murray, Herb and Eva, 25
Murray, Nora, 199

Murray, Stewart, 34, 113, 120, 128, 196–9, 202
  Aboriginal/non-Aboriginal divide, 137, 155, 196
  National Aboriginal and Torres Strait Islander Ex-Services Association, 198, 239
Murray Valley Cooperative, Robinvale, 223
Museum of Victoria, 207, 211–14, 229
  funeral tribute to Alick, 259
music, 10, 86–7, 119
  at Aboriginal Congresses, 128
  Lake Tyers, 119, 152
  at Manchester Unity Hall dances, 109
  see also gum leaf playing; singing

Nagle, Lyle, 21
Narbethong, 90
National Aboriginal and Islander Ex-Services Association, 198, 239
National Aboriginal Conference elections, 196–7
National Aboriginal Day Organisation Committee (NADOC/NAIDOC) week, 108, 217
  1983 celebrations, 102–3
  Aboriginal Balls, 115, 247
National Aboriginal Sports Foundation, 190
National Council of Aboriginal and Torres Strait Islander Women, 123
National Library of Australia, 255
National Reconciliation Week launch, 244
National Tribal Council, 139
Navajo Indians, 175, 176
  Tenario, 'Chief Little Wolf,' 59–60, 205
'Ned Kelly,' 59
Neilsen, Sandra, 158
Neo Café, Shepparton, 51–2
New Fitzroy Stadium, 24
New Guinea, 33, 256–8
New Mexico, 174
New South Wales, 41–2, 44–5, 46–7, 62, 73
  Sydney Show, 59, 95, 97
  see also Cummeragunja
New South Wales Aboriginal Protection Board, 106
New York, 174
New Zealand, 43, 172–3
Newfong, Archie and Edna, 92–3

Newfong (Thomson), Becky, 92–3, 249, 262
Newmerella, 158
newspaper boy, 18
Nicholls, Sir Doug, 106–8, *109*, 111–12, 226, 248–9
  Aboriginal/non-Aboriginal divide, 137, 139
  Aboriginal Welfare Board resignation, 116
  Aborigines Advancement League, 116, 121–2, 123, 127, 139; Alick's Life Member nomination, 140
  Australian Aborigines' League, 107, 113, 117–18
  Batman treaty, 125
  death, 202, 243
  Federal Council for the Aboriginal and Torres Strait Islanders (FCAATSI), 128–9
  Jackson's Track church services, 90
  Lake Tyers' closure fight, 116, 134
  Lake Tyers' land handed back, 186
  1967 referendum, 131–2
  'Save the Aborigines Committee,' 121
  see also football and Doug Nicholls
Nicholls, Lady Gladys, 107, 108, 111–12, 122–3, *123*, 243
1967 referendum, see referendum
Niven, Martha, 22
Noonuccal, Oodgeroo (Kath Walker), 92, 94, 129, 138, 243
Noor Captain Ambram Aston, 179–81, *183*, 249–51, 252, 258, 262
North Balwyn, 94
North Carlton, 4
North Coburg, 65
North Queensland, 34, 44, 92, 249
North Stradbroke Island, 33–4, 73, 92, *131*, 243, 249
Northcote, 6, 107, 109, 122–3, 202, 240
  'Doug Nicholls Centre,' 123, 128
  hostels in, 111, 122, 123
Northcote Football Ground (Oval/team), 106, 108, 121
  annual boomerang contest, 120
Northcote Town Hall, 114, 259–60
Northern Territory, 2, 93, 101, 126, *136*
  return of Uluru to traditional owners, 192–3
  World War II, 29–33
Nowa Nowa, 150, 152, 153, 158
  see also Lake Tyers

294   INDEX

Nyah Gift, 106

O'Brien, Tommy, 75
O'Donahue, Lowitja, 244, 260
Onus, Bill, 80, 90, 119–21, 148, 157, 226
   Aborigines Welfare Board member, 148
   Australian Aborigines' League, 114, 117, 119, 124, 127, 128
   boomerangs, 104, 119–20
   plaque donated to 'Doug Nicholls Centre,' 123
Onus, Eric, 22, 23, 80, 90, *110*, 212, 226
   in 'Corroboree Season 1949,' 119
   events organised with Alick, 108–9, 120
Onus, Judy, 90
Onus, Lin, 104, 243
Onus, Marjory Thorpe, 242
Onus, Mary, 90
Onus, Winnie, 22, 25, 90, *110*
Orang Asli, 181–2
Orbost, 24, 26, 127, 152, 158
Order of Australia, 199, 247–9
O'Rourke, Jim and Grace, 25
overseas travel, 40–1, 172–7, 179–84, 236–7
   indigenous football tour, 188–9
   in retirement, 249–53, 256–8
   WWII service, 29, 33, 35–8

Pahran, 85
Palin, Bert, 22
Pallaras, Alec, 35–6
Pallaras, Megthalia and Steve, 1
pan-Aboriginal identity, 126–7, 135–40
Papua New Guinea, 188–9
Parisi, Daniela, 200
Parisi, Yvonne, 68, 83, 87, 89, 260
Pascoe Vale, 81, 85–8, 94
   Returned Services League, 102
Patten, Herb, 121
Paulsen, Harry and Sylvia, 96
Paulsen's troupe, 53, 54, 59, 96
pay, *see* earnings
peanut selling, 18–20, 59
Pearl River Community, 176–7
Penrith, Harry, 139
Pepper, Philip, *192*
Perdrisat, Don, 208
Perkins, Charles, *239*
Perth, 1, 2, 187
Philippines, 181
Phoenix Indian Centre, 176

photograph collection, 11–12, 62, 92, 204–14, 229
   Day, Melva, 66
   used by Tatz, 210, 216
Pickford, Paul, 127
picnicking, 3, 89, 96
   at Jackson's Track, *113*
police, 52, 78, 124, 147, 152
police boys clubs, *see* youth clubs
political activists, 22–3, 107, 117–40, 154, 210–11
   Clark, Geoff, 169, 170
   Cummeragunja walk-off, 23, 65
   Lake Tyers closure fight, 116, 124, 127, 134–5, 142, 149
   see also Onus, Bill; Tucker, Margaret
politics, 123–4
Popjoy, Harry, *163*
Port Melbourne, 40
   Prince's Wharf, 204
Port Moresby, 33
postcards, *see* photograph collection
prejudice, 146–7
   see also racism
Premier's Department (Vic.), 164
Preston, 81
Preston Technical School, 217
public servant, 141, 143–86, 196–7
   genealogical knowledge used, 164–5, 217, 218, 220, 223
   redundancy, 170–1, 227
   retirement, 203
   see also Department of Aboriginal Affairs; Victorian Aborigines Welfare Board; Victorian Ministry of Aboriginal Affairs
public service rules, 166–7
publications, *see* writings and publications
Purfleet Mission, 46
PUSH, 174

Queenscliffe, 111
Queensland, 45, 73, 91–3, 234, 249
   DAA Mount Isa office, 177–9
   tent boxing and wrestling, 44, 48, 51, 52, 59, 61–2, 93
   during WWII, 33–5, 249
Queensland show train, 48

racism, 43, 45, 94, 178
   Robinvale, 146–7
   against Southern Europeans, 4–5, 13–14

United States, 176–7
  during WWII, 31–4
Red Cross Recreation Centres, 34
Redfern, 41
Reeves, Clarence ('Alabama Kid'), 41–2, 48, 62
referendum, 94, 131–2, 154, 162
  25th anniversary celebrations, 246–7
  30th anniversary celebrations, 244, 245
religion, 8–9, 28, 89, 90, 252–3, 259
  Asimina, 8–9, 17–18, 69
  Mormons, 183–4
  Nicholls, Doug, 107
Renkin, Peter, 159, 160, 161–2, 164, 166
research, 215–32, 240, 242–3
  see also genealogical knowledge
research grants, 170, 220–2, 226–8
researchers, assistance to, 210, 215–17
retirement, 203, 233–53
  from boomerang trade, 105
  from regular wrestling, 103
Returned Services League (RSL), 38, 198, 238–40, 254, 260
  Pascoe Vale, 102
  Robinvale, 147
Richards, Ron, 41, 44
Rickett's Point, picnicking at, 89, 96
Rickman, Joe, 151
Ritchie, Dave, 44
Ritchie, George, 44
Ritchie, Percy, 44, 45, 78
RMIT Greek–Australian Oral History Symposia, 240
Roach, Archie, 207–8, 241
road building, 31
robber, capture of, 184
Robinson, George Augustus, 190
Robinvale, 145, 146–7, 223
Roden, Lt-Colonel Phil, 257
Roe, Bill, 188
Rose, Lionel, 212
Ross, Maude, 64
Royal Children's Hospital, Melbourne, 60, 158
Royal Commission into Aboriginal Deaths in Custody (RCADIC), 124, 152, 171
Royal Easter Show, Sydney, 59, 95, 97
Royal Parade, Pascoe Vale South, 81, 85–8, 94
Rule, Len, 149
Rumbalara, 124, 133–4, 142
Russell, Fran, 127
Russell Street

Golden Fleece Hotel, 57
  hamburger shop, 75–9, 119
Ryan, Senator Susan, 197

Sabadine, Tony, 178–9
Sabah, 251, 252
St Phillip's Street, 84–5
St Vincent's Private Hospital, 259
salesman, 238
  boomerang trade, 104–5, 167, 238
  fruit and vegetables, 80–3, 95, 108, 132
  Jackomos, Andrew (Andreas), 2
  peanuts, 18–20, 59
  RSL badges and poppies, 38, 239–40
  spruiking ('gees'), 50–5, 60–1
Sampson, John, 48–9, 51
Sanders, George, 100
Sands, Ritchie, 44, 45, 78
Saunders, Reg, 192
Savage, James, 241–2
Savage, Maryann, 34
Savage, Phyllis (Lily), 34
Savage family, Cairns, 34, 92
'Save the Aborigines Committee,' 121
Save the Children Fund, 147
'Save the Lake Tyers Campaign,' 124, 127
school children, letters of inquiry from, 216
schooling, see education
schools, educational talks in, 199–200, 217
Scott, James, 119
Scott, Vera, 26
Second World War, see World War II
segregation, 31–2, 34, 45
self-determination, 155, 160–1
  American First Nation peoples, 176
Sharman, 'Old Jimmy,' 57, 58, 77, 87
Sharman, 'Young Jimmy,' 50, 57, 95, 96–7, 120, 230, 237
  Alick's boomerang sales, 104
Sharman troupe, 48–52, 55, 57–9, 65, 100
  closed, 102
  after marriage, 77, 95, 124
  Nicholls' season with, 106
  at Shepparton, 51–2, 124
Shell Company, 40
Shepparton, 65, 70–1, 124, 236
Shepparton Show, 70, 96, 102, 124
  'Greek café' routine, 51–2
Shields Motor Company, 21, 22
showgrounds life, 41–63, 103–4, 237–8
Showmen's Guild, 45, 104
Shrimpton, Jean, 88

Sibley, George, 61
Sideshow Alley, 73, 229–32, 242–3, 255
Sigley, Ernie, 101
singing, 10, 86, 166
  at Alick's funeral, 260
  Williams, Irwin 'Tiger,' 59
'Sir Douglas Nicholls Cup,' 187–8, 190
Smith, Cecilia, 61–2
Smith, James (Jimmy), 32, 33
Smith, Sissie, 240
Smoke Signals, 123, 216
South Australia, 185, 187, 202
  see also Adelaide
South Eastern Land Council, 220
spirituality, see religion
sport and sportsmen, 106, 108
  Aboriginal Sporting Hall of Fame, 216
  see also boxing and wrestling; football; youth clubs
'Spring House,' 65
spruiking and spruikers, 50–5, 60–1
'Squizzy,' 57
Stadiums Ltd, 97, 98
stamp collector, 204
Station Street, 16, 83
Statistics Bureau, 167–70
Stegley Foundation, 221–2
Stephen, Sir Ninian, 192, 246
Stevens, Cora, 158
Stewart, Frank, 154–5
story teller, 52–3
Stradbroke Island, 33–4, 73, 92, 131, 243, 249
Strathpine, 33
Sumatra, 251
Swan Hill, 56, 64, 143–9, 223
Swan Hill Aboriginal Welfare Committee, 148
Sydney, 40–1
Sydney Show, 59, 95, 97

'takes,' 54–5
'Tanderra,' 111–12, 216
Tarakan, 35
Tasmania, 97, 98
  with Paulsen's troupe, 53, 54, 96
  Truginini's cremated remains, scattering of, 190–1
Tatz, Colin, 125, 127, 136, 137, 262
  Aboriginal Sporting Hall of Fame, 216
  Aborigines Welfare Board member, 134–5, 142–3, 148, 149, 153
  Alick as research assistant, 210, 216, 219

televised wrestling, 101–2
television appearances, 98, 101, 134, 255
  in Brunei, 180, 250
Tenario, 'Chief Little Wolf,' 59–60, 205
tent boxing and wrestling, see boxing and wrestling
Terrick, Jessie, 22
Terrick, Willy, 22
Thomas, Alice, 109
Thomas, George and Agnes, 25
Thomson, Becky, 92–3, 249, 262
Thomson, Donald, 142
Thorpe, E., 148
Thorpe Onus, Marjory, 242
Tinaroo Dam, 249
Tongerie, George, 262
Torres Strait Islands and Islanders, 34–5, 178, 243–4
  National Council of Aboriginal and Torres Strait Islander Women, 123
  Savage family, 34, 92
  see also Federal Council for Aboriginal and Torres Strait Islanders
Townsville, 58
travel, 40–63, 172–93
  for Aborigines' Advancement League, 133, 172–3, 190–1, 243
  for Aborigines Welfare Board, 144–51
  for Australian Bureau of Statistics, 168–70
  to conferences and courses, 129, 161, 162, 172–7, 187, 191
  for Department of Aboriginal Affairs (DAA), 164–5, 166–7, 173–82, 193, 199–200, 217
  on family holidays, 90, 91–3, 96, 101, 112, 136
  hitchhikers, 24–5, 150–1, 166
  honeymoon, 73
  meeting Merle when, 65–6
  for Ministry of Aboriginal Affairs, 157–9
  with Nicholls, 118, 129
  in retirement, 236–7, 245, 249, 255
  World War II, 31–9
  as youth, 24–6
  see also motor vehicles; overseas travel
Treaty of Waitangi, 173
Trinity Beach, 34
Truganini, scattering of cremated remains of, 190–1
Tuck, Patrick, 199
Tucker, Margaret, 70, 117, 119, 212, 243
  Aboriginal Debutante Ball, 116, 119

Aborigines Welfare Board member, 128, 142, 143
Alick's writings about, 116, 226
see also Dyer, Mollie
Tupper, Fred, 97
Turner, Alec, 32, 33
2/1st Battalion, 28–33
2/12th Battalion, 34
2/14th Battalion, 33–8, 249
   Anzac Day, 38, 79, 238
   'The Last Parade,' 256–8

Uluru, return to traditional owners, 192–3
United Kingdom, *see* Britain
United States, 174–7, 183–4, 233, 241–2
   servicemen in Brisbane, WWII, 34
   see also First Nation peoples

Valadian, Margaret, 173
Victorian Aboriginal Advancement League, 121–3, 160, 193, 198, 216, 217, 240, 241
   Aboriginal Affairs Advisory Council membership, 155
   Aboriginal Balls, 114, 115
   Aboriginal/non-Aboriginal divide, 137, 139–40
   Alick's *Identity* article, 226
   award for services to, 247–9
   fundraising, 114, 116, 121
   Lake Tyers inquiry, 134–5, 149
   life membership, 140, 248–9
   Merle's membership, 121, 126, 140, *198*, 236
   testimonial for Alick's retirement from DAA, 203
   travel representing, 133, 172–3, 190–1, 243
   Victoria vs SA football march, 187
   women's auxiliary, 244
   see also Australian Aborigines' League
Victorian Aboriginal Advancement League, employment with, 132–4, 141, 143, 146
   family members, 140
   study tour to New Zealand, 172–3
Victorian *Aboriginal Affairs Act* (1967), 153
Victorian Aboriginal Affairs Advisory Council, 155, 160, 196
Victorian Aboriginal Child Care Agency (VACCA), 193–6, 234

Victorian Aboriginal Legal Service, 242, 247
Victorian Aboriginal policy, 128, 153, 155–6, 160–1, 164
   assimilation, 121, 134, 142, 146, 241–2
   land hand backs, 185–6
   'mixed descent,' 117, 118, 149
   see also child removal
Victorian Aboriginal Protection Board, 117, 118, 121, 149, 186
Victorian Aboriginals Lands Act 1970, 185–6
Victorian Aborigines Welfare Board, 141–53, 218, 241–2
   Aboriginal representatives on, 116, 128, 141–2
   housing, 127, 133–4, 141
   Huggard, Charlie, 124, 142
   Lake Tyers' closure attempt, 116, 124, 127, 134–5
   reports to Aboriginal Congresses, 126, 127
Victorian country shows, 56, 65, 95, 97, 103
   boomerang sales at, 104
   see also Shepparton Show
Victorian Department of Education, 200, 217
Victorian Department of Health, 217
Victorian Department of Innovation, Industry and Regional Development, 233
Victorian Department of Social Welfare, 194
Victorian Football Association, 187
Victorian Justice Department, 233–4
Victorian Ministry of Aboriginal Affairs, 142, 153–63, 164, 171, 199, 218
   Alick's children's, 233, 234
   photographic collection, 206
   support for Indigenous football, 187–8, 189
   see also Department of Aboriginal Affairs; Worthy, Reg
Victorian Premier's Department, 164
Vilate, Mary and Vito, 183–4
Violet Grove, 202–3, 236, 237, 256

wages, *see* earnings
Waitangi Treaty, 173
Walker, Kath, 92, 94, 129, 138, 243
Walker, Yolanda, 196, 233, 235, 236, 259, 260

Walker (Blow), Walda, 86–7, 88, 236, 262
Wallace, Daryl, 239
Walsh, Frank, 22
Walsh, Hilton, 148
Wamba Wamba, 34, 56, 144, 164
Wandin family, 22
war, 38, 226, 229, 230
  see also World War II
Warburton Ranges Mission, 121
Warracknabeal Gift, 106
Warrnambool, 126, 187, 190
Washington DC, 174
'Watch This Space,' 134
Webb, Crusher, 100
weight, 46, 100
Werribee Football Association, 187
West Coburg Baptist Church, 89
West Melbourne Stadium, 19–20, 59, 97–8
Westcott, Joey, *30*
Western Australia, 1, 2, 187
  Warburton Ranges Mission, 121
White, Frank, 143, 148, 153
White, Leo, 87
White Australia Policy, 4, 62
Whitlam, Gough, 244
Whitlam Government, 123–4, 162
Whyman, Beverley, 241–2
Wild Cat Corporation, 174
Williams, Bindi, 103
Williams, Harry, 109, 120
Williams, Iris, 120
Williams, Irwin ('Tiger'), 58–9, 205
Williams, Mervyn, 120, 212
Wilson, Johnny, 43
Wirrpunda, Margaret, 123, *198*

Wittingslow, Tom, 102
Woodenbong Aboriginal Mission, 58
Woorinen, 145
work, *see* employment
World War I, 226
World War II, 27–38, 206, 225, 249, *261*
  Aboriginal labourers, 32–3
  Aboriginal servicemen, 28, 33, 107, 198, 262
Worthy, Reg, *150*, 154–6, 158, 159–61, 162–3, 170–1
  indigenous football, support for, 187, 189
wrestling, *see* boxing and wrestling
writing, 7
writings and publications, 170, 224–32, 242–3, 247, 255
  'Aboriginal News,' 115–16
  papers at Greek–Australian Oral History Symposia, 240
  with Tatz, 216
Wynnum, 92–3

Yarra Bank, 23
York, Barry, 162, 177, 204, 242–3, 255
Yorta Yorta, 225
Yorta Yorta land claim, 222–3
Young, Alice, 109
Young, 'Taggie,' 57
youth, *see* childhood and youth
youth clubs, 98, 110–11
  Exhibition Club, 20, 21, 24
youth hostels, 94, 111–12, 122, 123, 216
Yuendumu Sports carnivals, 190

Zable, Arnold, 260